MARVEL KNIGHTS

CAPTAIN AMERICA

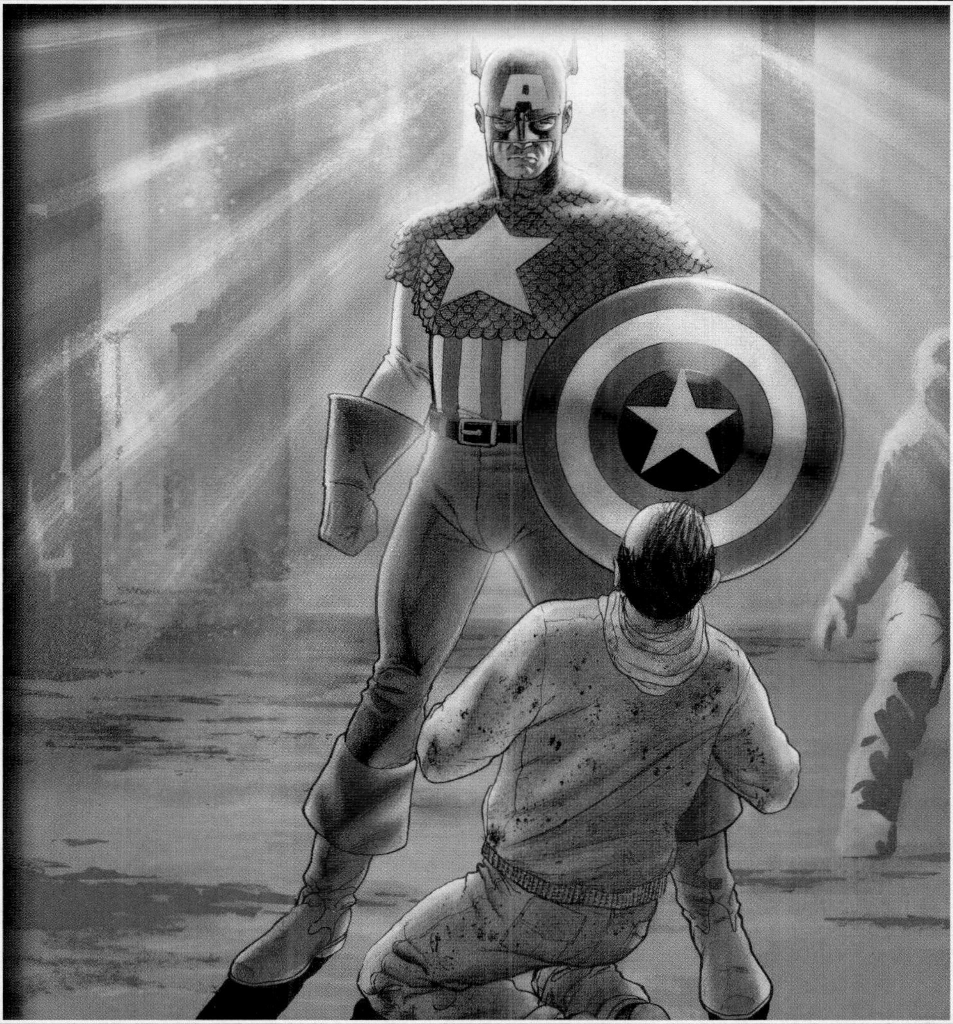

THE NEW DEAL

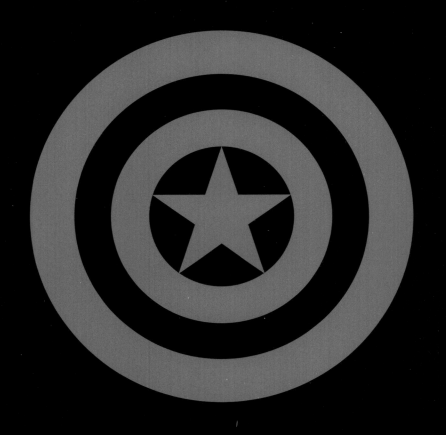

MARVEL KNIGHTS

CAPTAIN AMERICA
THE NEW DEAL

JOHN NEY RIEBER
Writer

JOHN CASSADAY
Artist

DAVE STEWART
Colorist

RICHARD STARKINGS & COMICRAFT'S **WES ABBOTT**
Letterer

NICK LOWE
Assistant Editor

STUART MOORE & **JOE QUESADA**
Editors

KELLY LAMY
Associate Managing Editor

NANCI DAKESIAN
Managing Editor

Captain America created by Joe Simon & Jack Kirby

Collection Editor **MARK D. BEAZLEY**
Assistant Editor **CAITLIN O'CONNELL**
Associate Managing Editor **KATERI WOODY**
Associate Manager, Digital Assets **JOE HOCHSTEIN**
Senior Editor, Special Projects **JENNIFER GRÜNWALD**
VP Production & Special Projects **JEFF YOUNGQUIST**
Book Designers **ADAM DEL RE**
SVP Print, Sales & Marketing **DAVID GABRIEL**

Editor In Chief **C.B. CEBULSKI**
Chief Creative Officer **JOE QUESADA**
President **DAN BUCKLEY**
Executive Producer **ALAN FINE**

GHTS CAPTAIN AMERICA BY RIEBER & CASSADAY: THE NEW DEAL. Contains material originally published in magazine form as CAPTAIN AMERICA #1-6. First printing 2018. ISBN 978-1-302-91402-8. Published b
LDWIDE, INC., a subsidiary of MARVEL ENTERTAINMENT, LLC. OFFICE OF PUBLICATION: 135 West 50th Street, New York, NY 10020. Copyright © 2018 MARVEL No similarity between any of the names, characters, persons
ions in this magazine with those of any living or dead person or institution is intended, and any such similarity which may exist is purely coincidental. **Printed in the U.S.A.** DAN BUCKLEY, President, Marvel Entertainmen
blisher; JOE QUESADA, Chief Creative Officer; TOM BREVOORT, SVP of Publishing; DAVID BOGART, SVP of Business Affairs & Operations, Publishing & Partnership; DAVID GABRIEL, SVP of Sales & Marketing, Publishin
UIST, VP of Production & Special Projects; DAN CARR, Executive Director of Publishing Technology; ALEX MORALES, Director of Publishing Operations; DAN EDINGTON, Managing Editor; SUSAN CRESPI, Productio
N LEE, Chairman Emeritus. For information regarding advertising in Marvel Comics or on Marvel.com, please contact Vit DeBellis, Custom Solutions & Integrated Advertising Manager, at vdebellis@marvel.com. For Marv
nquiries, please call 888-511-5480. **Manufactured between 9/21/2018 and 10/23/2018 by LSC COMMUNICATIONS INC., KENDALLVILLE, IN, USA.**

3 2 1

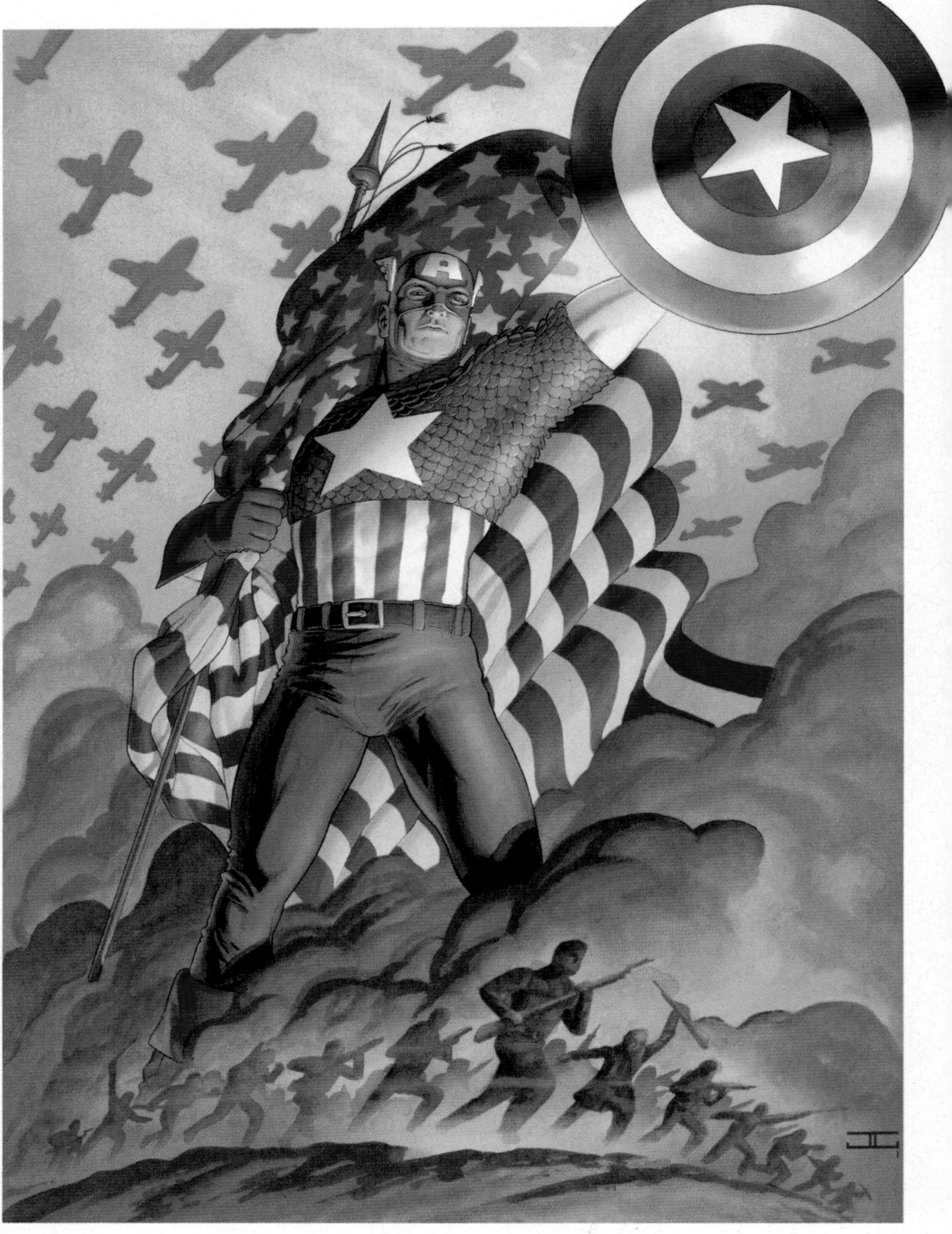

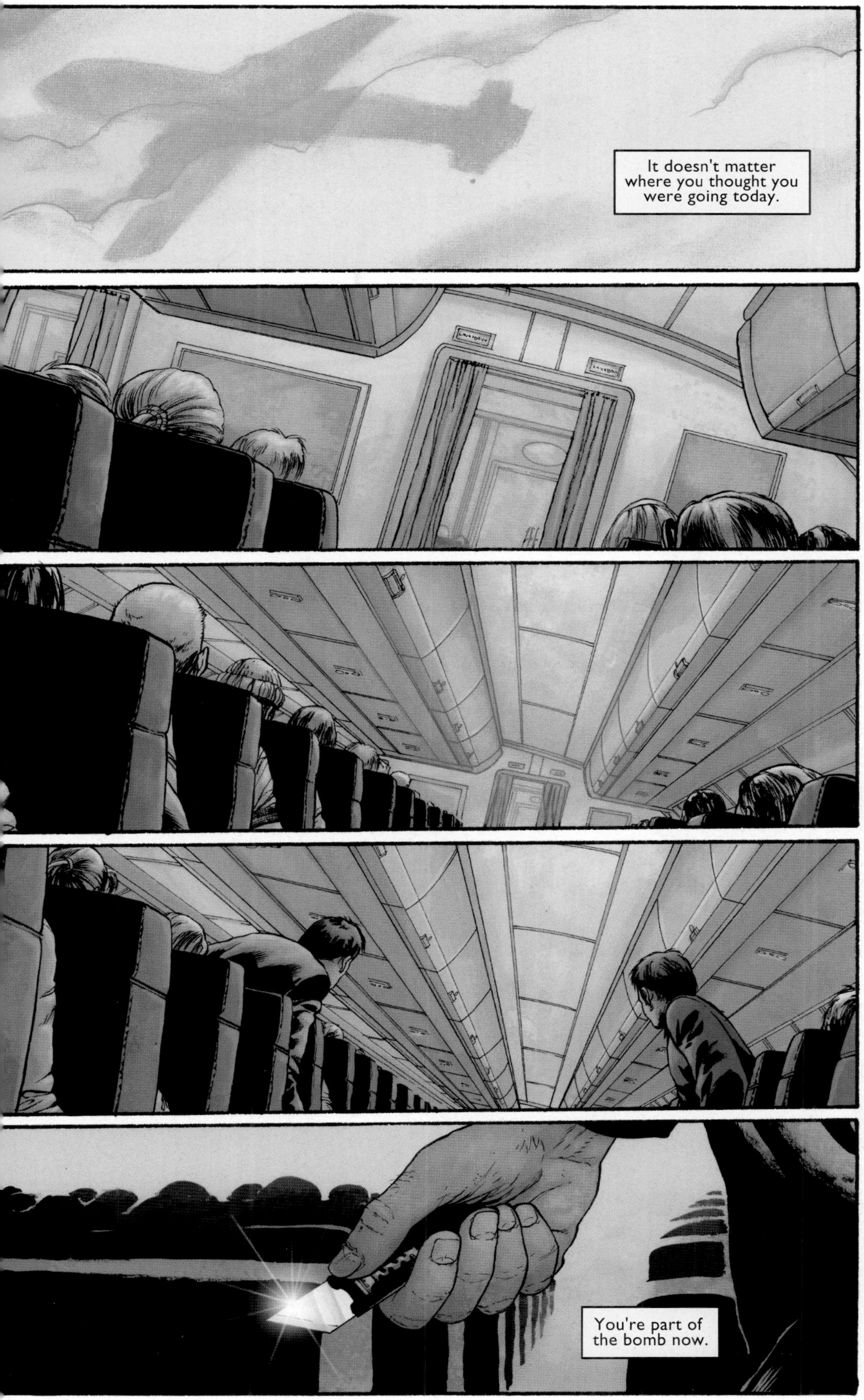
It doesn't matter where you thought you were going today.
You're part of the bomb now.

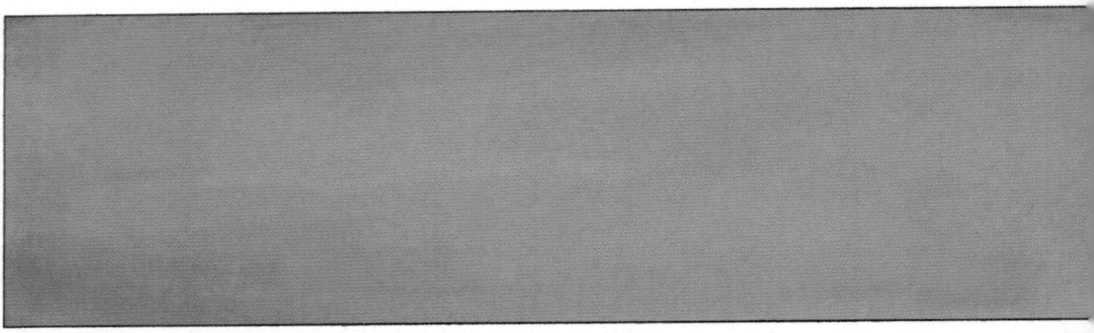

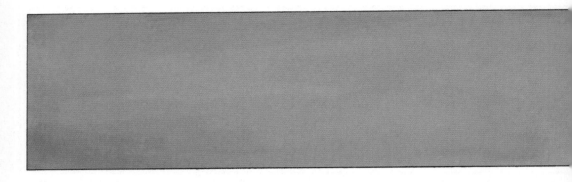

And somewhere in the world --

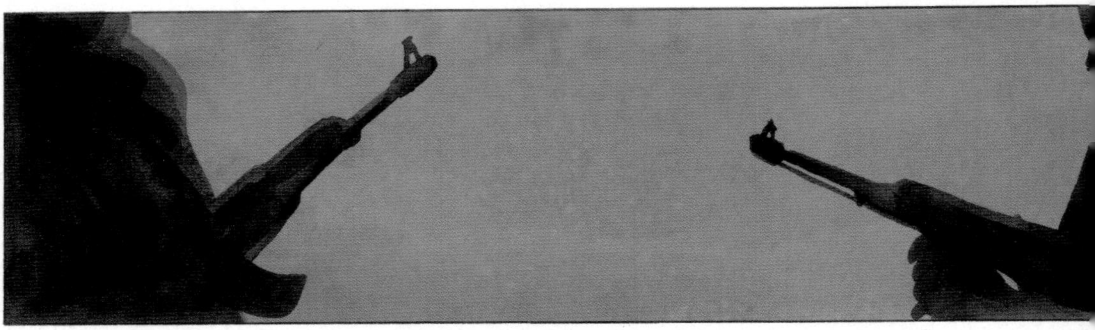

A handful of men with famished eyes sit around a radio --

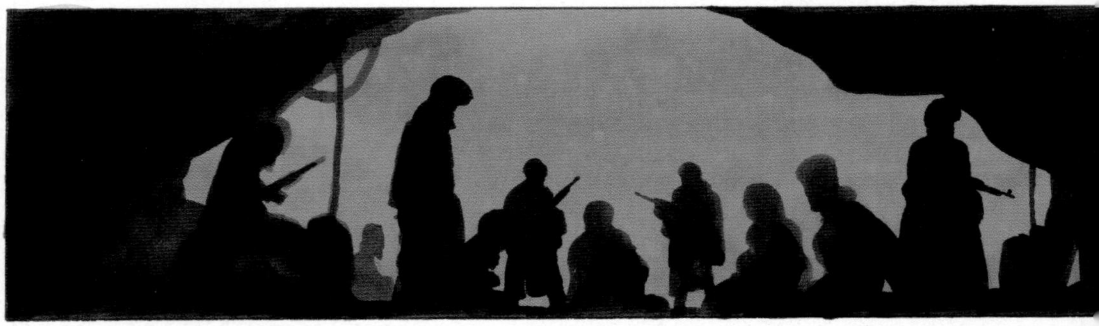

Or a telephone.

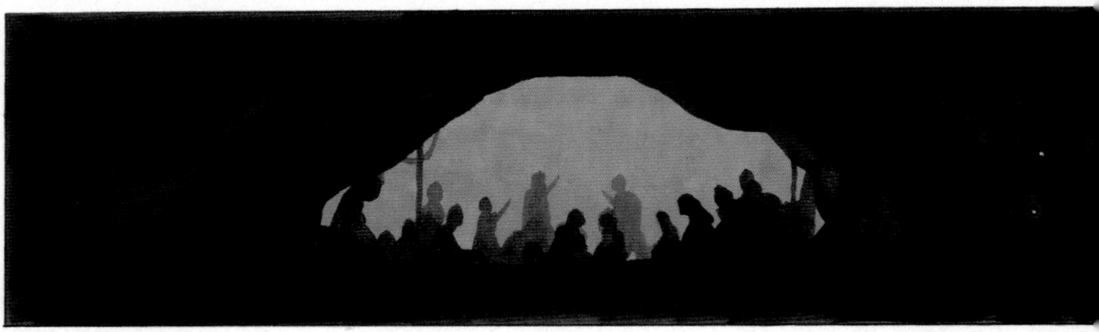

Waiting.

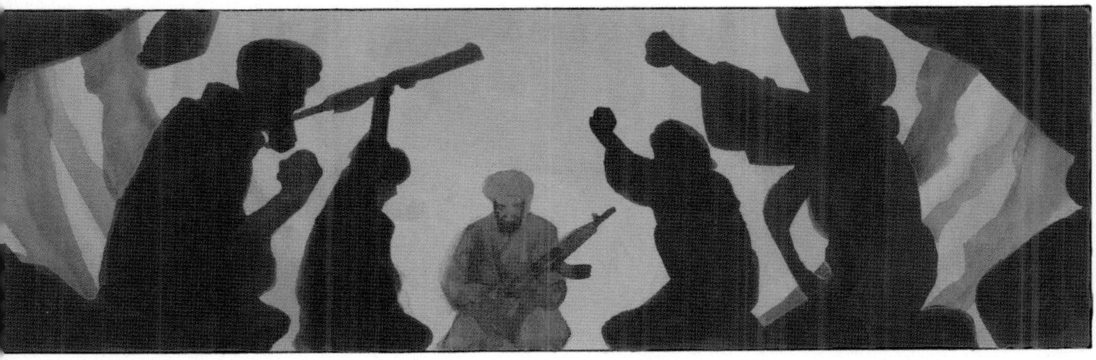

Twenty minutes --

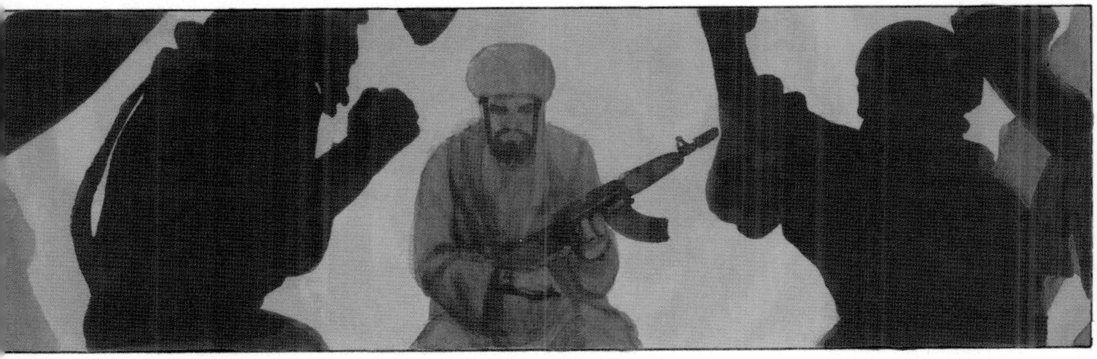

Four thousand murders later --

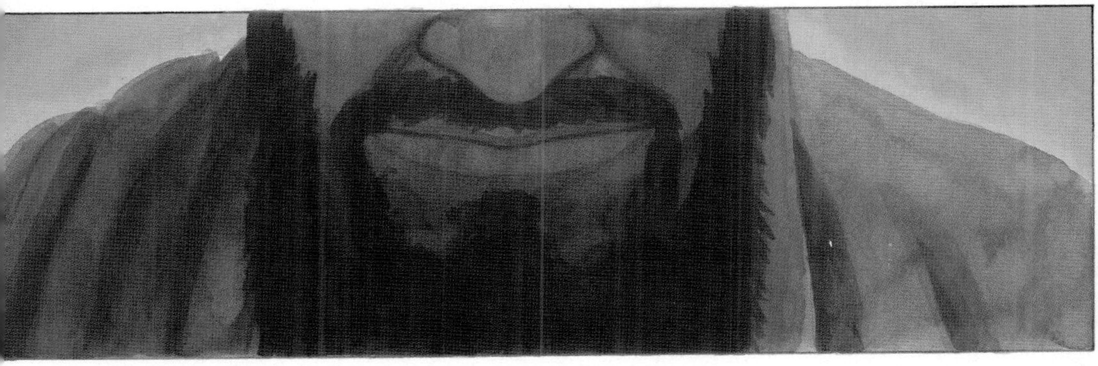

They praise God for the blood that stains their hands.

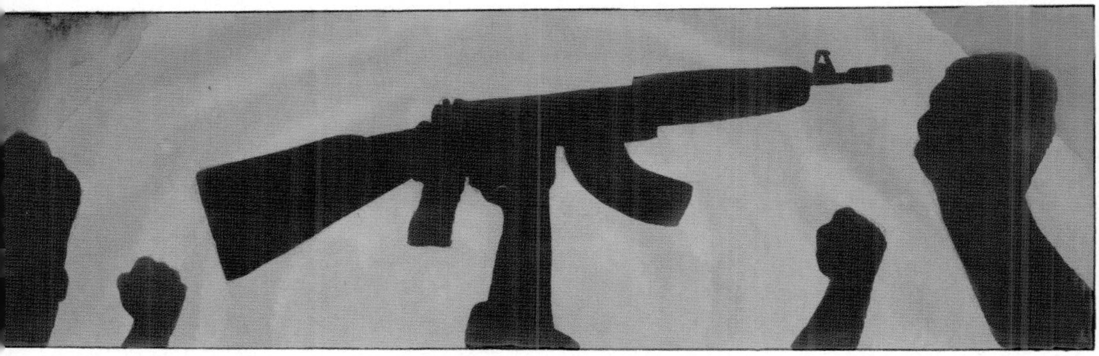

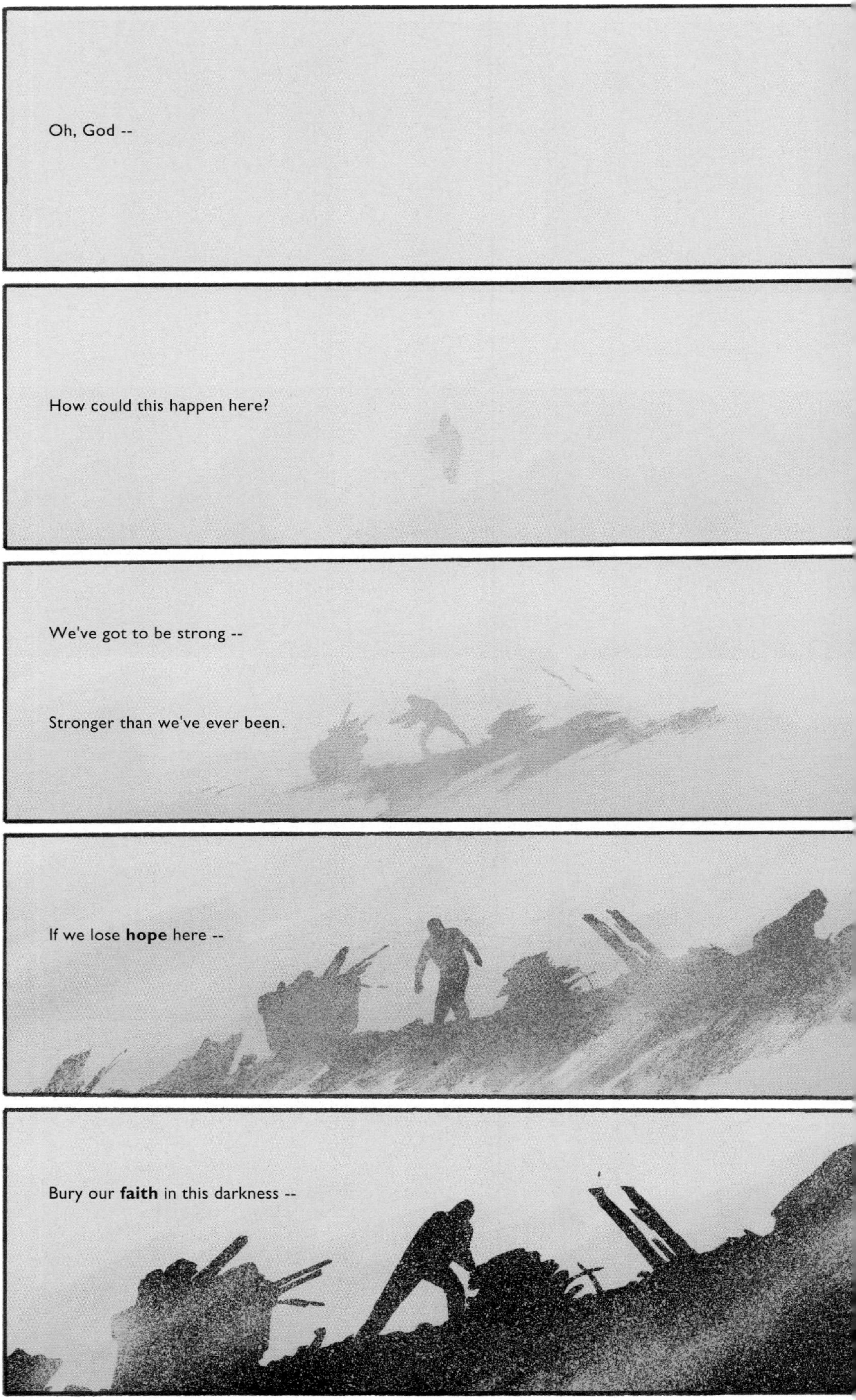
Oh, God --
How could this happen here?
We've got to be strong --
Stronger than we've ever been.
If we lose **hope** here --
Bury our **faith** in this darkness --

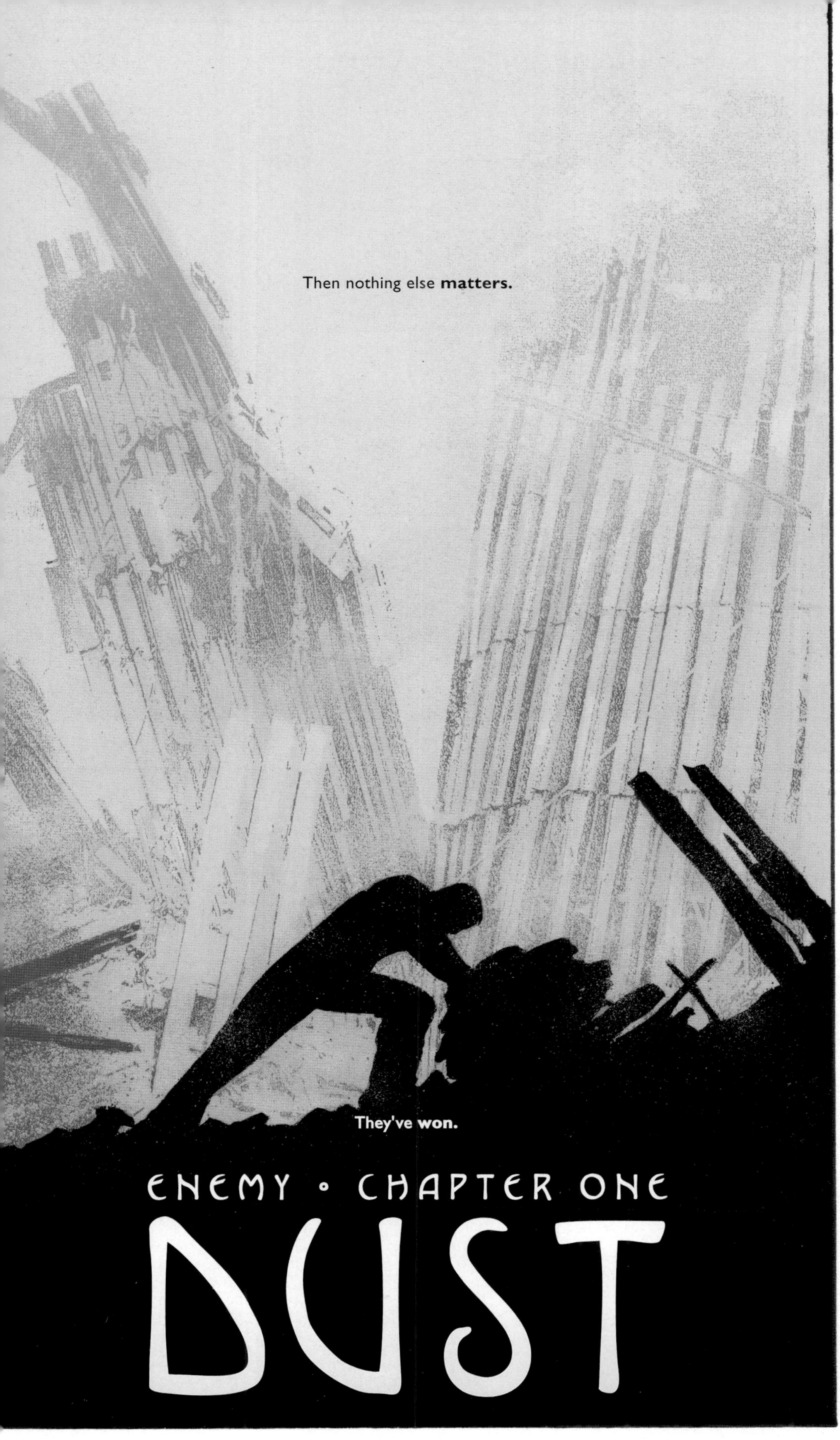
Then nothing else **matters.**
They've won.
ENEMY • CHAPTER ONE
DUST

This time --

This time --

Let it not be

Too late.

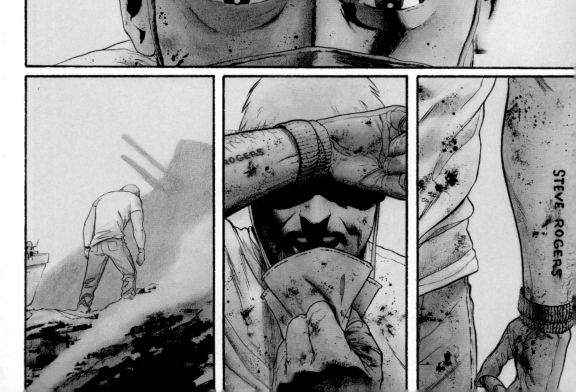

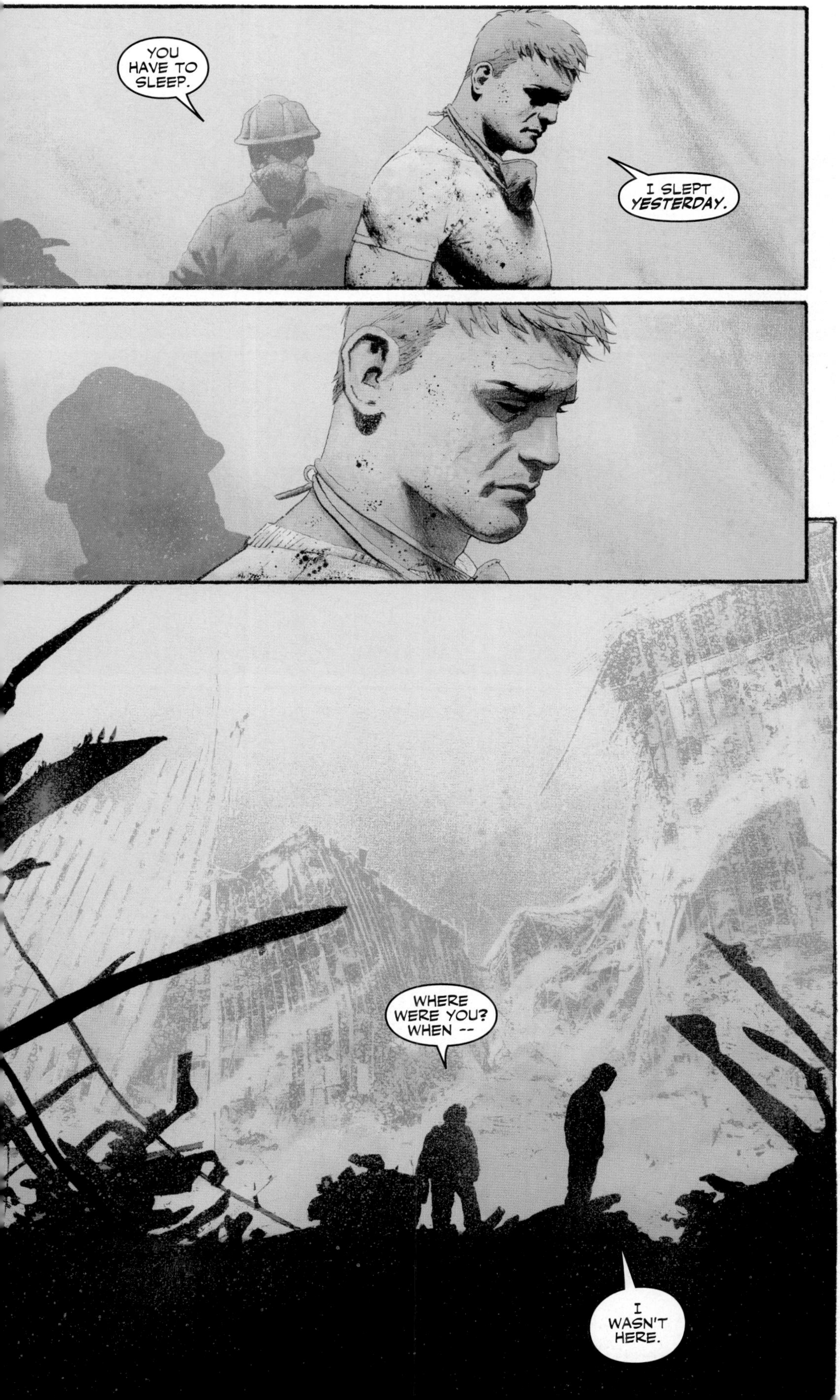
YOU HAVE TO SLEEP.
I SLEPT YESTERDAY.
WHERE WERE YOU? WHEN --
I WASN'T HERE.

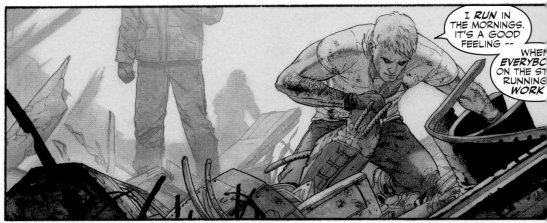

I *RUN* IN THE MORNINGS. IT'S A GOOD FEELING -- WHEN *EVERYBO* ON THE ST RUNNING *WORK*

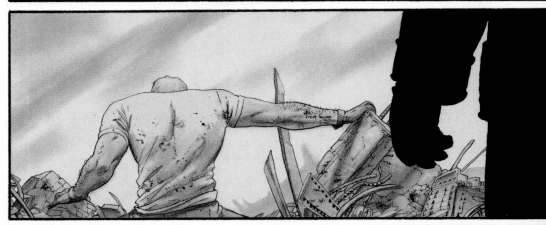

I SAW A MAN AND A WOMAN --

WHEN I'D RUN HERE FROM THE PARK.

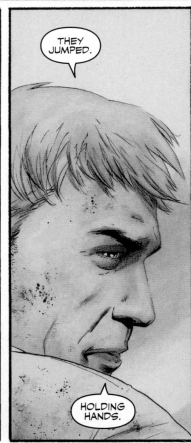

THEY JUMPED.

HOLDING HANDS.

I'LL GET A STRETCHER.

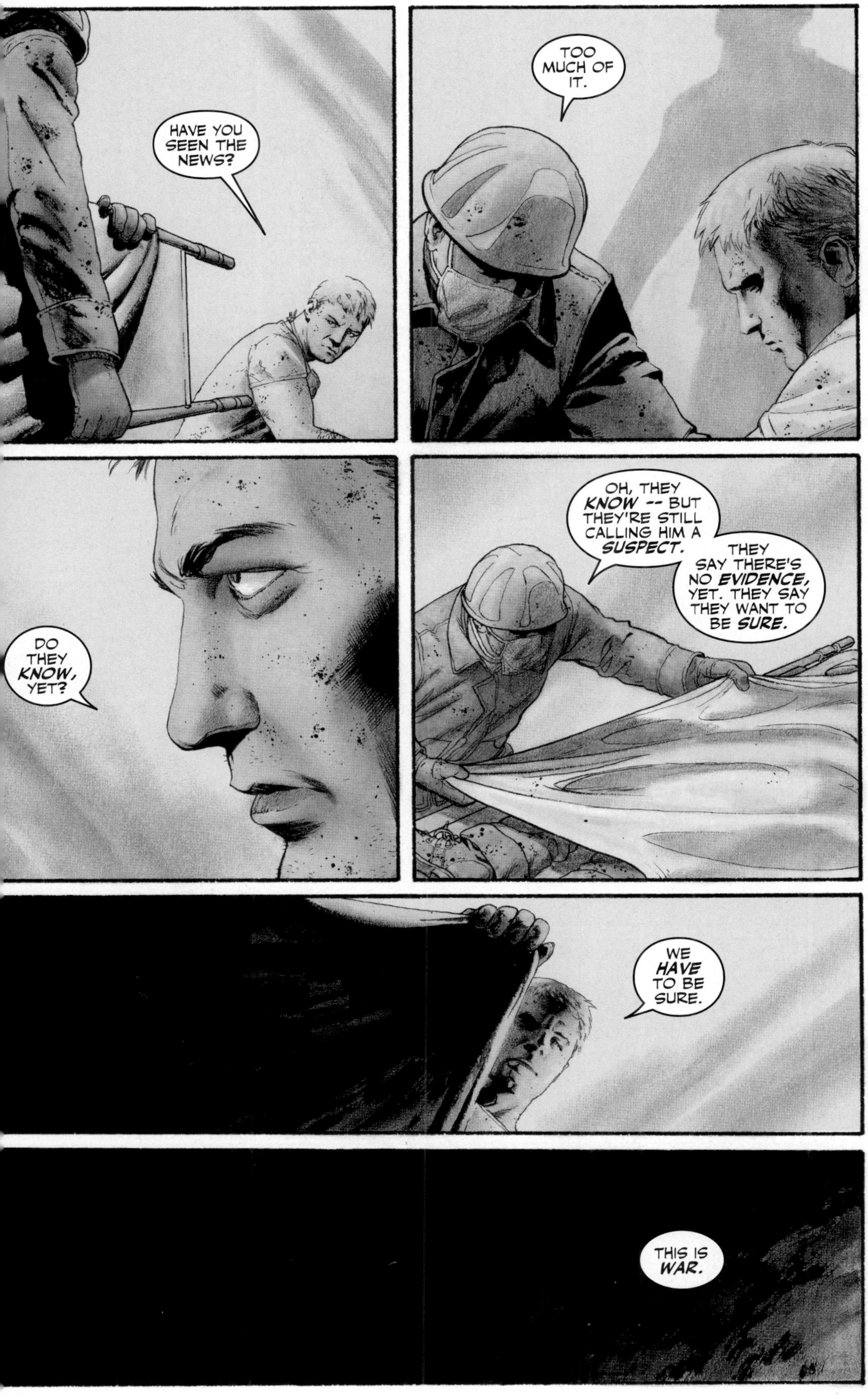
HAVE YOU SEEN THE NEWS?
TOO MUCH OF IT.
DO THEY KNOW, YET?
OH, THEY KNOW -- BUT THEY'RE STILL CALLING HIM A SUSPECT.
THEY SAY THERE'S NO EVIDENCE, YET. THEY SAY THEY WANT TO BE SURE.
WE HAVE TO BE SURE.
THIS IS WAR.

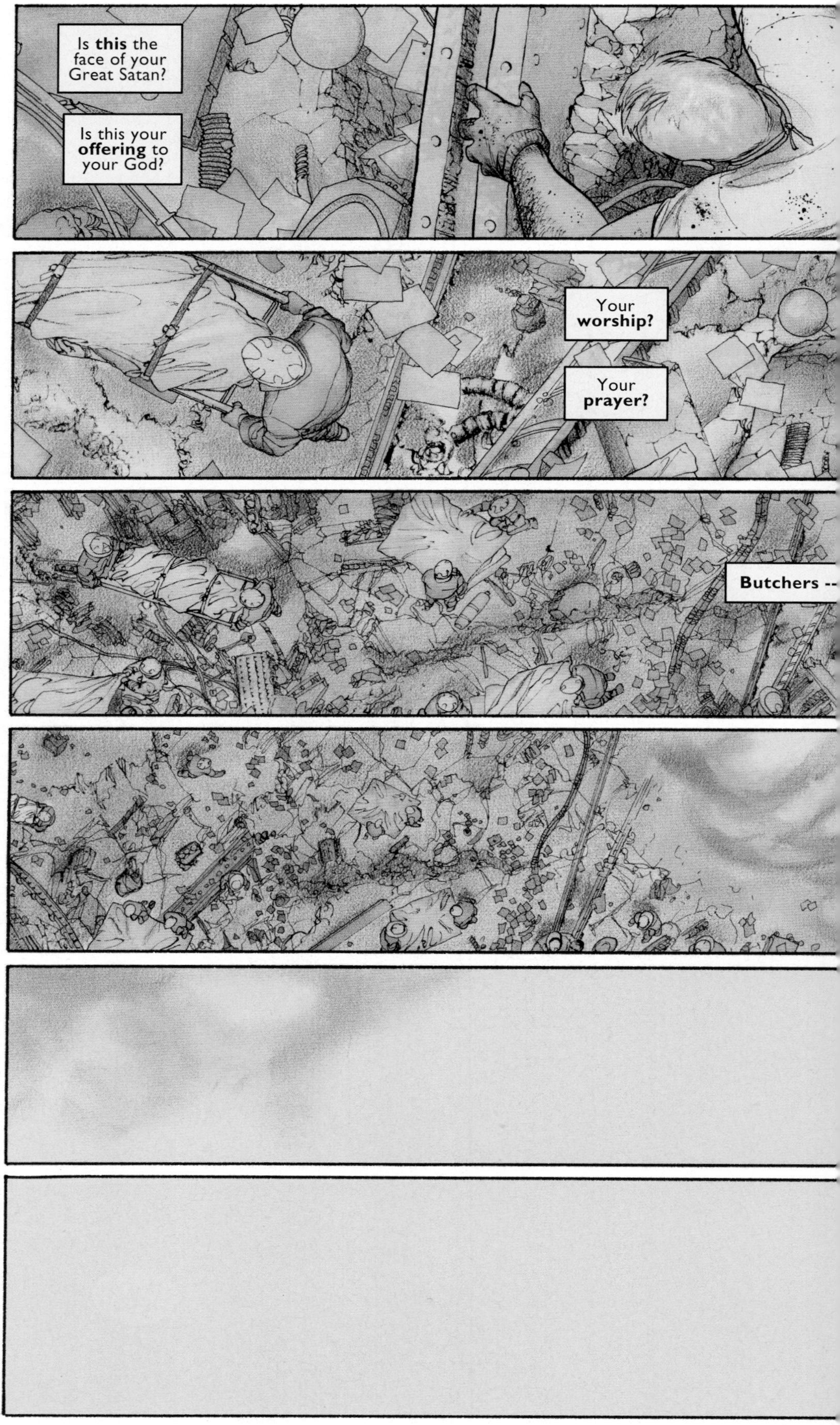
Is this the face of your Great Satan?
Is this your offering to your God?
Your worship?
Your prayer?
Butchers --

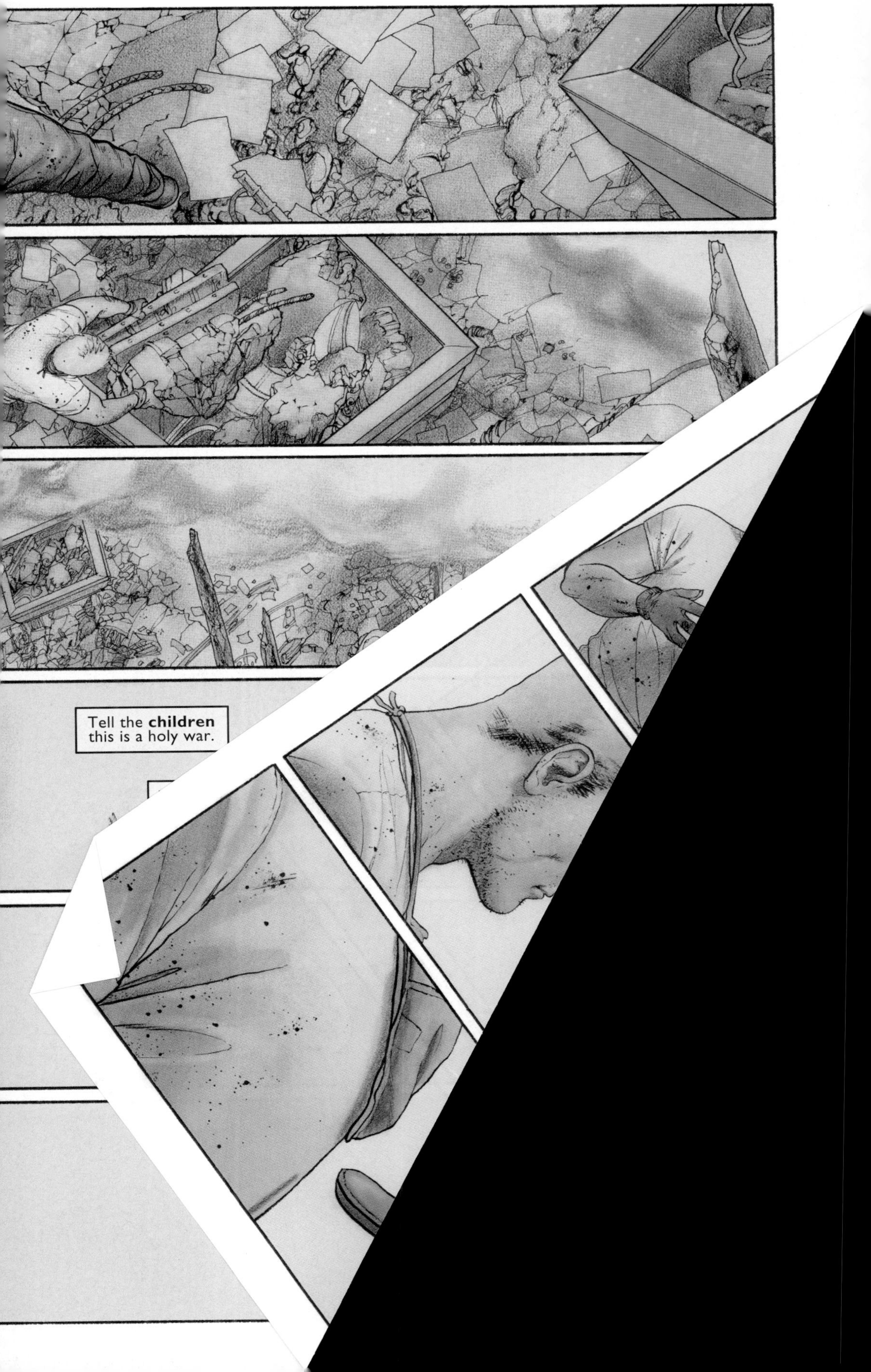
Tell the **children** this is a holy war.

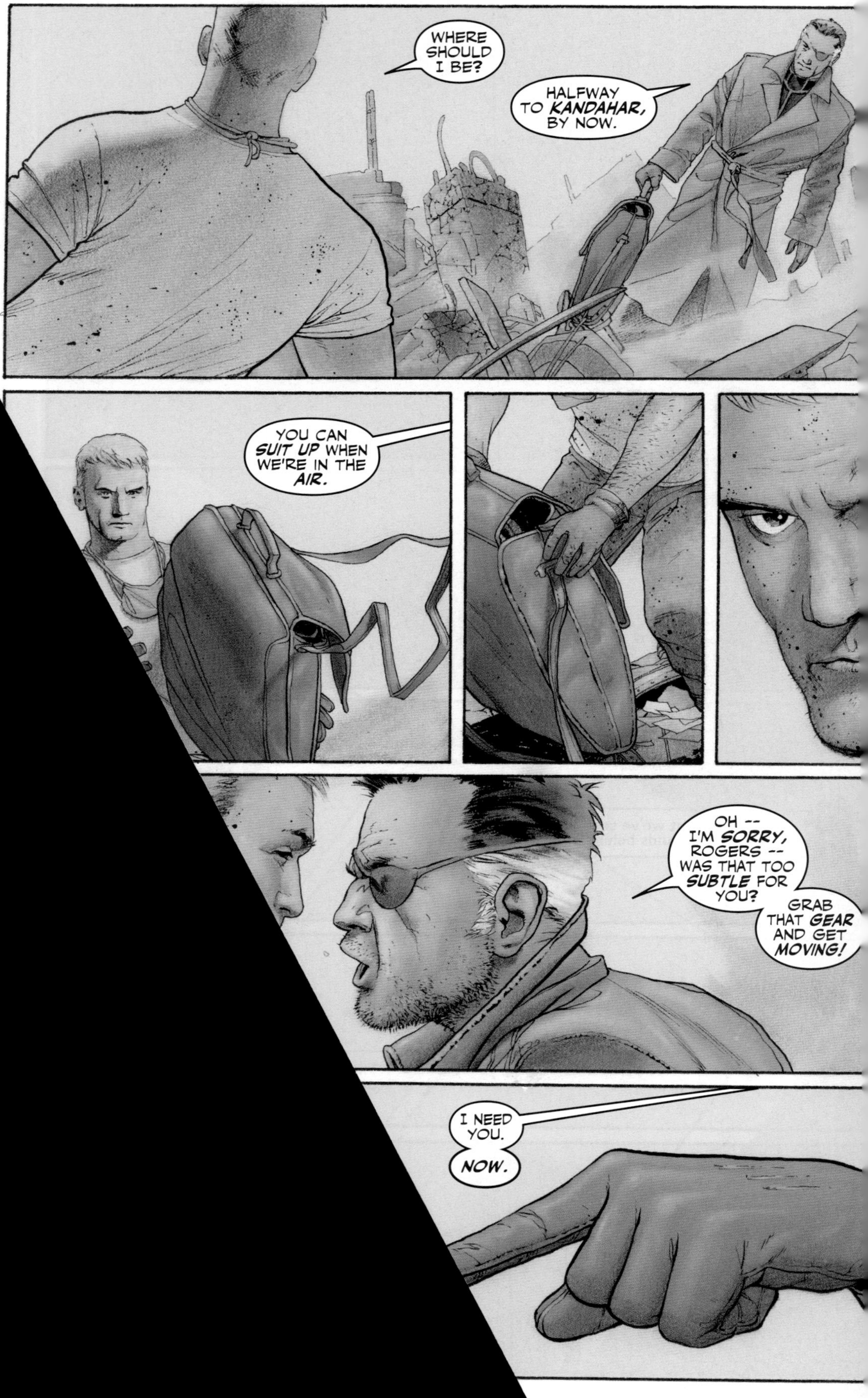
WHERE SHOULD I BE?
HALFWAY TO ***KANDAHAR,*** BY NOW.
YOU CAN ***SUIT UP*** WHEN WE'RE IN THE ***AIR.***
OH -- I'M ***SORRY,*** ROGERS -- WAS THAT TOO ***SUBTLE*** FOR YOU?
GRAB THAT ***GEAR*** AND GET ***MOVING!***
I NEED YOU.
NOW.

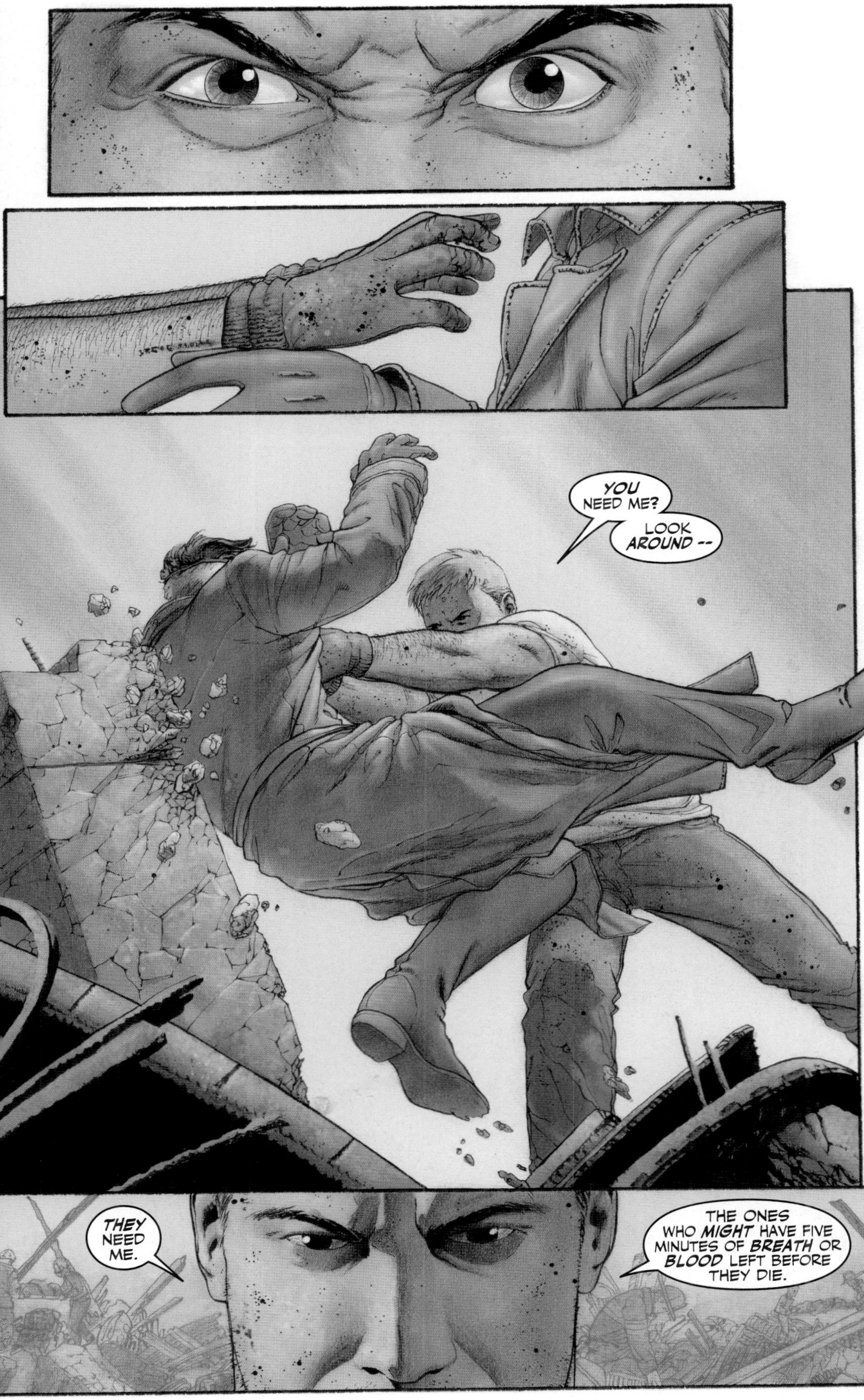
YOU NEED ME?
LOOK AROUND --
THEY NEED ME.
THE ONES WHO MIGHT HAVE FIVE MINUTES OF BREATH OR BLOOD LEFT BEFORE THEY DIE.

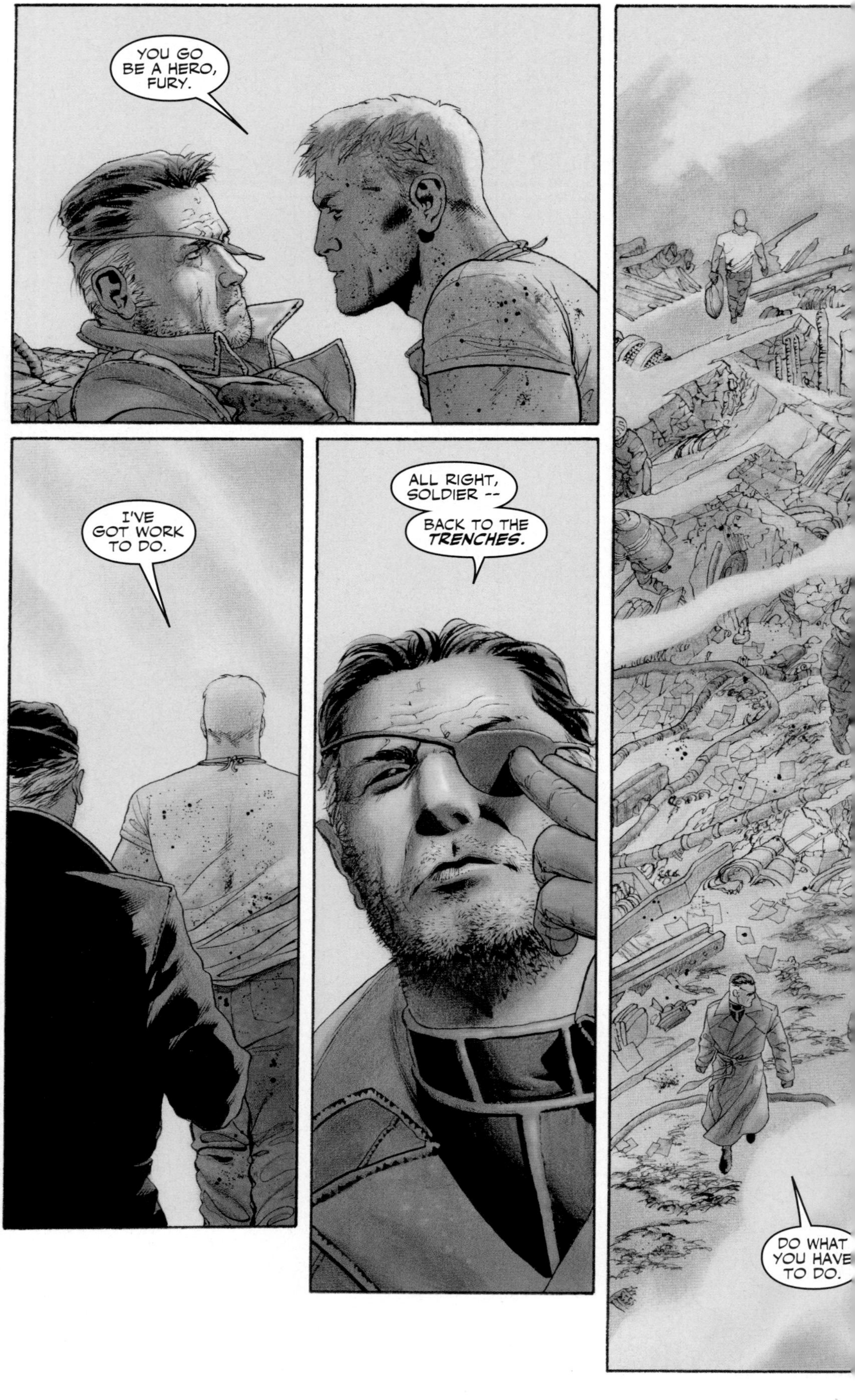
YOU GO BE A HERO, FURY.
I'VE GOT WORK TO DO.
ALL RIGHT, SOLDIER --
BACK TO THE TRENCHES.
DO WHAT YOU HAVE TO DO.

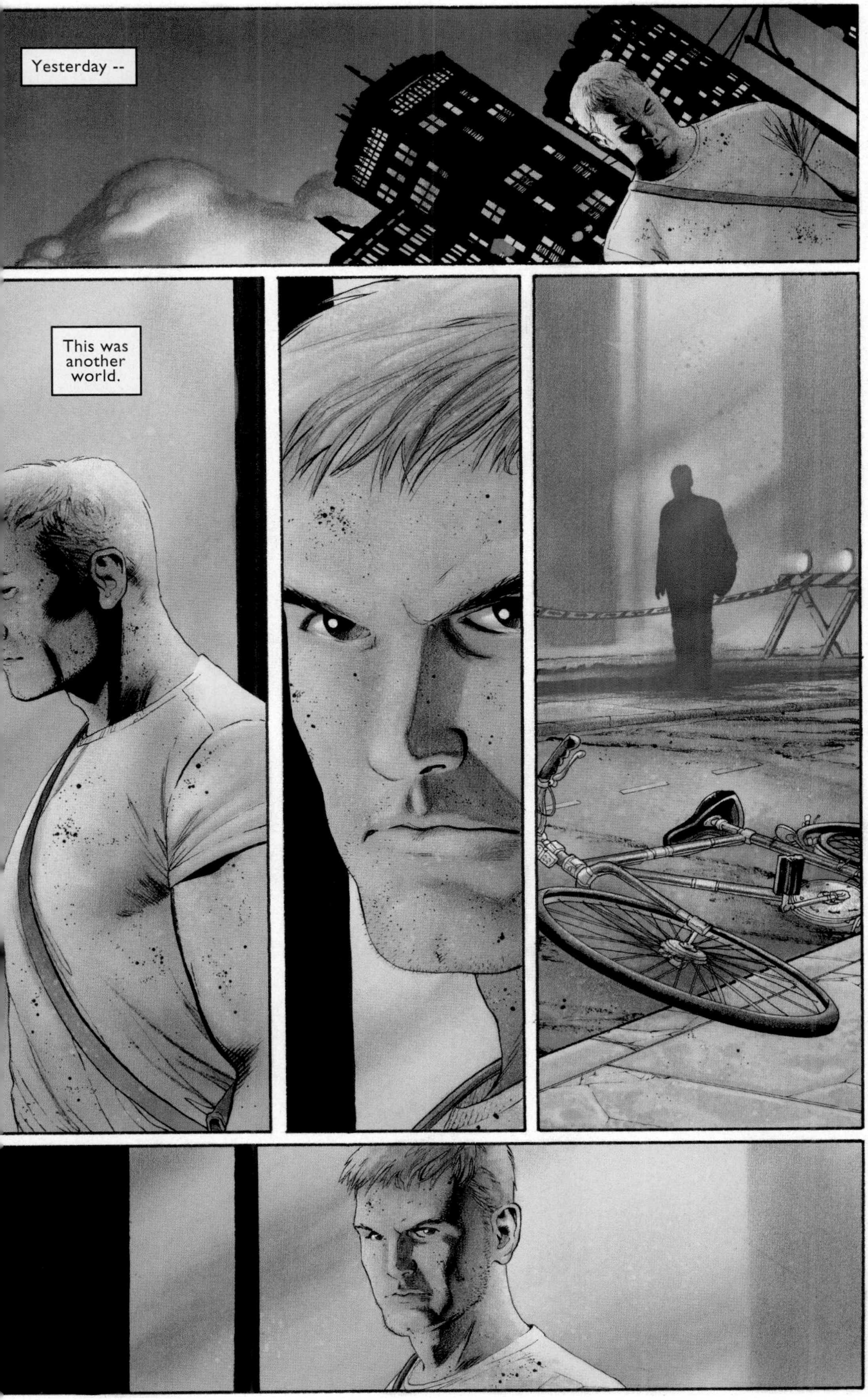
Yesterday --
This was another world.

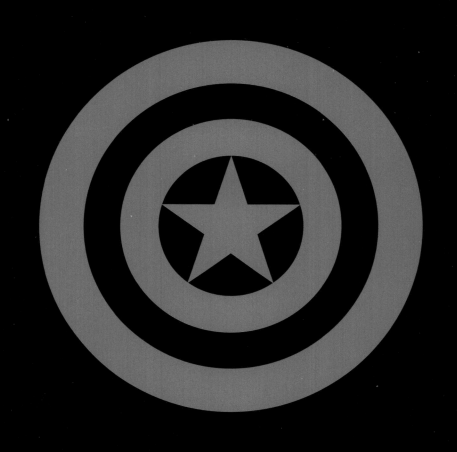

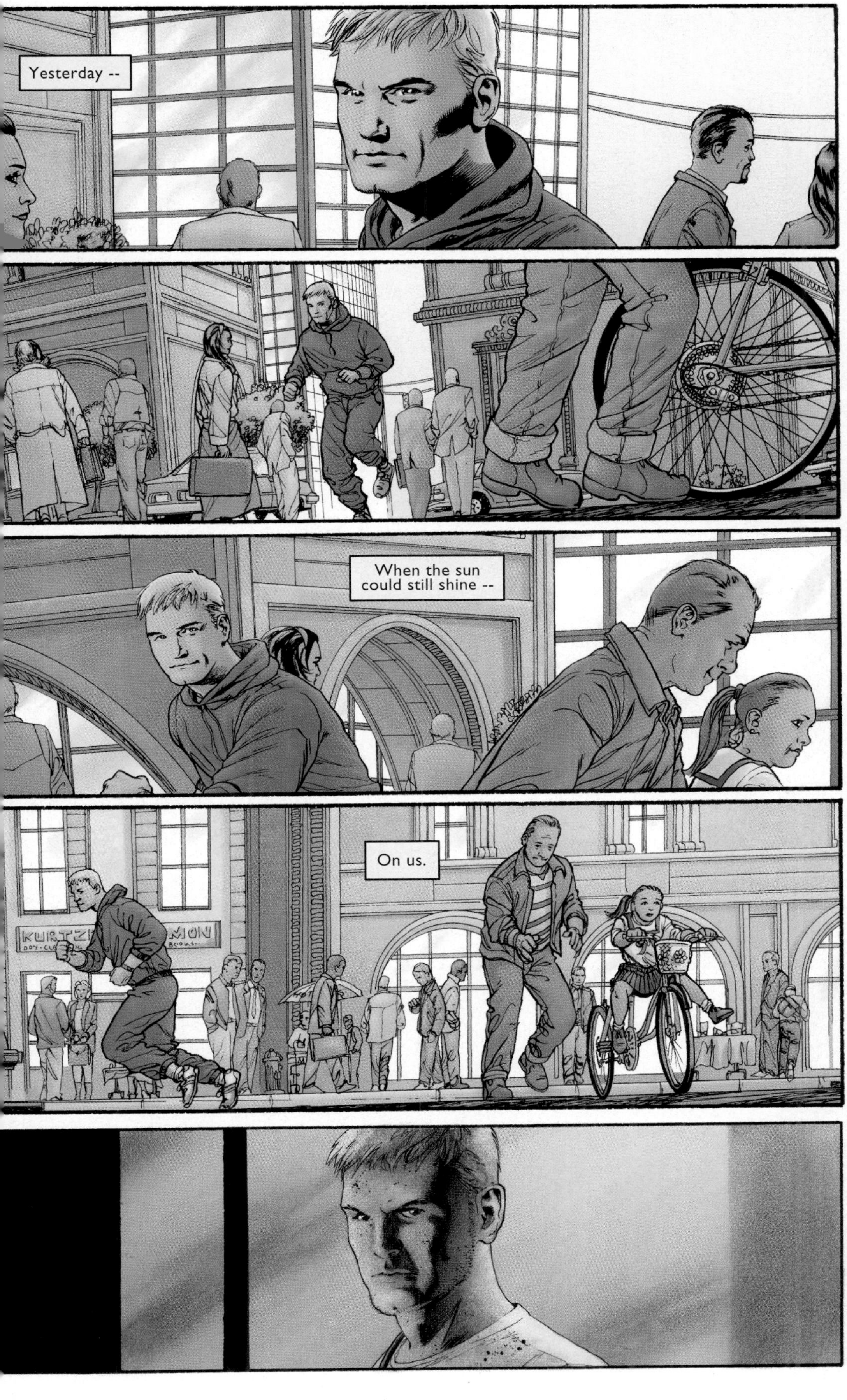
Yesterday --
When the sun could still shine --
On us.

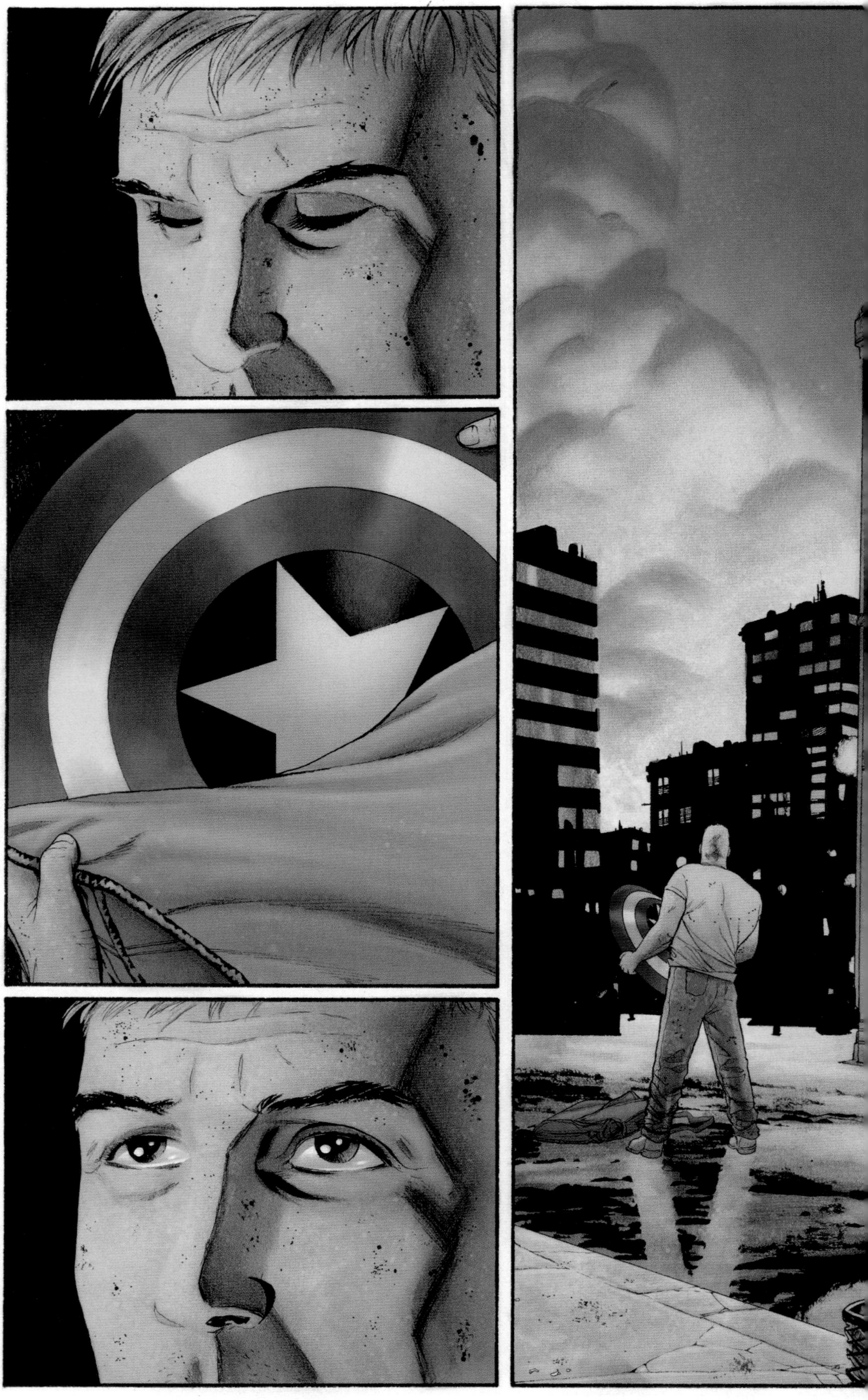

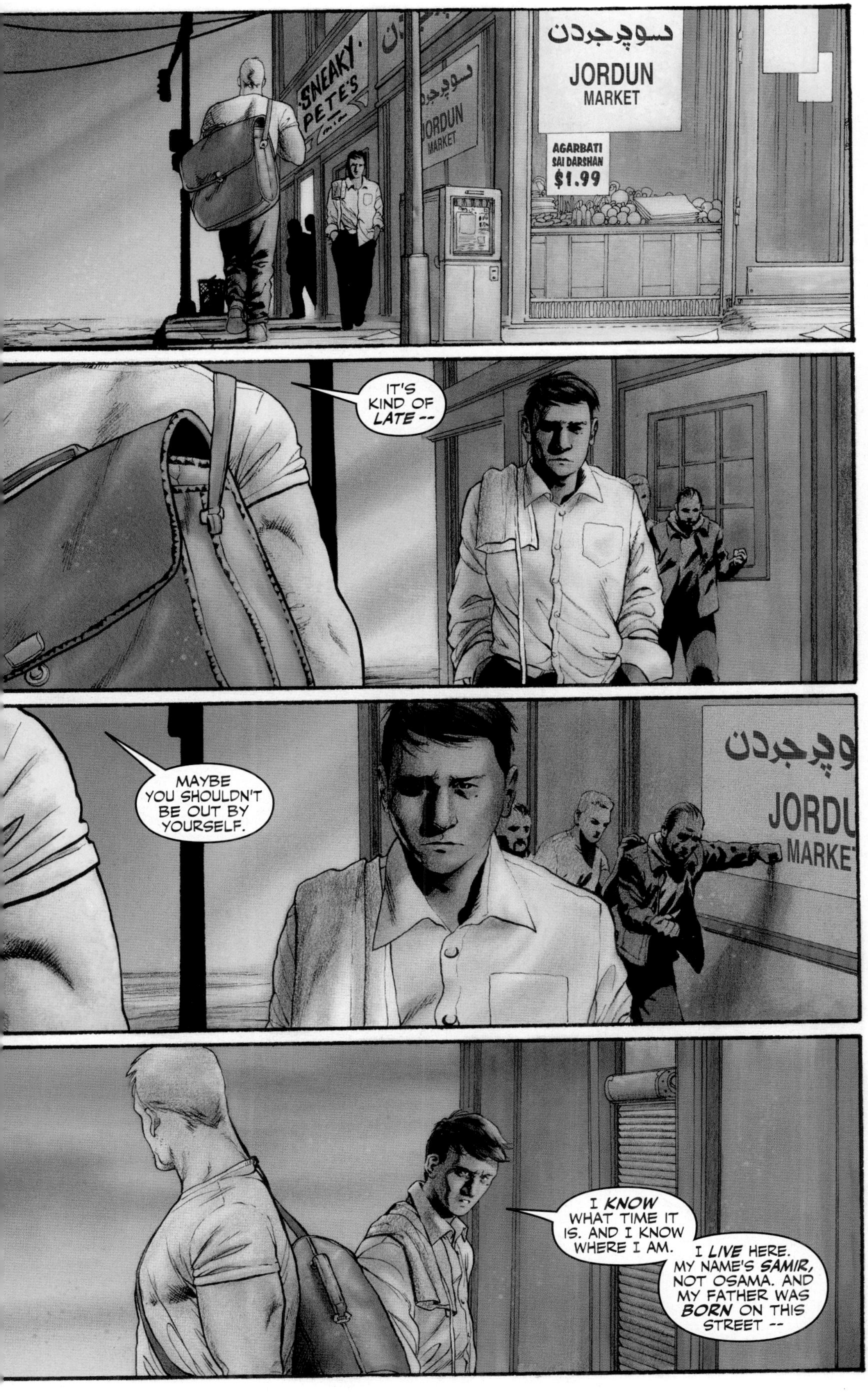
SNEAKY PETE'S
سوپرجردن
JORDUN MARKET
AGARBATI SAI DARSHAN $1.99
IT'S KIND OF *LATE* --
MAYBE YOU SHOULDN'T BE OUT BY YOURSELF.
I *KNOW* WHAT TIME IT IS. AND I KNOW WHERE I AM.
I *LIVE* HERE. MY NAME'S *SAMIR,* NOT OSAMA. AND MY FATHER WAS *BORN* ON THIS STREET --

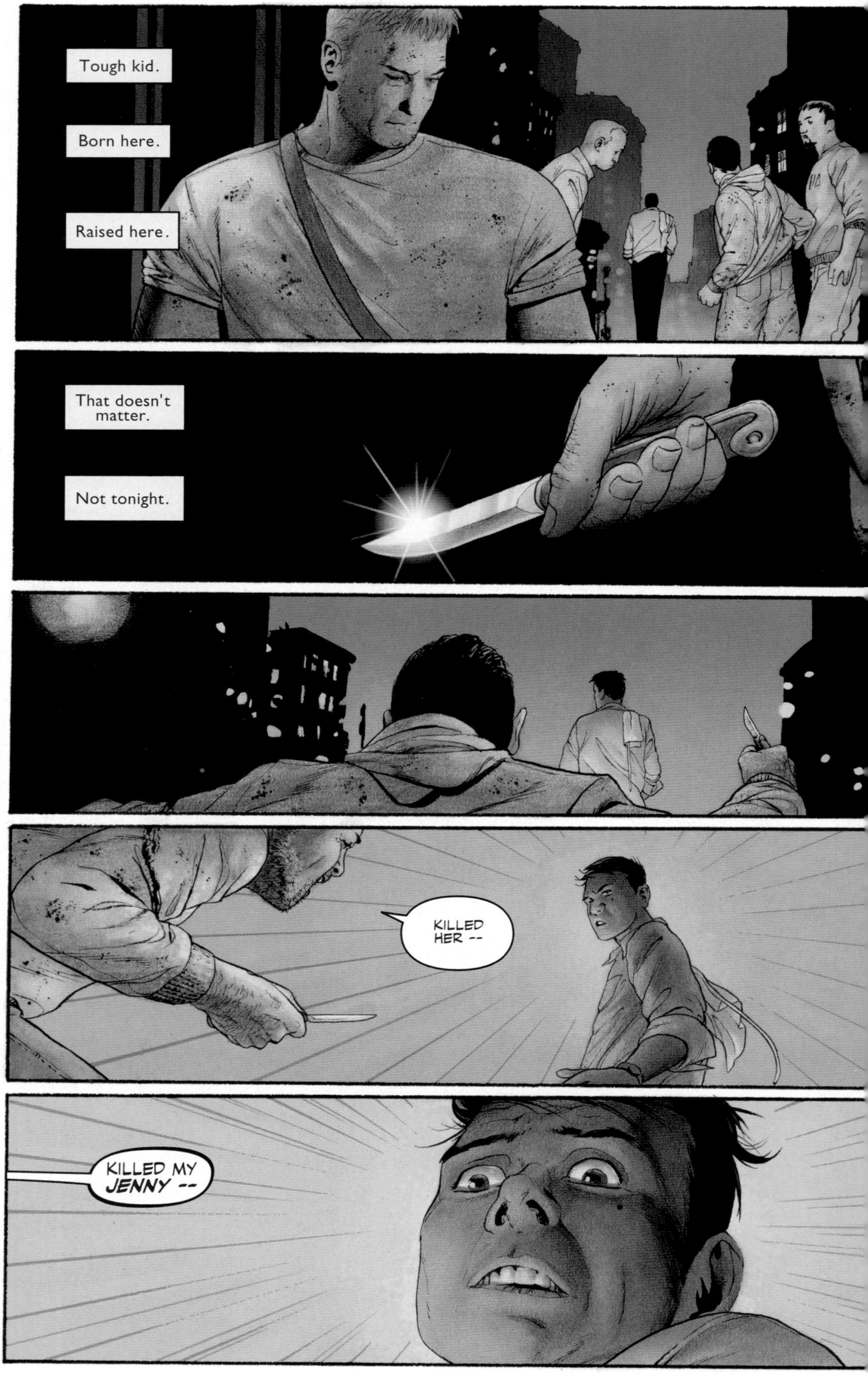
Tough kid.
Born here.
Raised here.
That doesn't matter.
Not tonight.
KILLED HER --
KILLED MY JENNY --

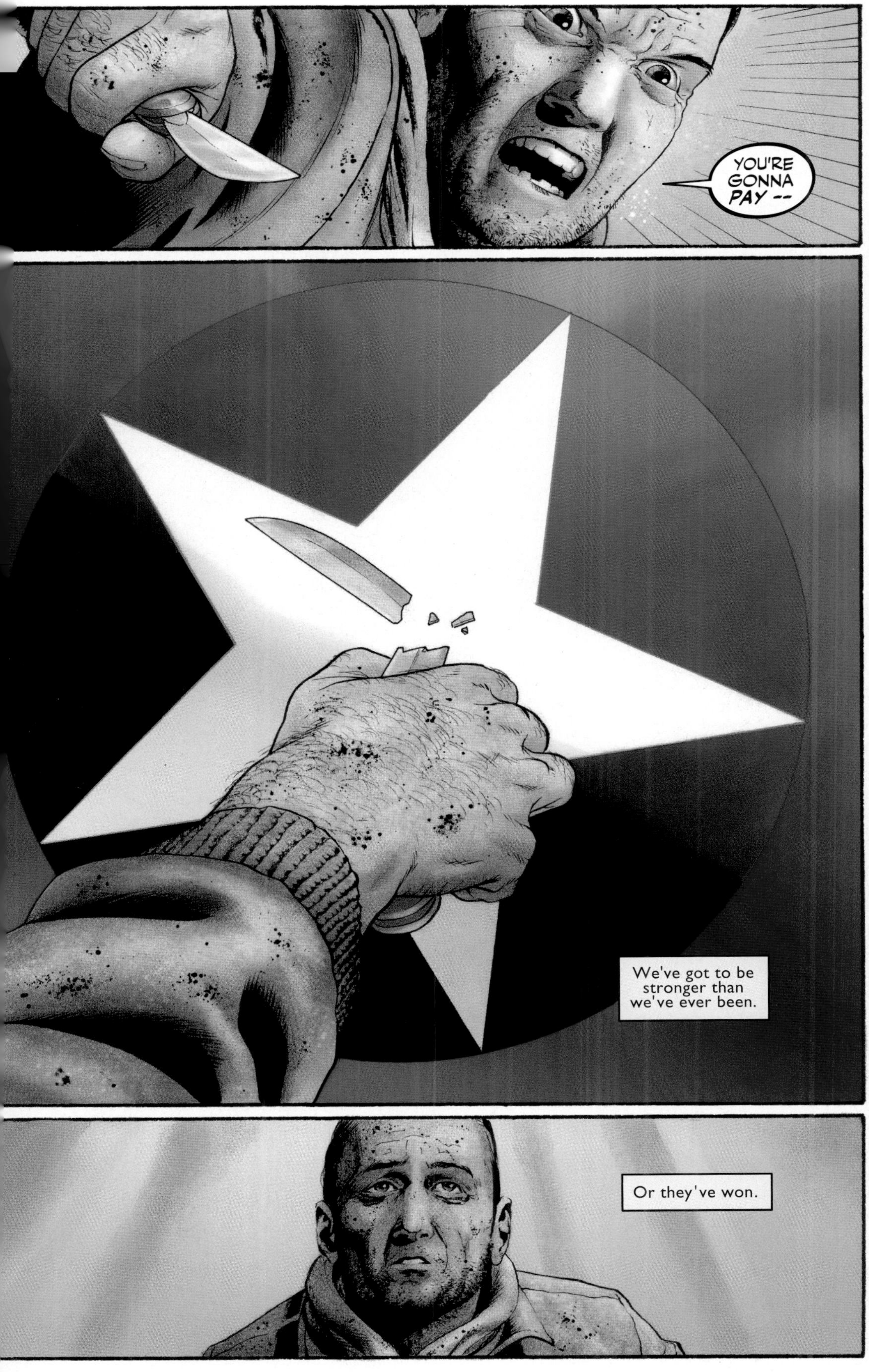
YOU'RE GONNA PAY --
We've got to be stronger than we've ever been.
Or they've won.

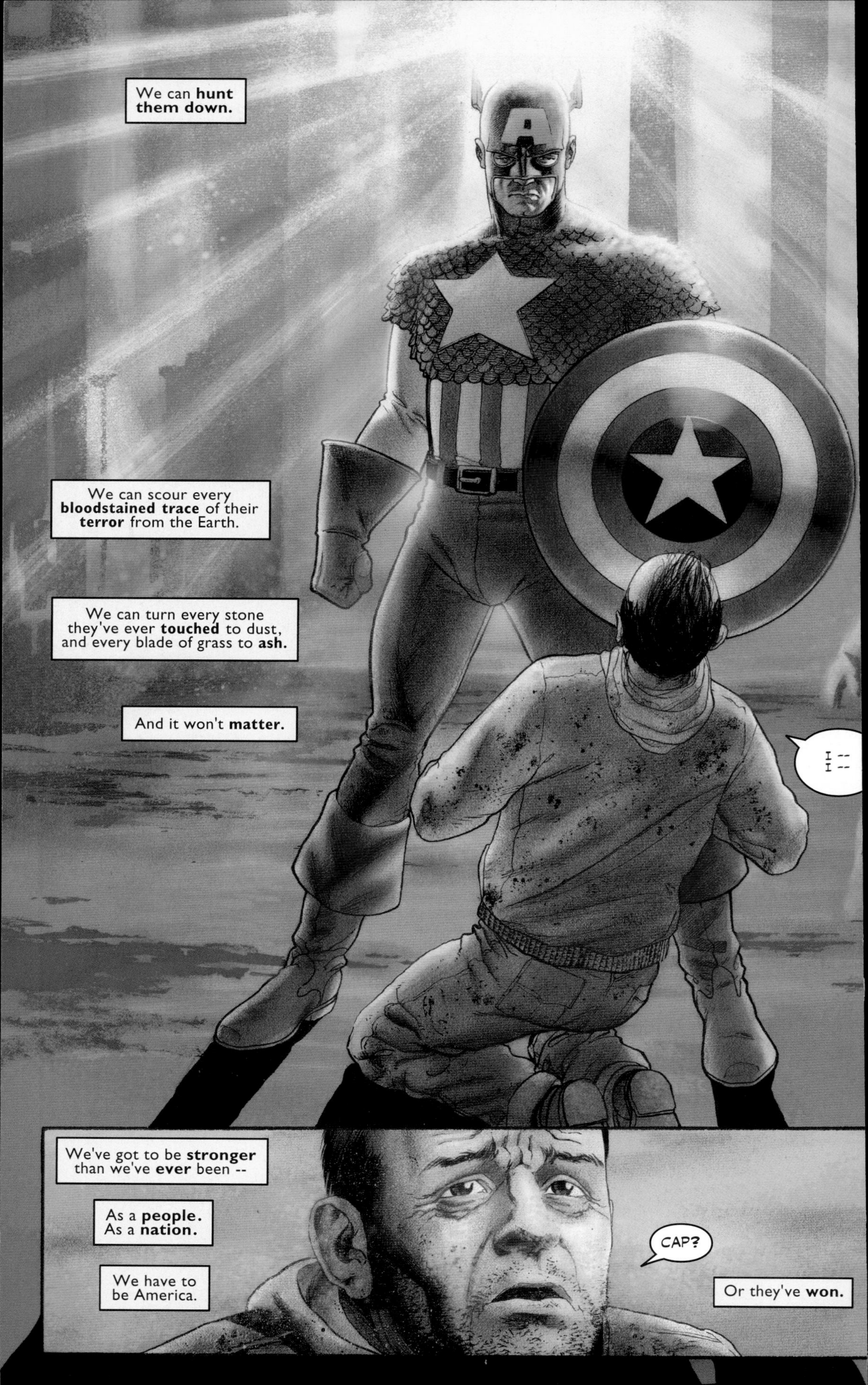

We can **hunt them down.**
We can scour every **bloodstained trace** of their **terror** from the Earth.
We can turn every stone they've ever **touched** to dust, and every blade of grass to **ash.**
And it won't **matter.**
I -- I --
We've got to be **stronger** than we've **ever** been --
As a **people.** As a **nation.**
We have to be America.
CAP?
Or they've **won.**

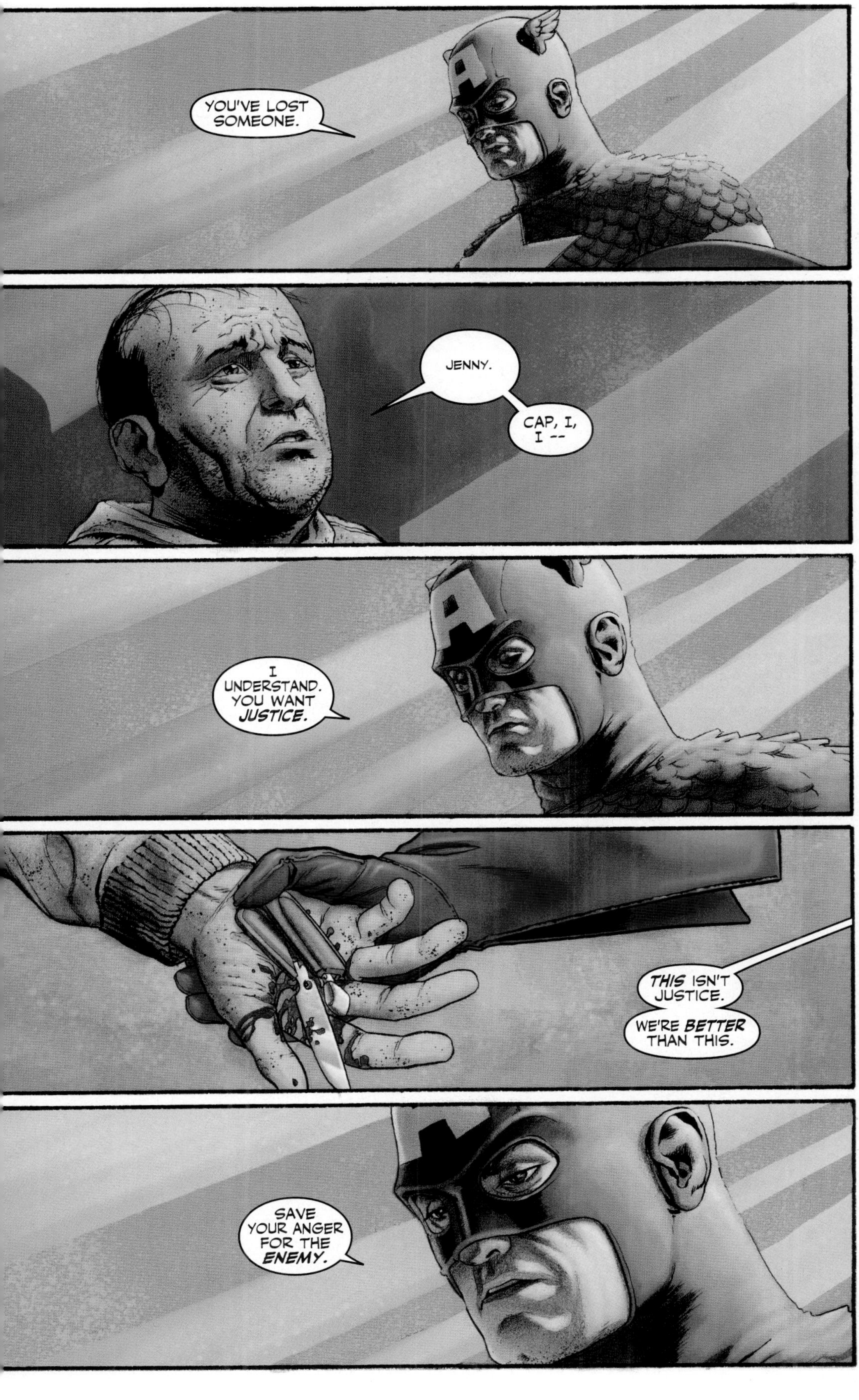
YOU'VE LOST SOMEONE.
JENNY.
CAP, I, I --
I UNDERSTAND. YOU WANT JUSTICE.
THIS ISN'T JUSTICE.
WE'RE BETTER THAN THIS.
SAVE YOUR ANGER FOR THE ENEMY.

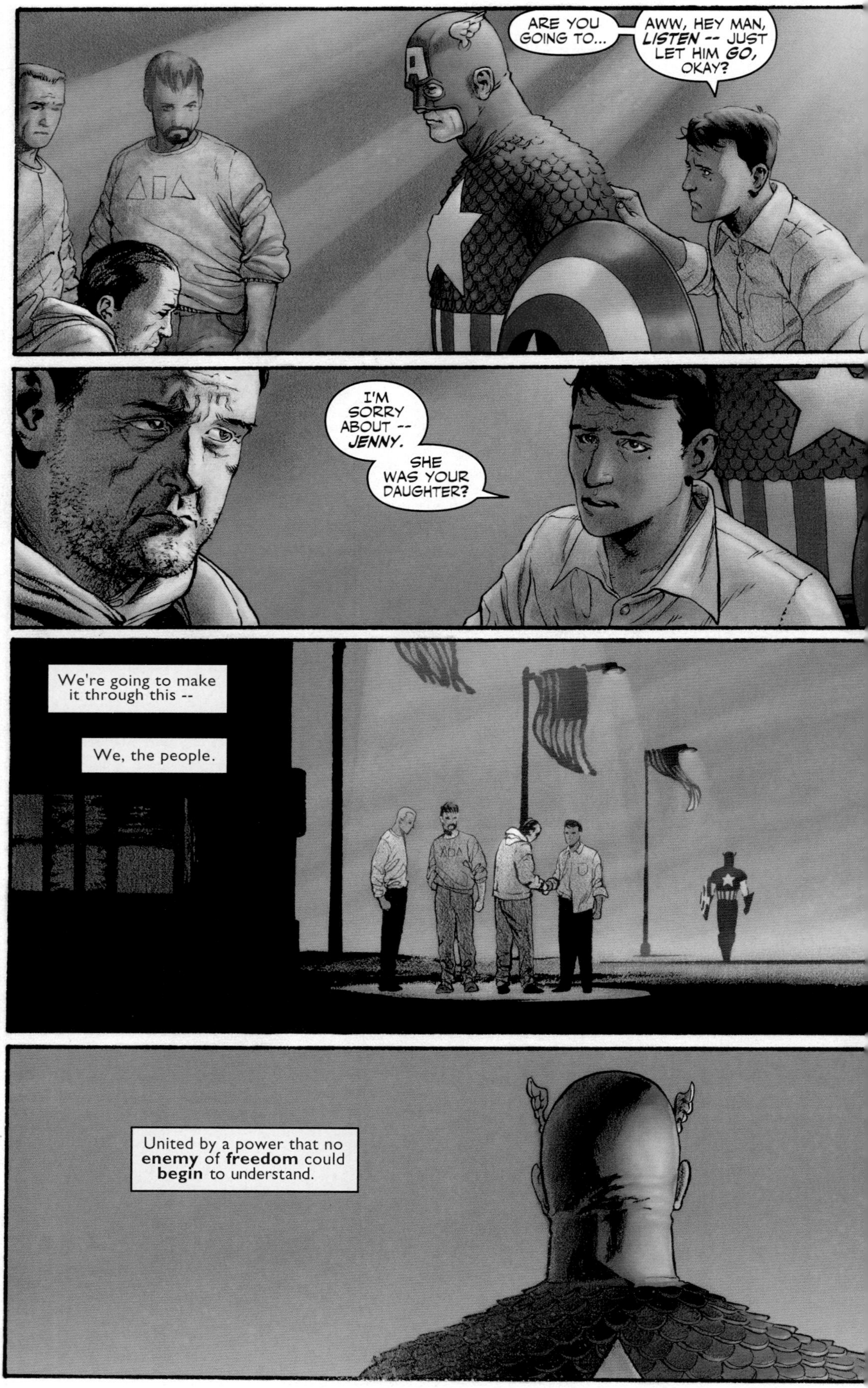
ARE YOU GOING TO...
AWW, HEY MAN, LISTEN -- JUST LET HIM GO, OKAY?
I'M SORRY ABOUT -- JENNY.
SHE WAS YOUR DAUGHTER?
We're going to make it through this --
We, the people.
United by a power that no enemy of freedom could begin to understand.

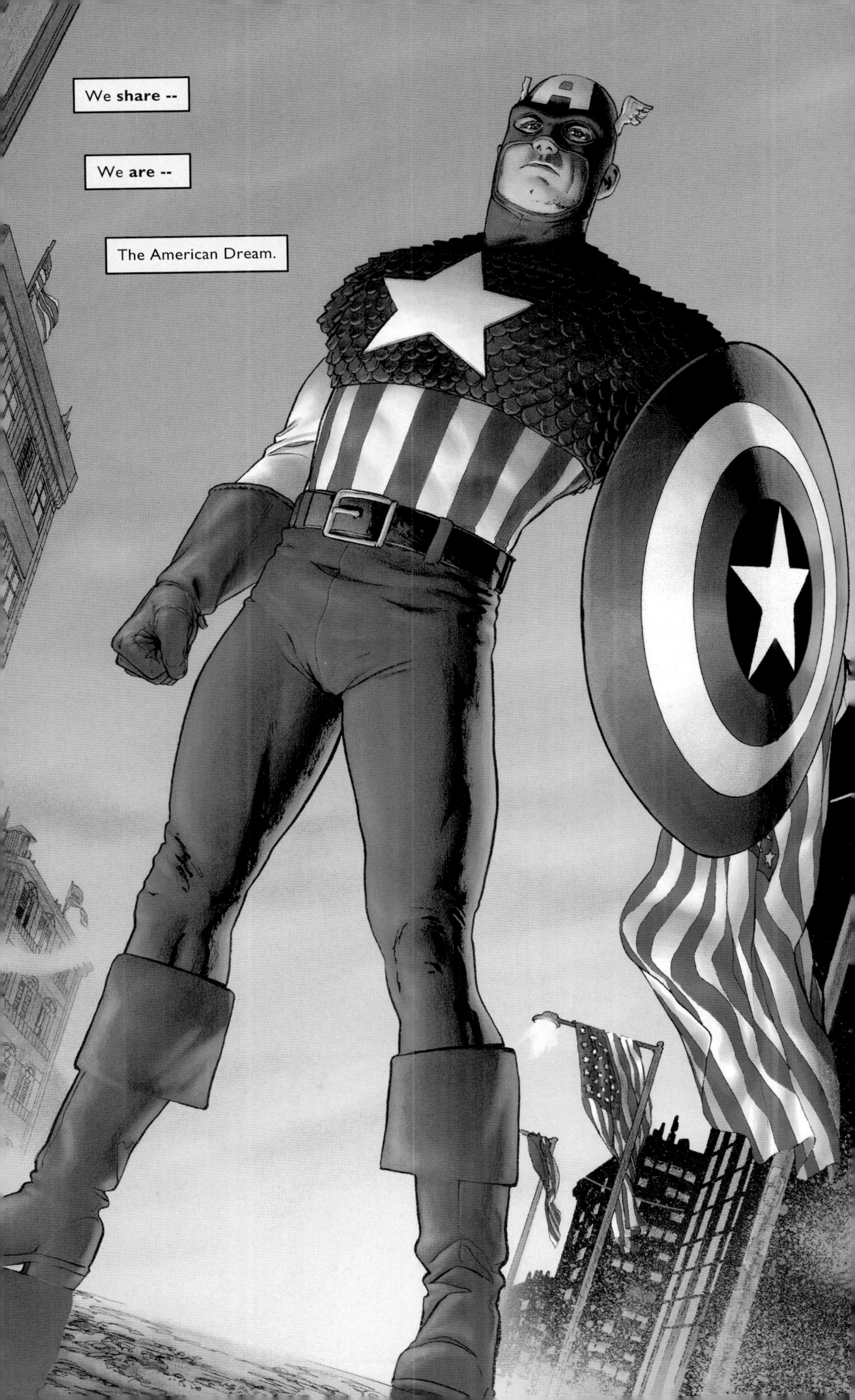
We share --
We are --
The American Dream.

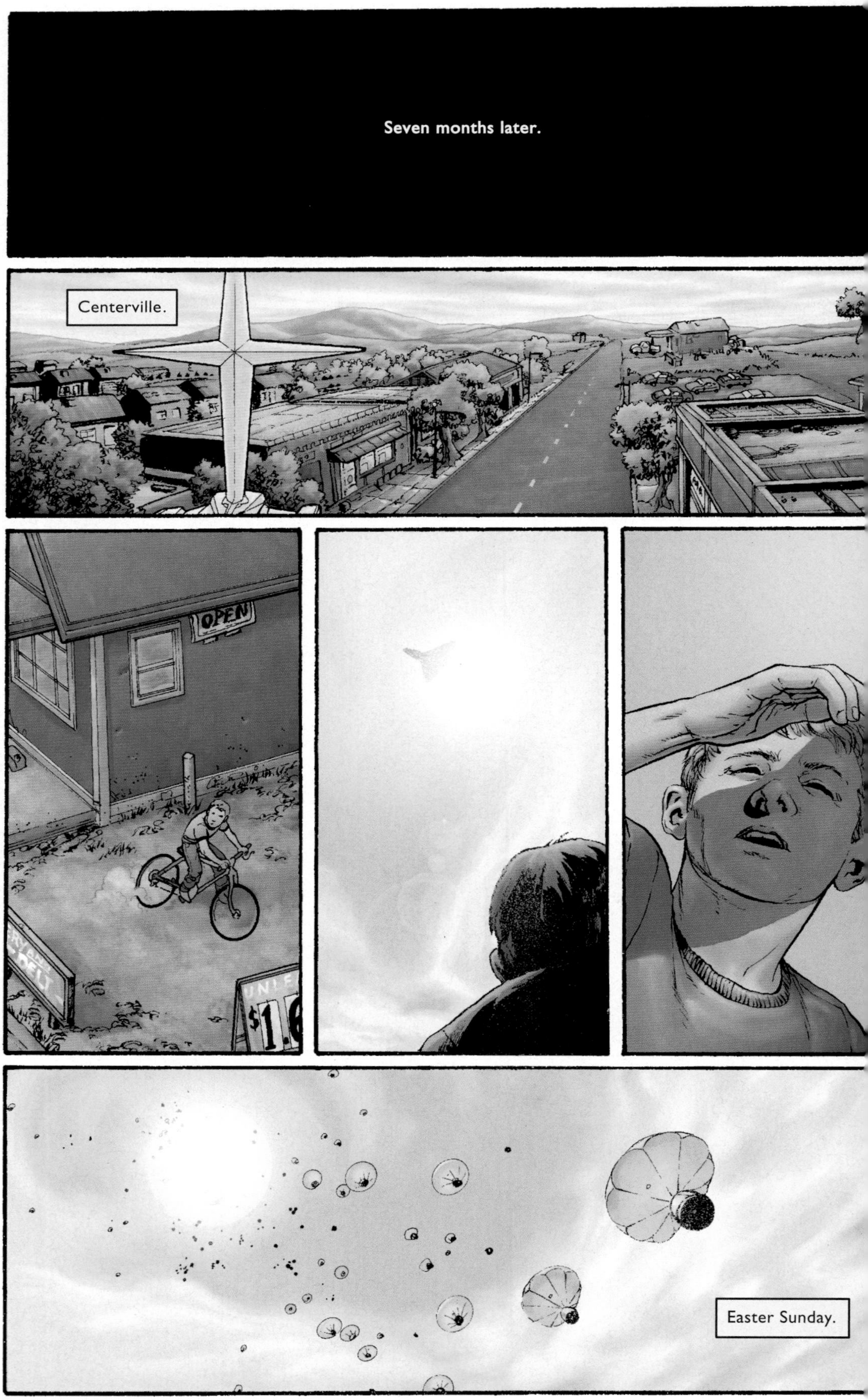
Seven months later.
Centerville.
OPEN
Easter Sunday.

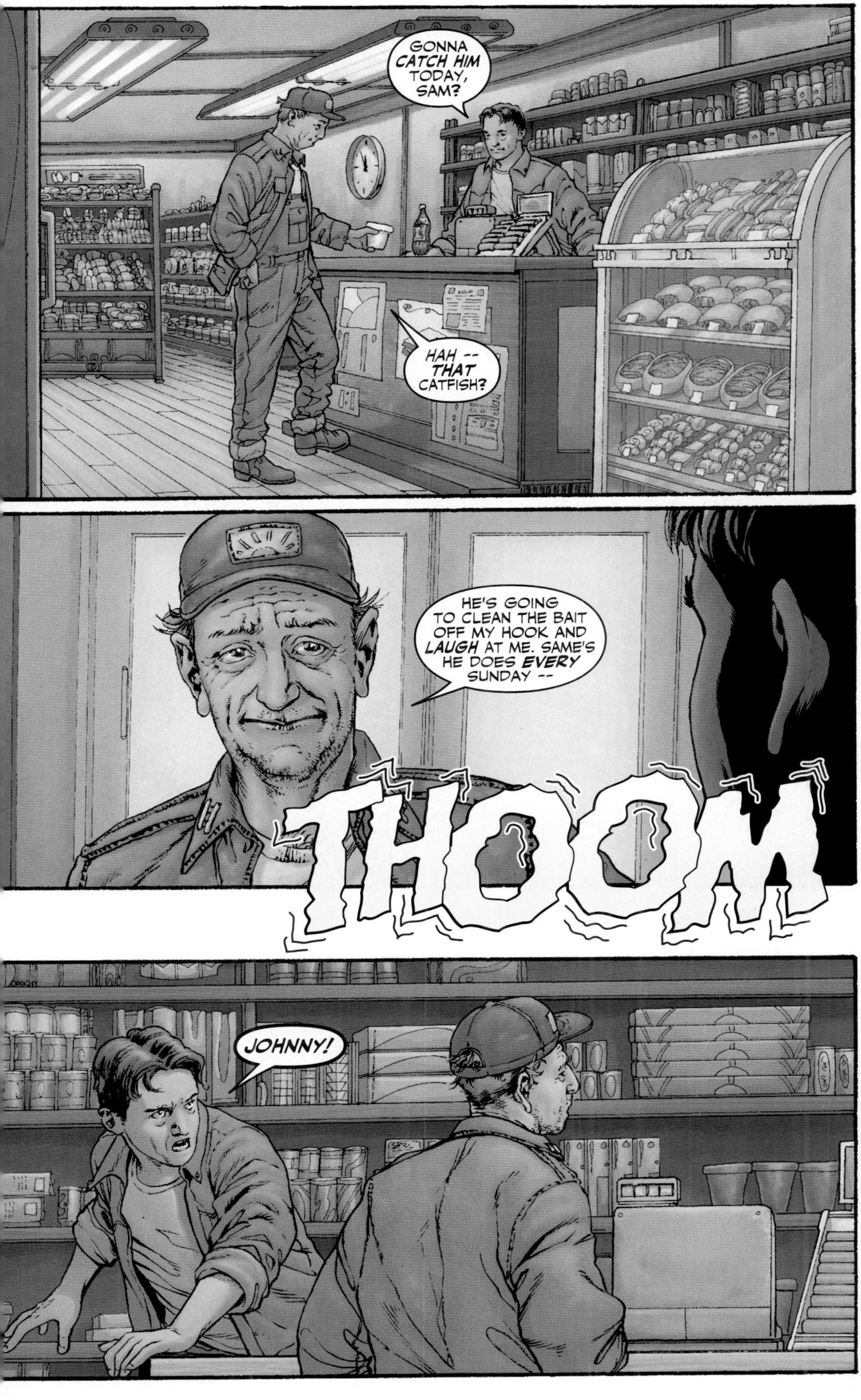
GONNA CATCH HIM TODAY, SAM?
HAH -- THAT CATFISH?
HE'S GOING TO CLEAN THE BAIT OFF MY HOOK AND LAUGH AT ME. SAME'S HE DOES EVERY SUNDAY --
THOOM
JOHNNY!

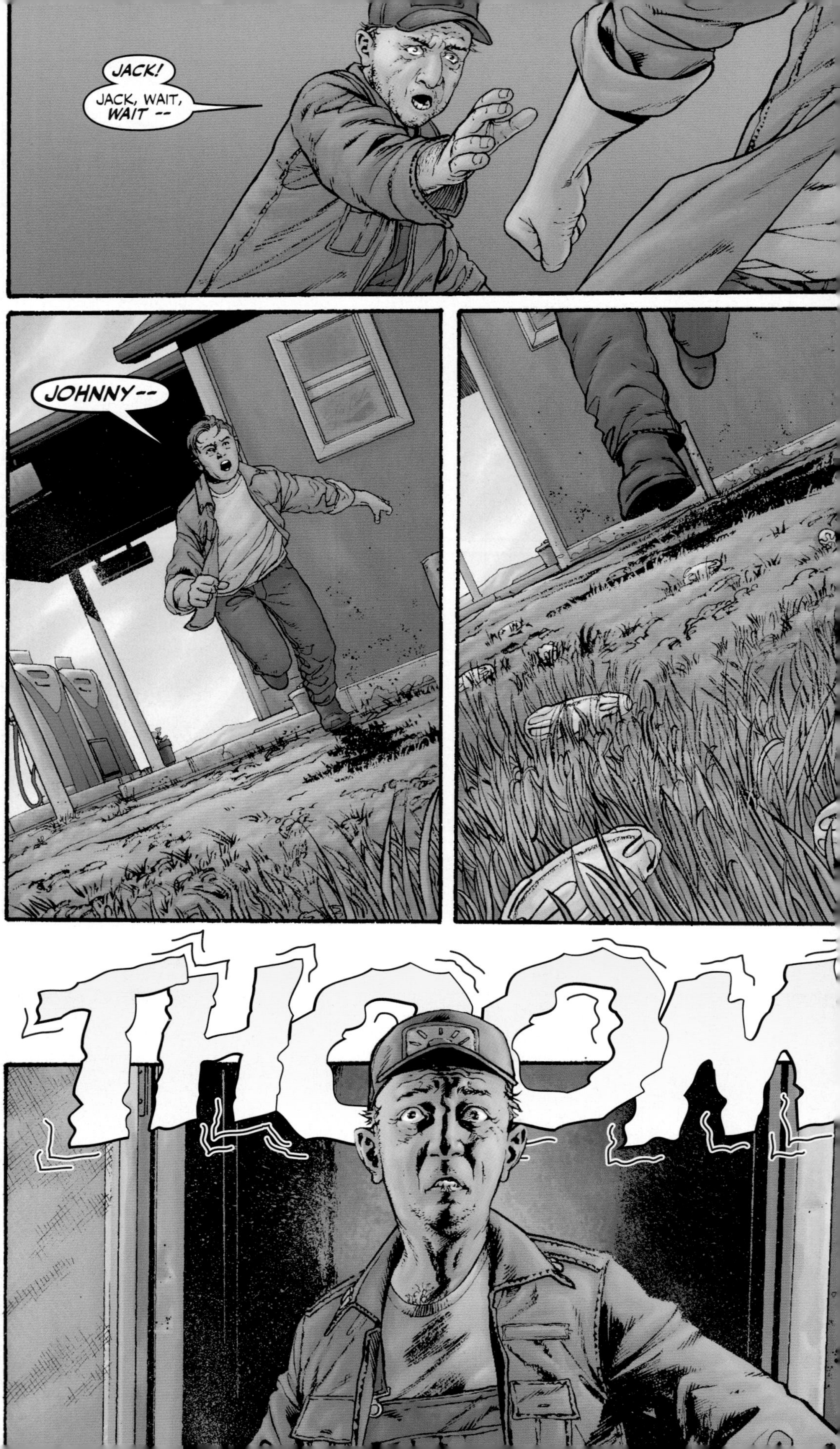
JACK!
JACK, WAIT, WAIT --
JOHNNY--
THOOM

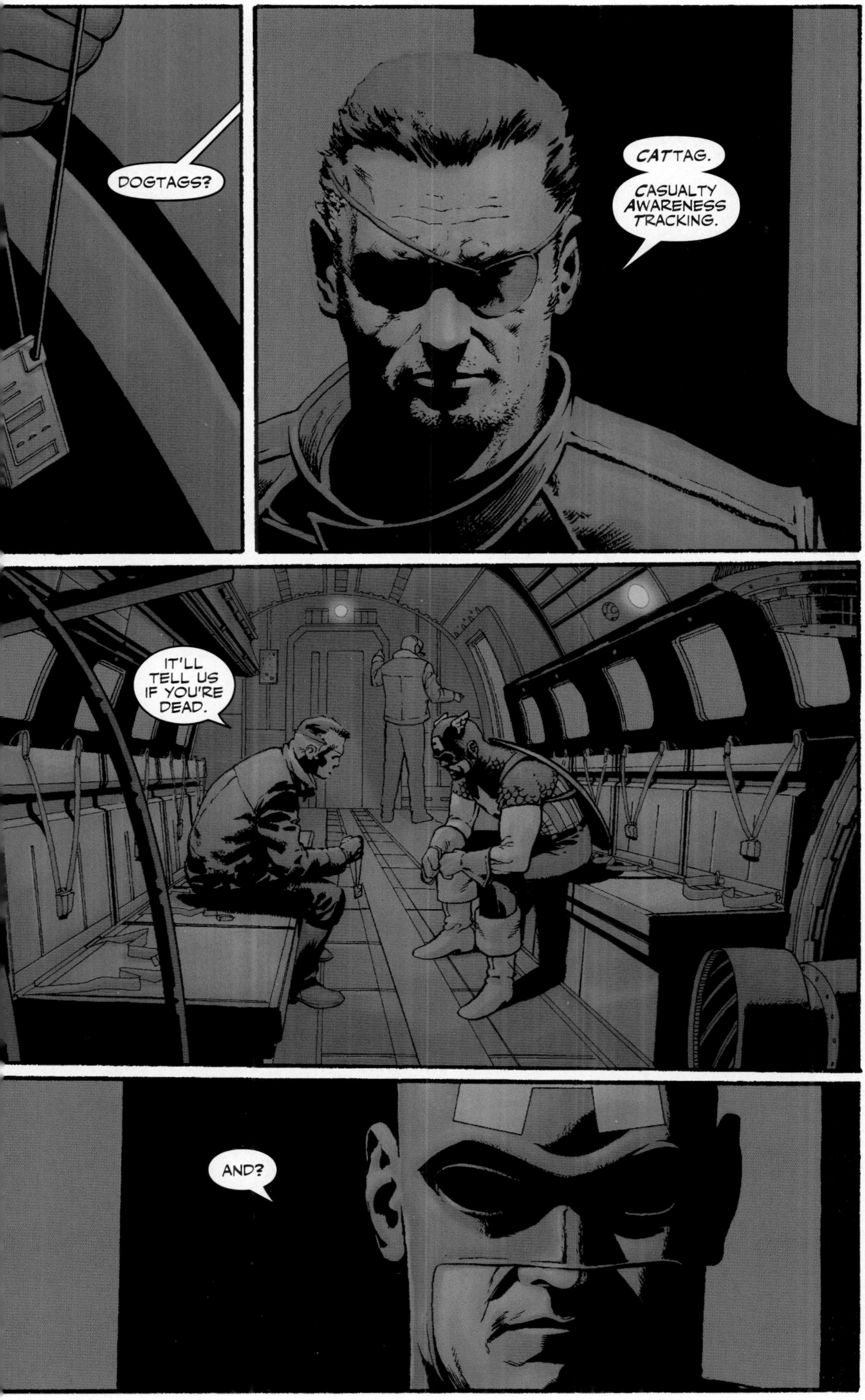
DOGTAGS?
CATTAG.
CASUALTY AWARENESS TRACKING.
IT'LL TELL US IF YOU'RE DEAD.
AND?

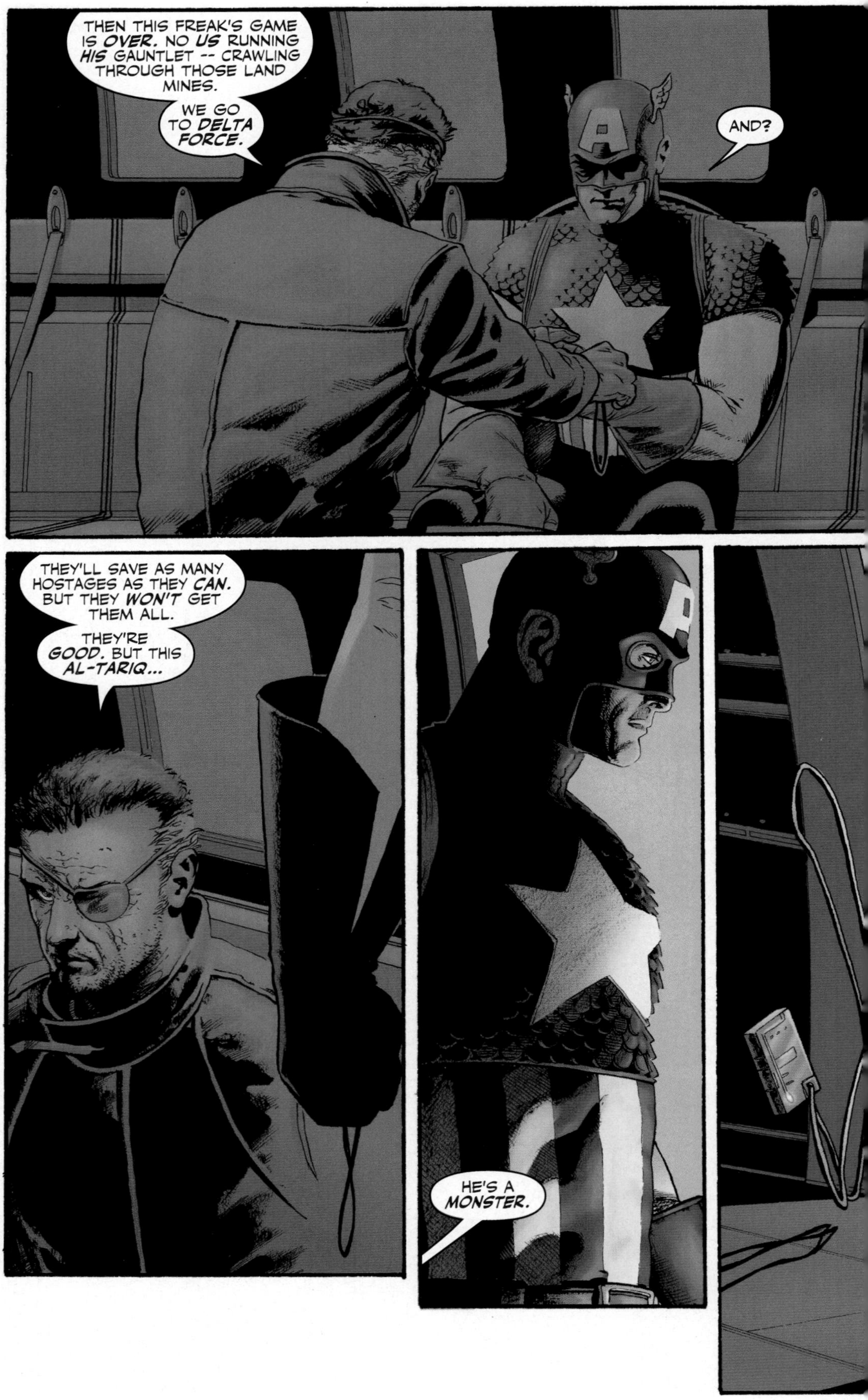
THEN THIS FREAK'S GAME IS *OVER*. NO *US* RUNNING *HIS* GAUNTLET -- CRAWLING THROUGH THOSE LAND MINES.
WE GO TO *DELTA FORCE*.
AND?
THEY'LL SAVE AS MANY HOSTAGES AS THEY *CAN*. BUT THEY *WON'T* GET THEM ALL.
THEY'RE *GOOD*. BUT THIS *AL-TARIQ*...
HE'S A *MONSTER*.

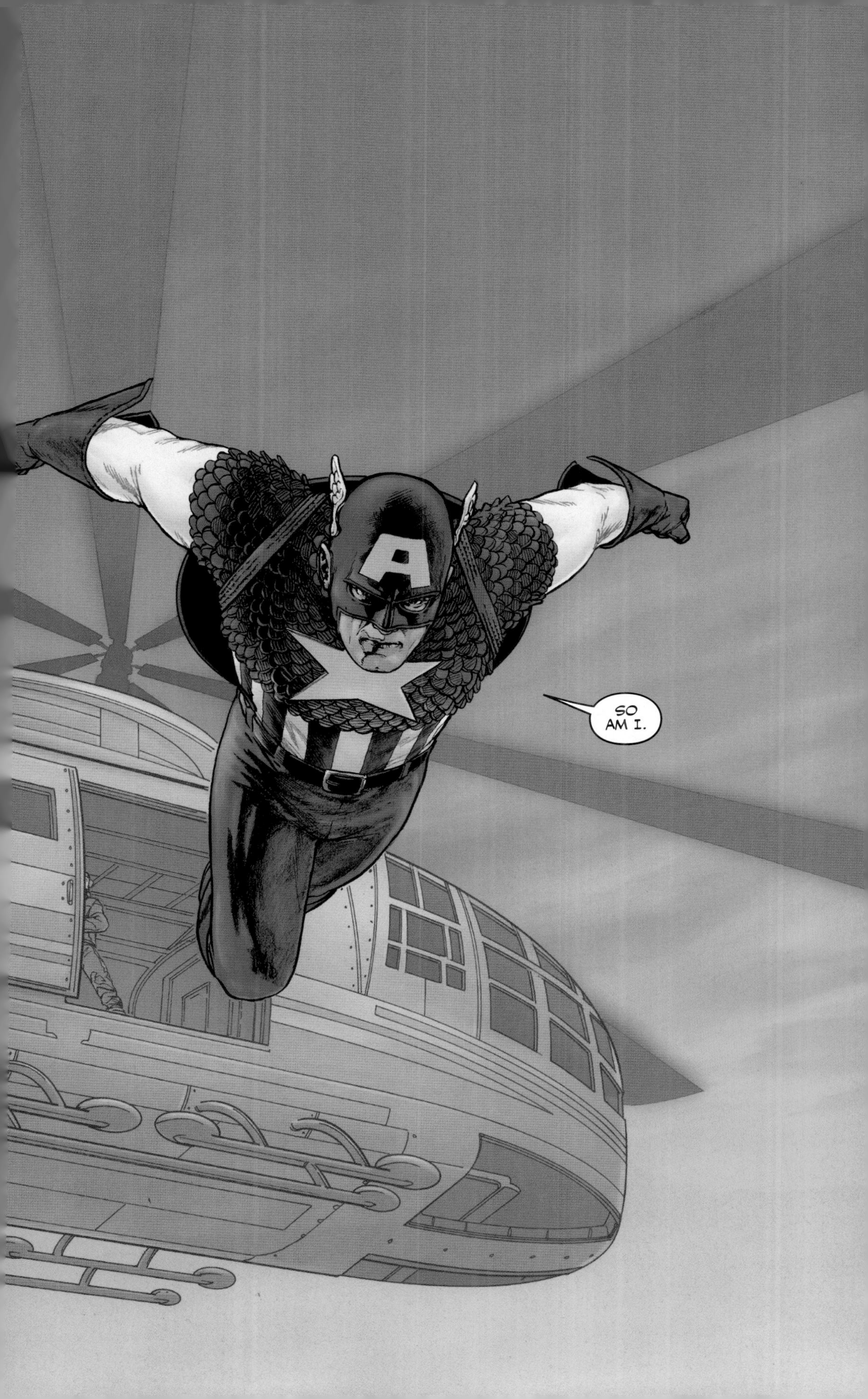
SO AM I.

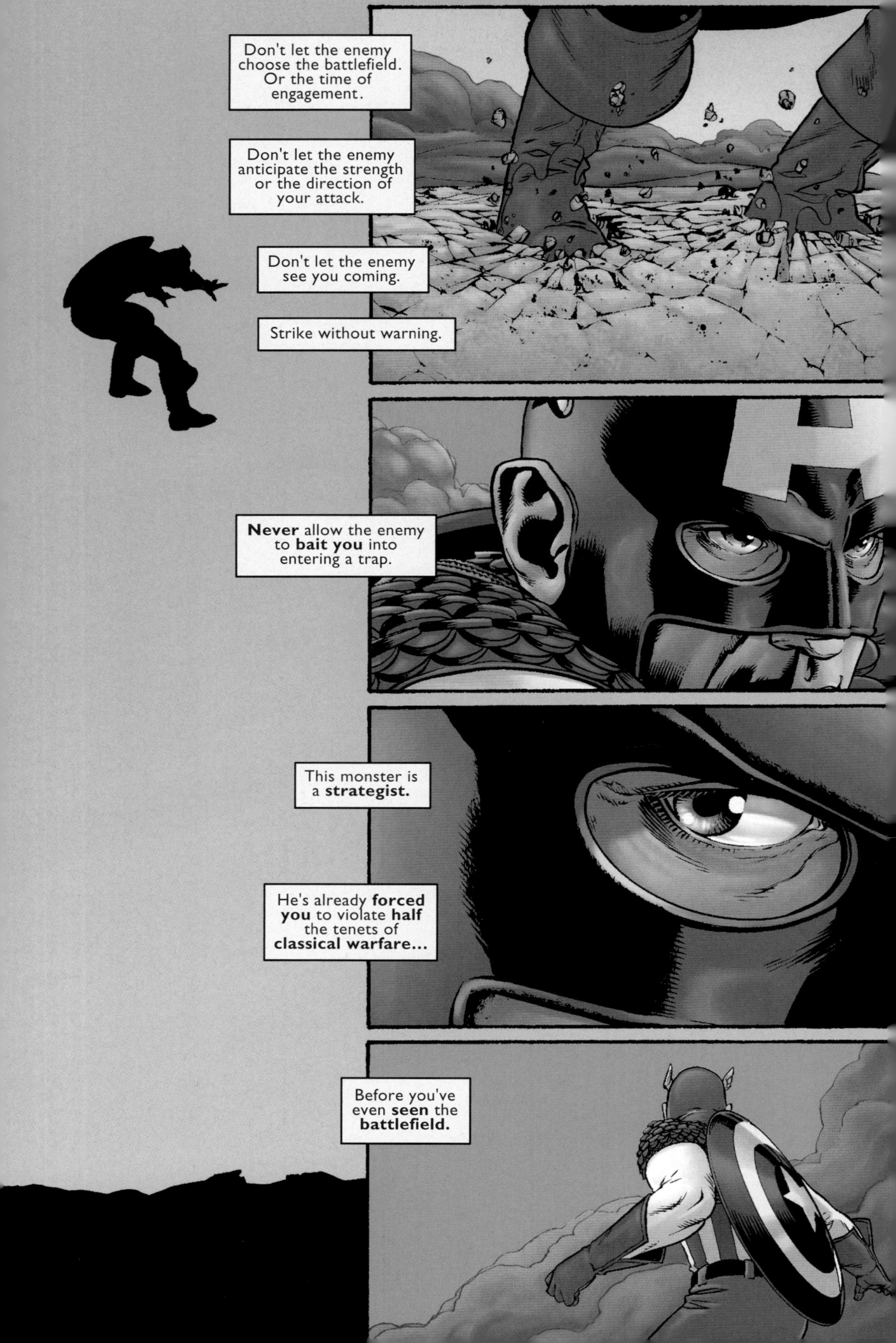
Don't let the enemy choose the battlefield. Or the time of engagement.
Don't let the enemy anticipate the strength or the direction of your attack.
Don't let the enemy see you coming.
Strike without warning.
Never allow the enemy to **bait you** into entering a trap.
This monster is a **strategist.**
He's already **forced you** to violate **half** the tenets of **classical warfare...**
Before you've even **seen** the **battlefield.**

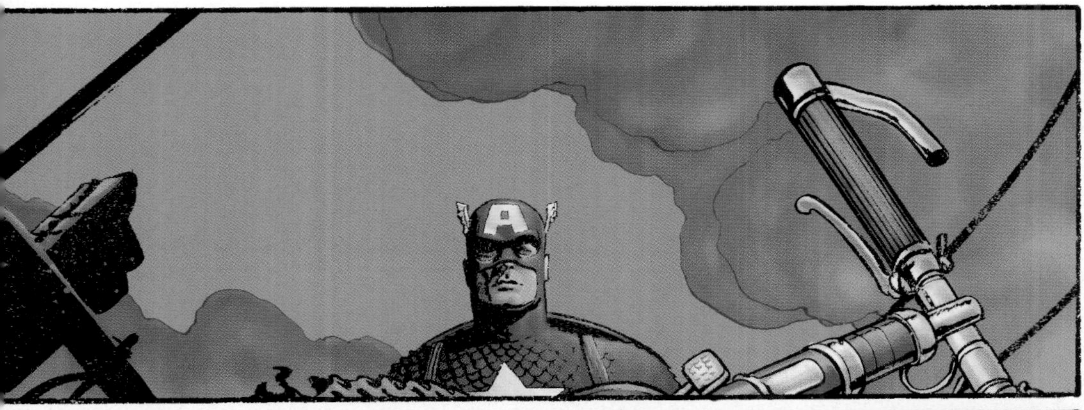

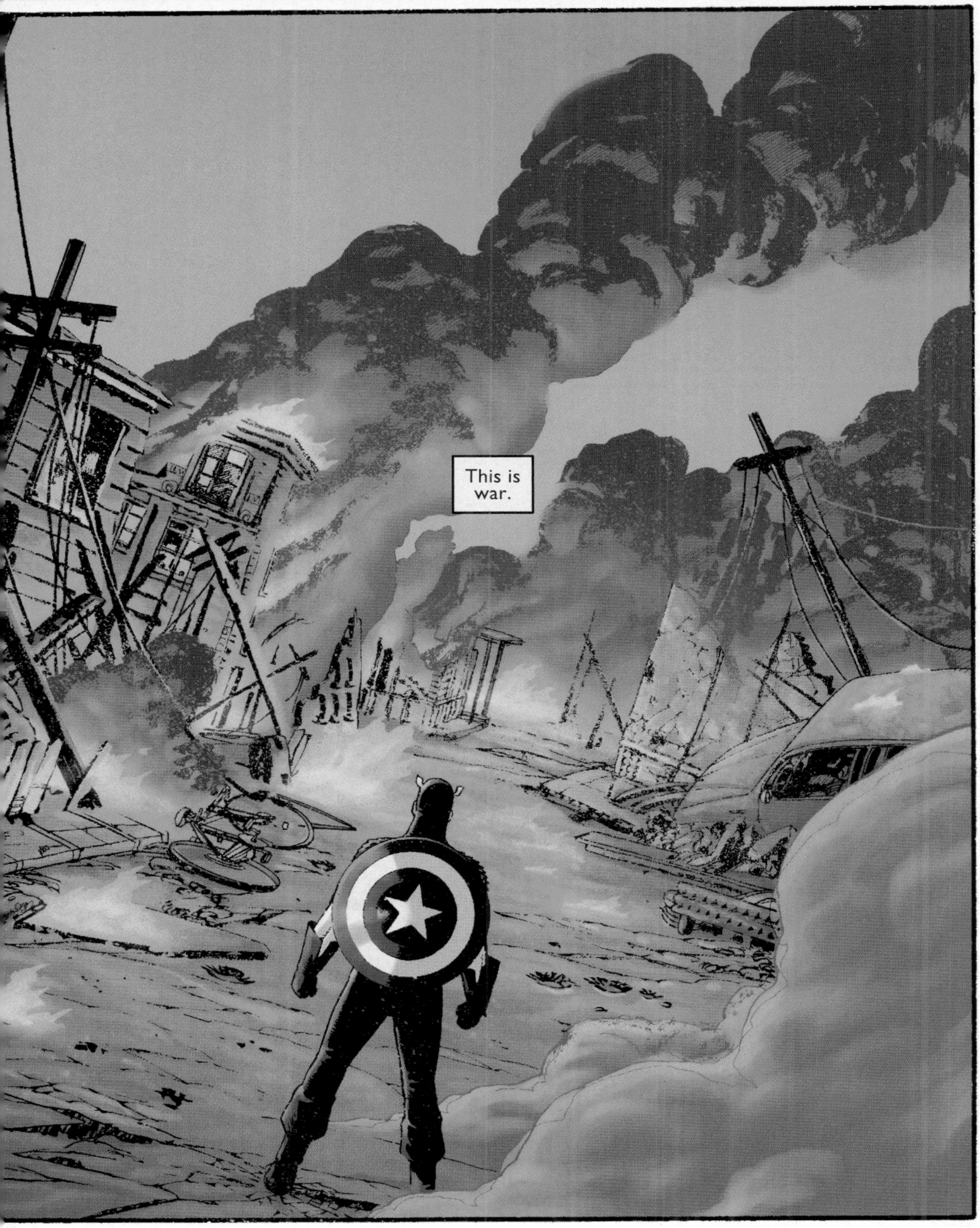
This is war.

But it's never the **wars** that bleed and burn and die.

It's the **people.**

A boy --

A girl --

A **child.**

Playing. On Sunday morning...

Never even **saw** the mine.

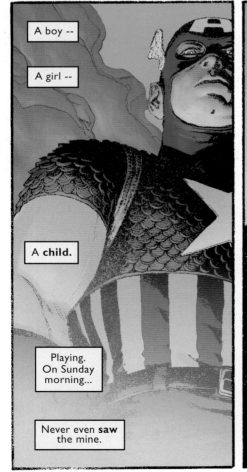

But they're not here.

There's no blood on the bike or on the ground.

So maybe --

Maybe **this time** --

You're not too late.

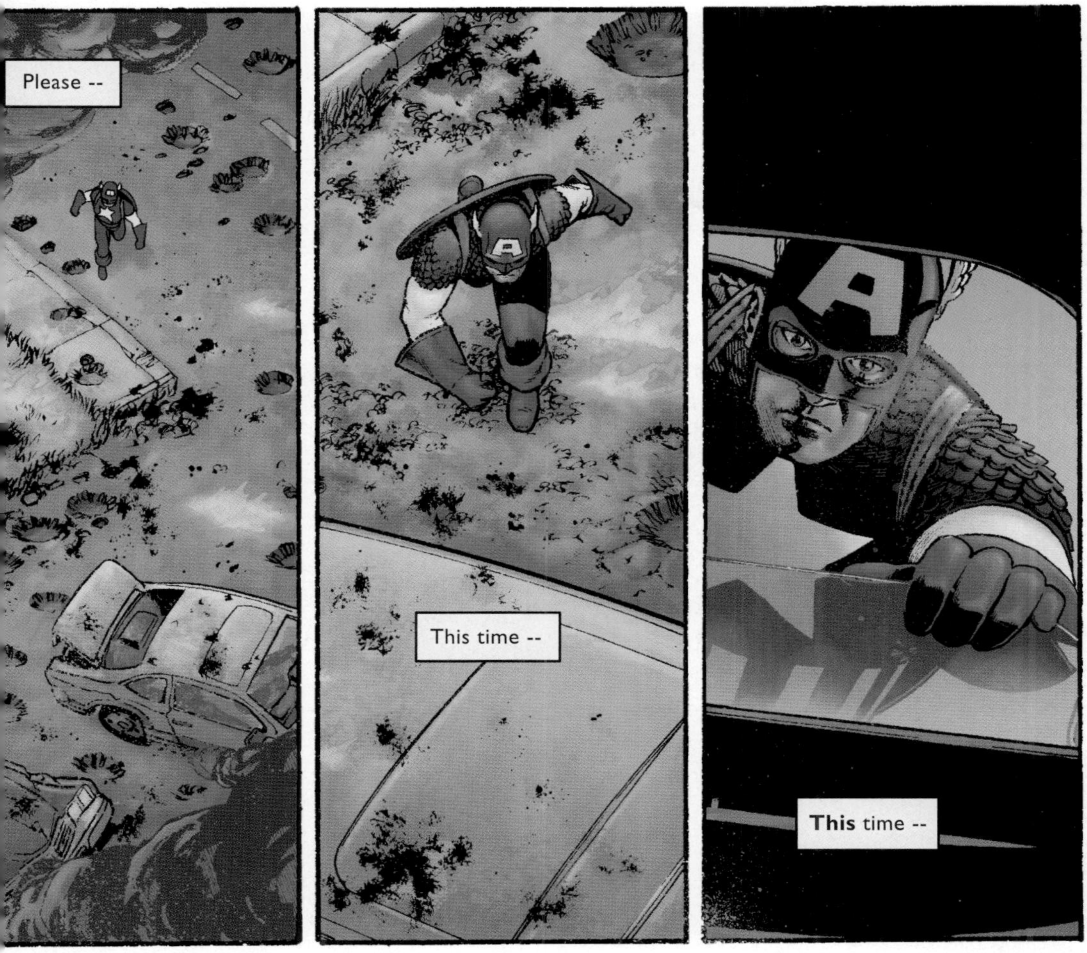
Please --
This time --
This time --

Let it not be --

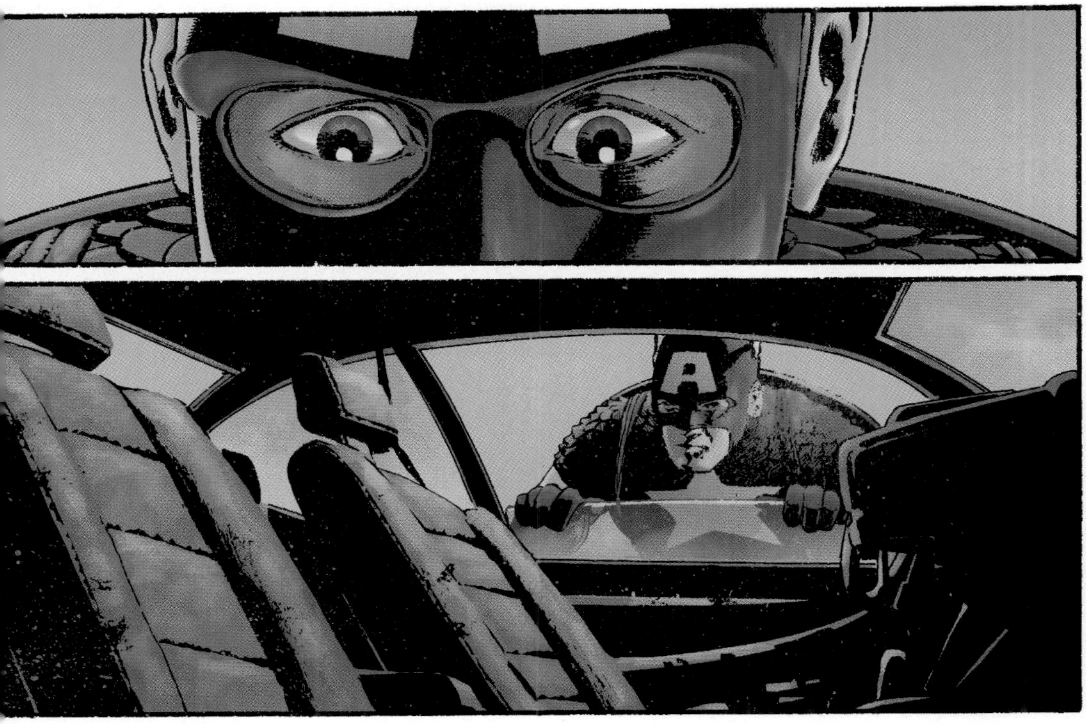

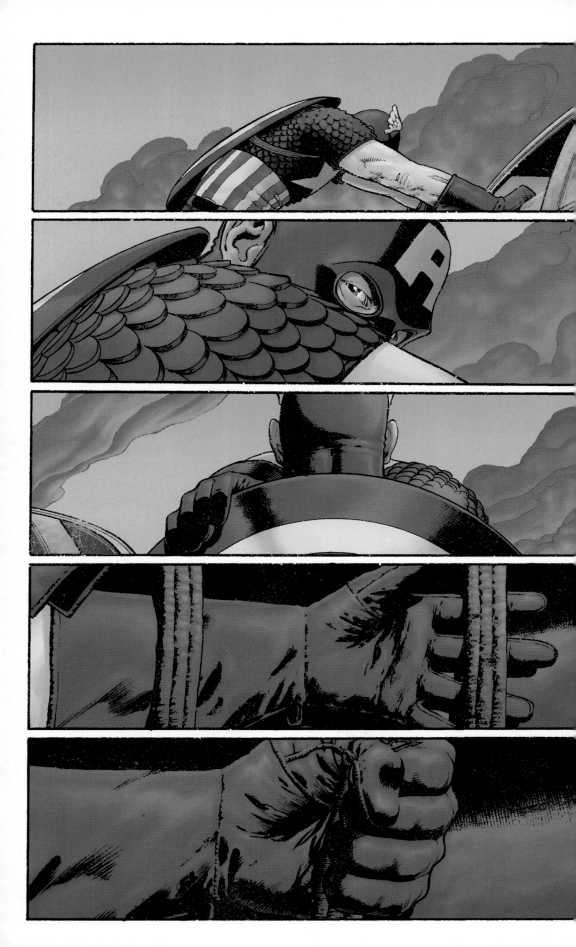

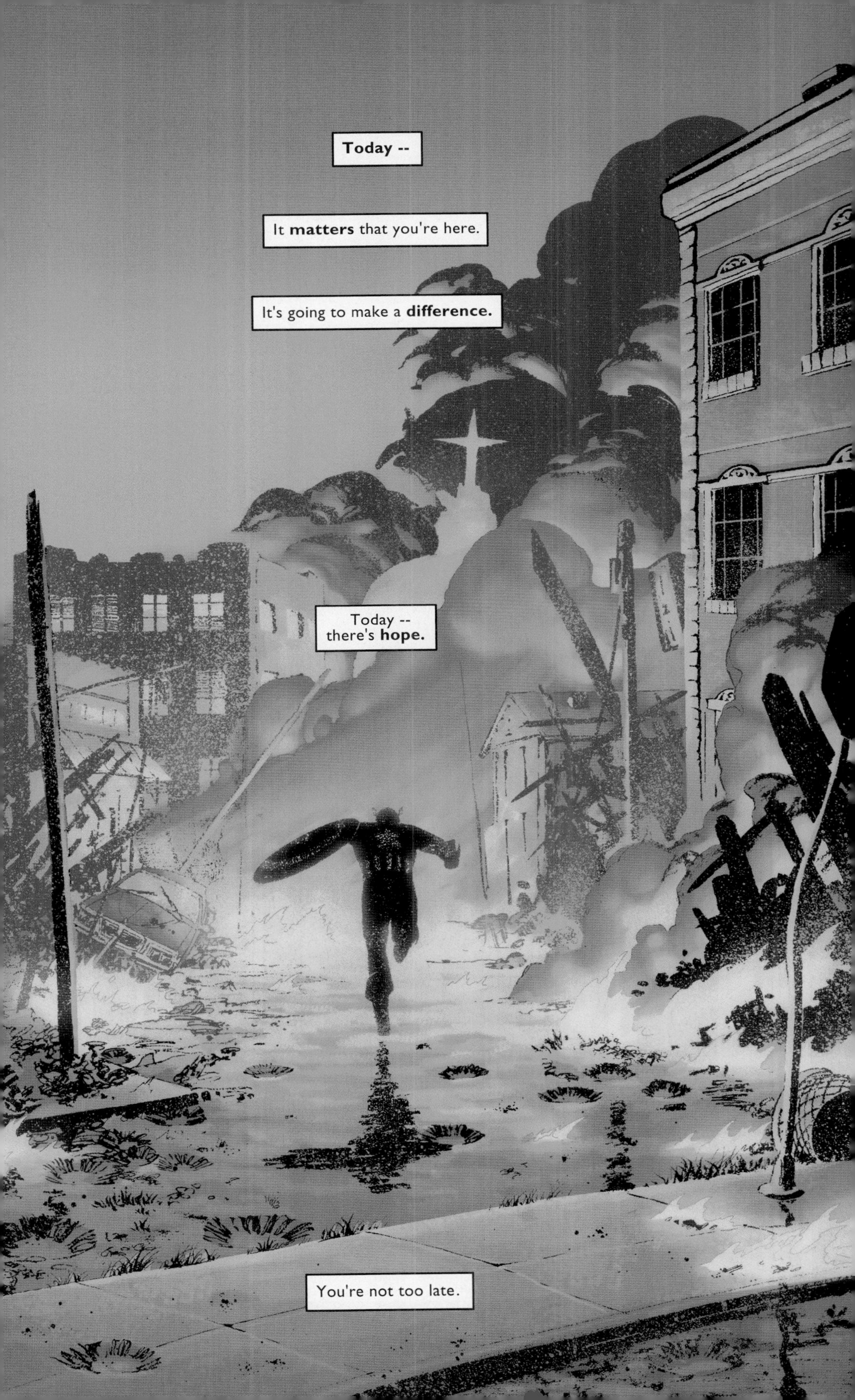
Today --
It matters that you're here.
It's going to make a difference.
Today -- there's hope.
You're not too late.

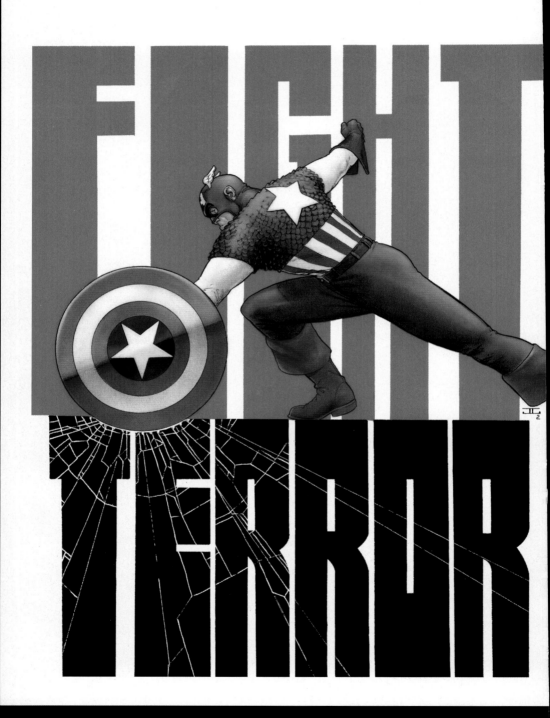

2 ENEMY, CHAPTER TWO: ONE NATION

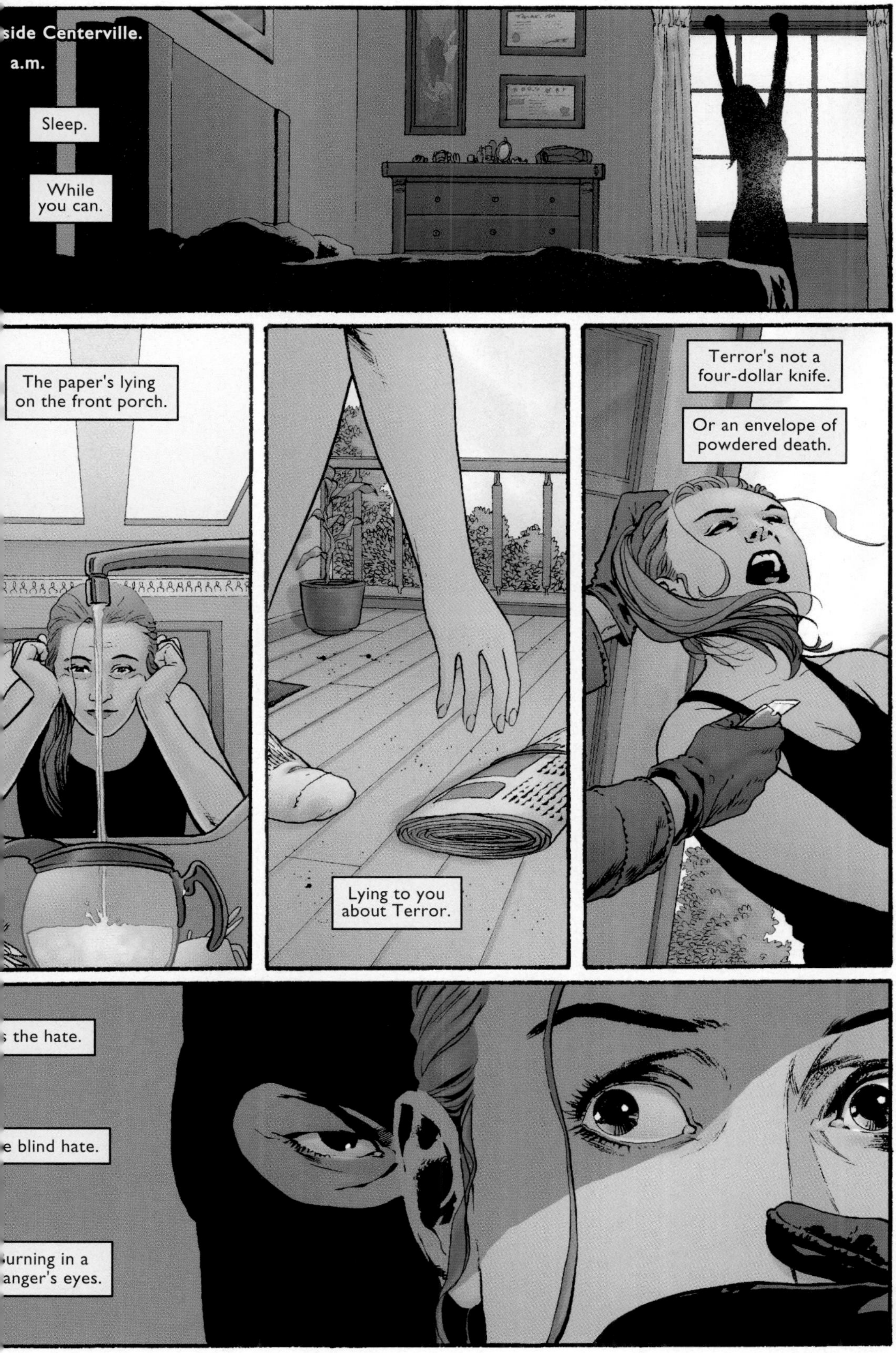
side Centerville.
a.m.
Sleep.
While you can.
The paper's lying on the front porch.
Lying to you about Terror.
Terror's not a four-dollar knife.
Or an envelope of powdered death.
the hate.
e blind hate.
urning in a
anger's eyes.

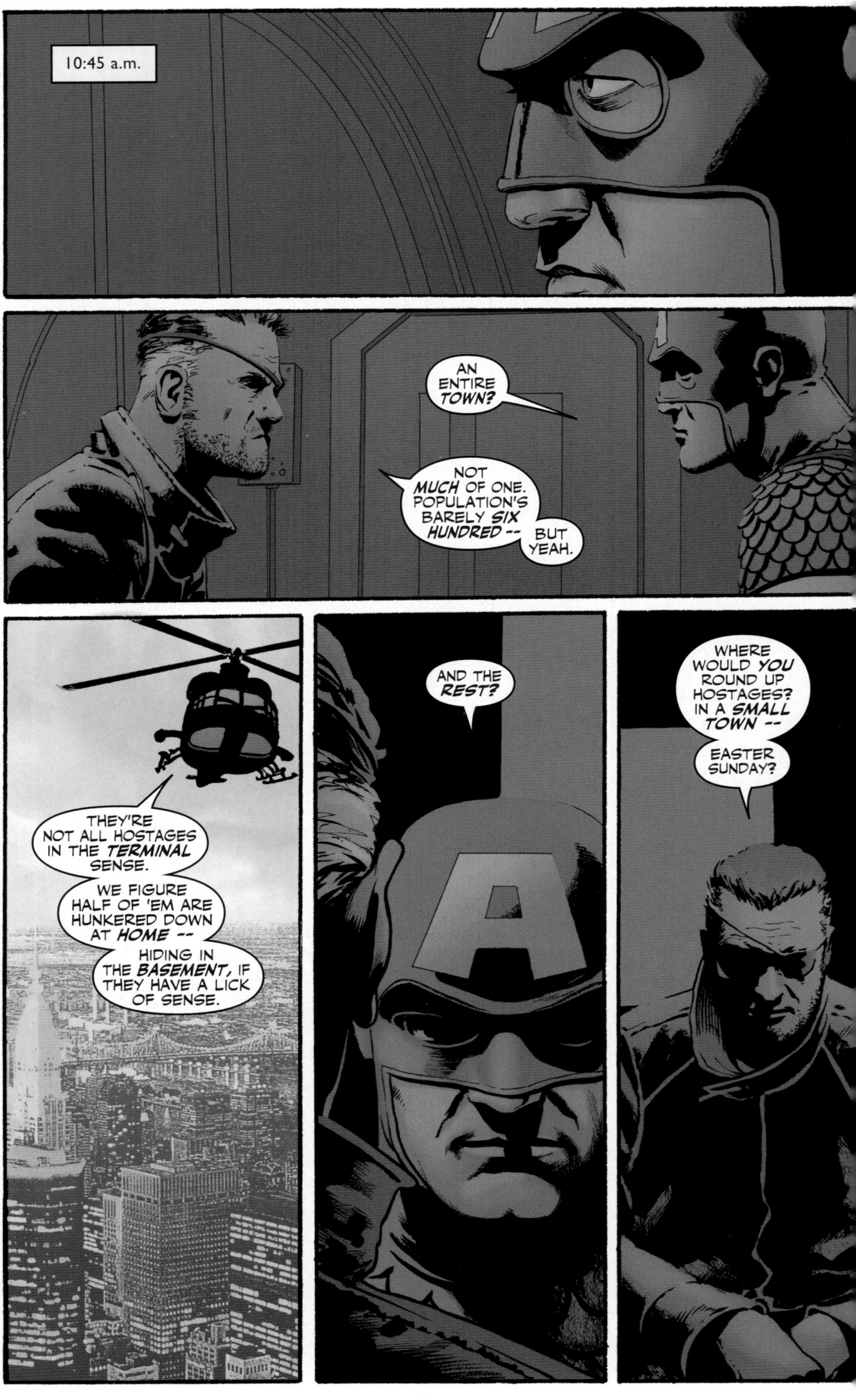
10:45 a.m.
AN ENTIRE TOWN?
NOT MUCH OF ONE. POPULATION'S BARELY SIX HUNDRED --
BUT YEAH.
THEY'RE NOT ALL HOSTAGES IN THE TERMINAL SENSE.
WE FIGURE HALF OF 'EM ARE HUNKERED DOWN AT HOME --
HIDING IN THE BASEMENT, IF THEY HAVE A LICK OF SENSE.
AND THE REST?
WHERE WOULD YOU ROUND UP HOSTAGES? IN A SMALL TOWN --
EASTER SUNDAY?

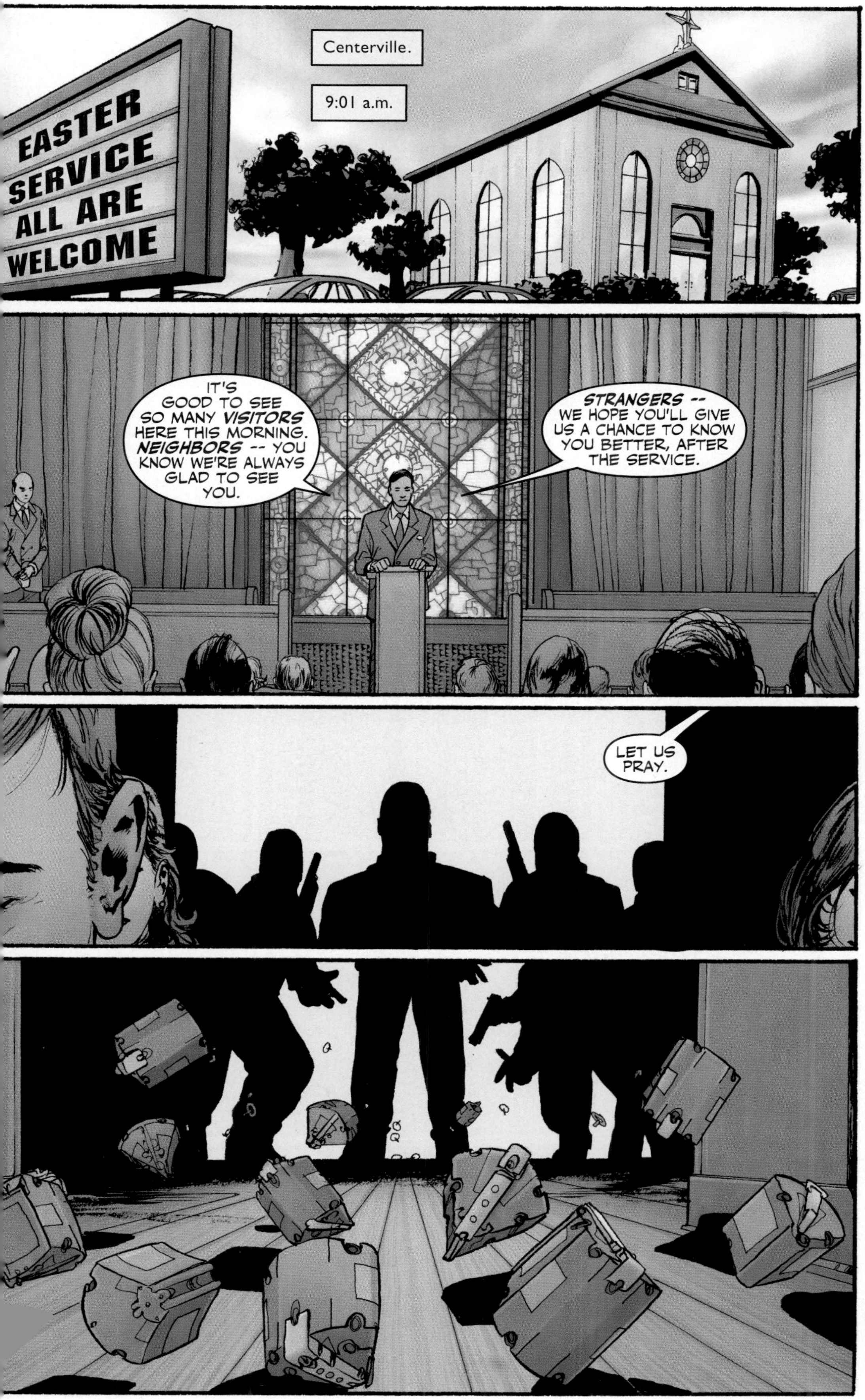

EASTER SERVICE ALL ARE WELCOME
Centerville.
9:01 a.m.
IT'S GOOD TO SEE SO MANY VISITORS HERE THIS MORNING. NEIGHBORS -- YOU KNOW WE'RE ALWAYS GLAD TO SEE YOU.
STRANGERS -- WE HOPE YOU'LL GIVE US A CHANCE TO KNOW YOU BETTER, AFTER THE SERVICE.
LET US PRAY.

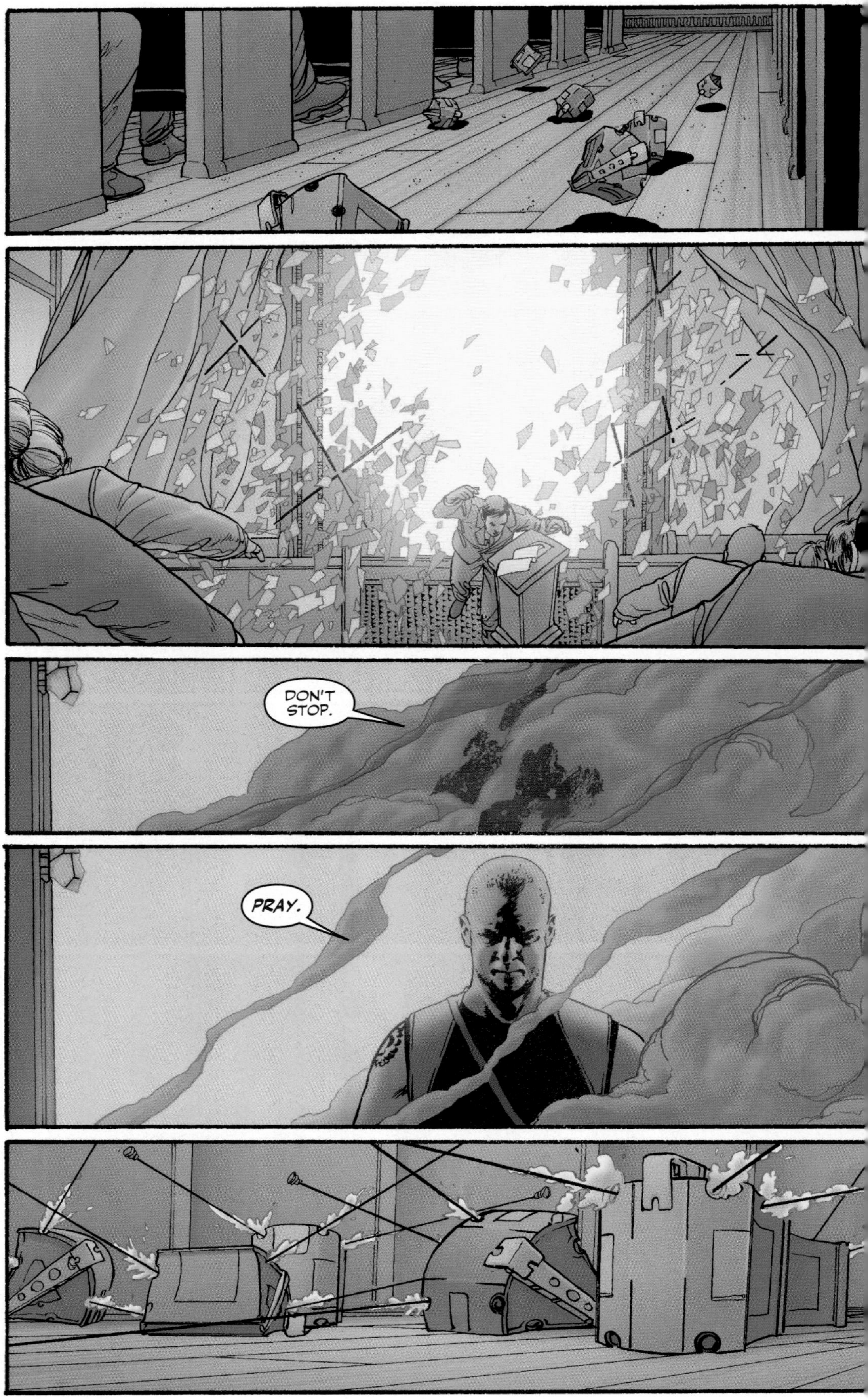
DON'T STOP.
PRAY.

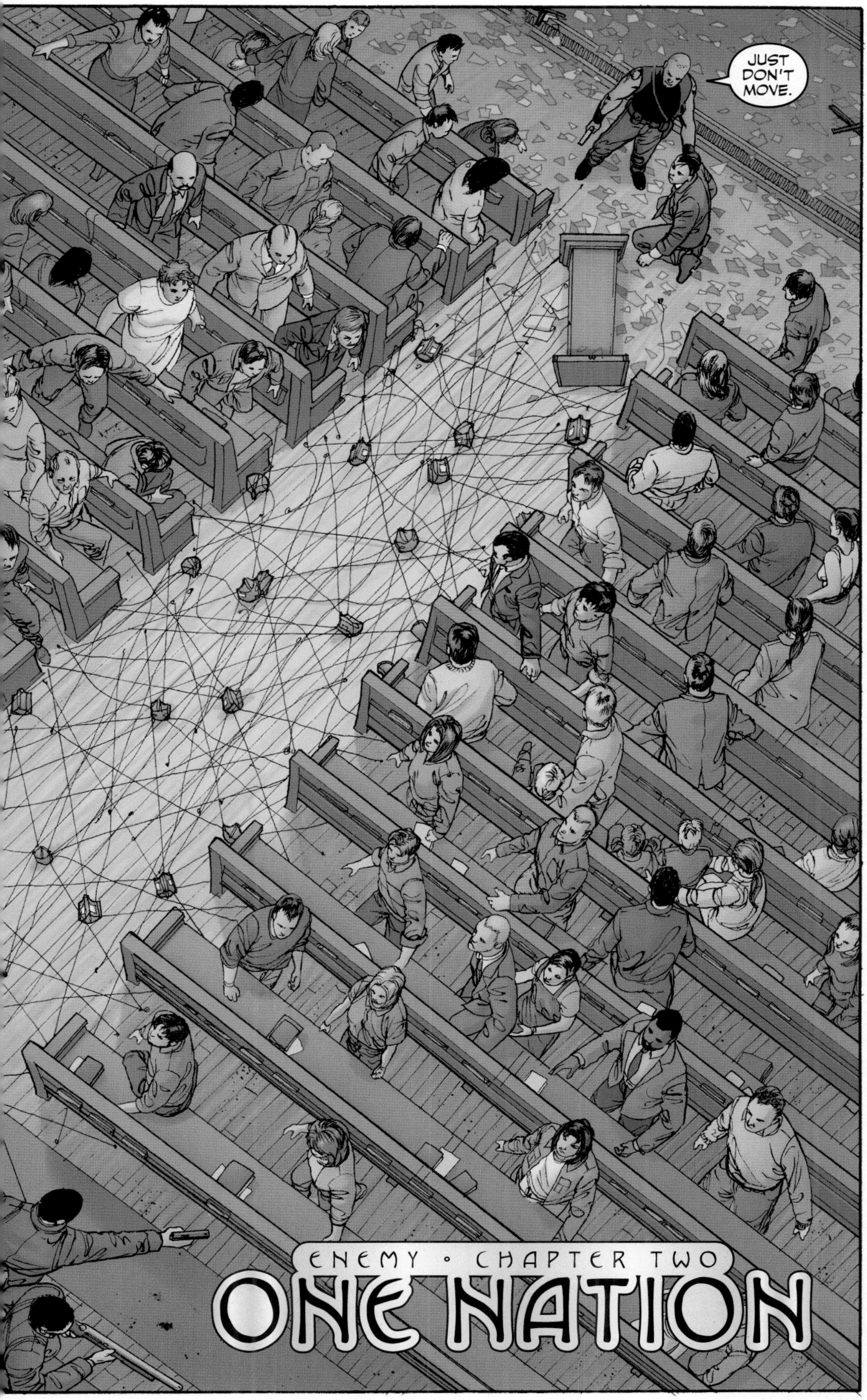

JUST DON'T MOVE.
ENEMY • CHAPTER TWO
ONE NATION

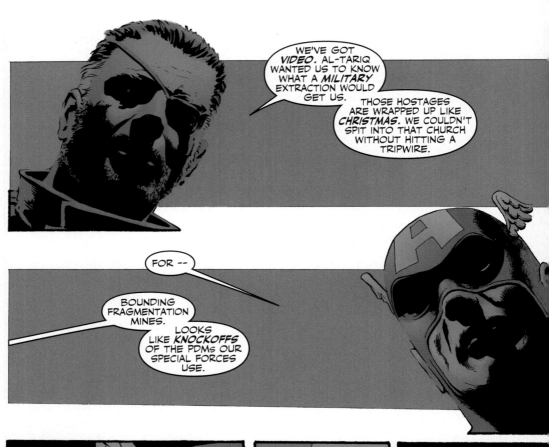

WE'VE GOT *VIDEO*. AL-TARIQ WANTED US TO KNOW WHAT A *MILITARY* EXTRACTION WOULD GET US.

THOSE HOSTAGES ARE WRAPPED UP LIKE *CHRISTMAS*. WE COULDN'T SPIT INTO THAT CHURCH WITHOUT HITTING A TRIPWIRE.

FOR --

BOUNDING FRAGMENTATION MINES. LOOKS LIKE *KNOCKOFFS* OF THE PDMs OUR SPECIAL FORCES USE.

WHAT DOES HE WANT?

IF NO ONE SETS THEM OFF, THEY'LL *STILL* DETONATE. SELF-DESTRUCT --

FOUR HOURS AFTER ARMING. THAT GIVES US *TWO HOURS*.

WHAT DOES HE WANT.

YOU.

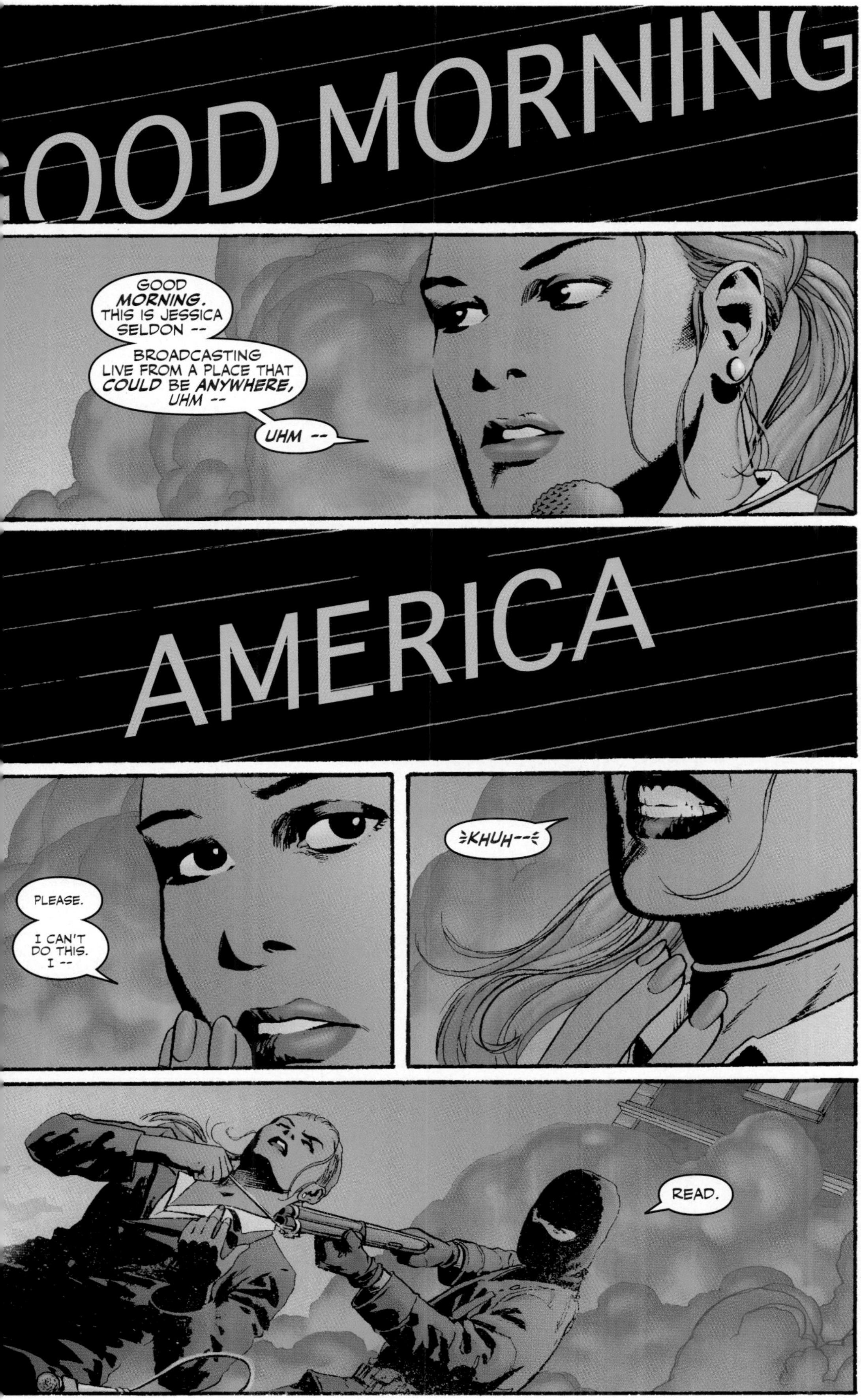
GOOD MORNING
GOOD MORNING. THIS IS JESSICA SELDON --
BROADCASTING LIVE FROM A PLACE THAT COULD BE ANYWHERE, UHM --
UHM --
AMERICA
PLEASE.
I CAN'T DO THIS. I --
KHUH--
READ.

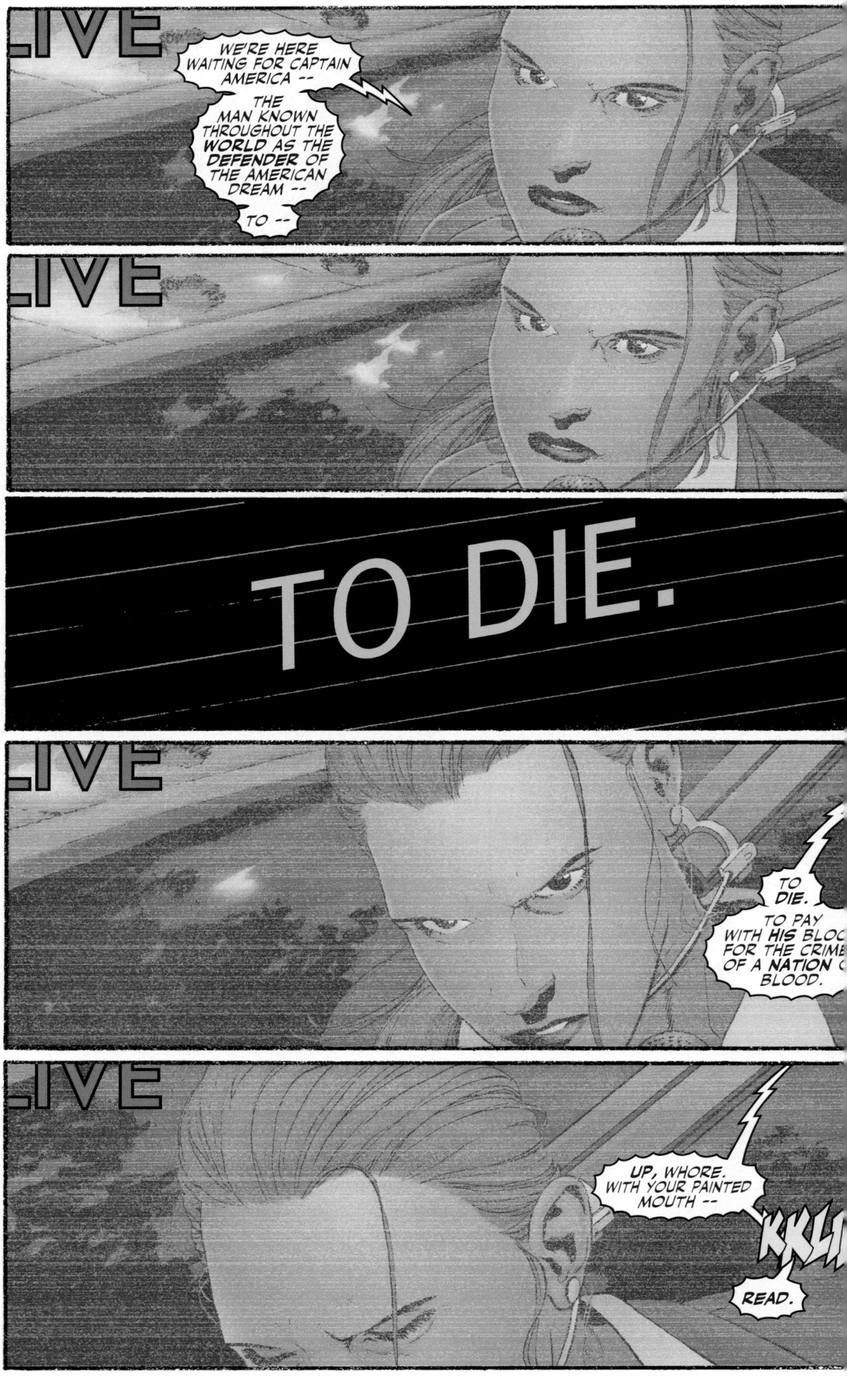
LIVE
WE'RE HERE WAITING FOR CAPTAIN AMERICA --
THE MAN KNOWN THROUGHOUT THE WORLD AS THE DEFENDER OF THE AMERICAN DREAM --
TO --
LIVE
TO DIE.
LIVE
TO DIE.
LIVE
UP, WHORE. WITH YOUR PAINTED MOUTH --
READ.

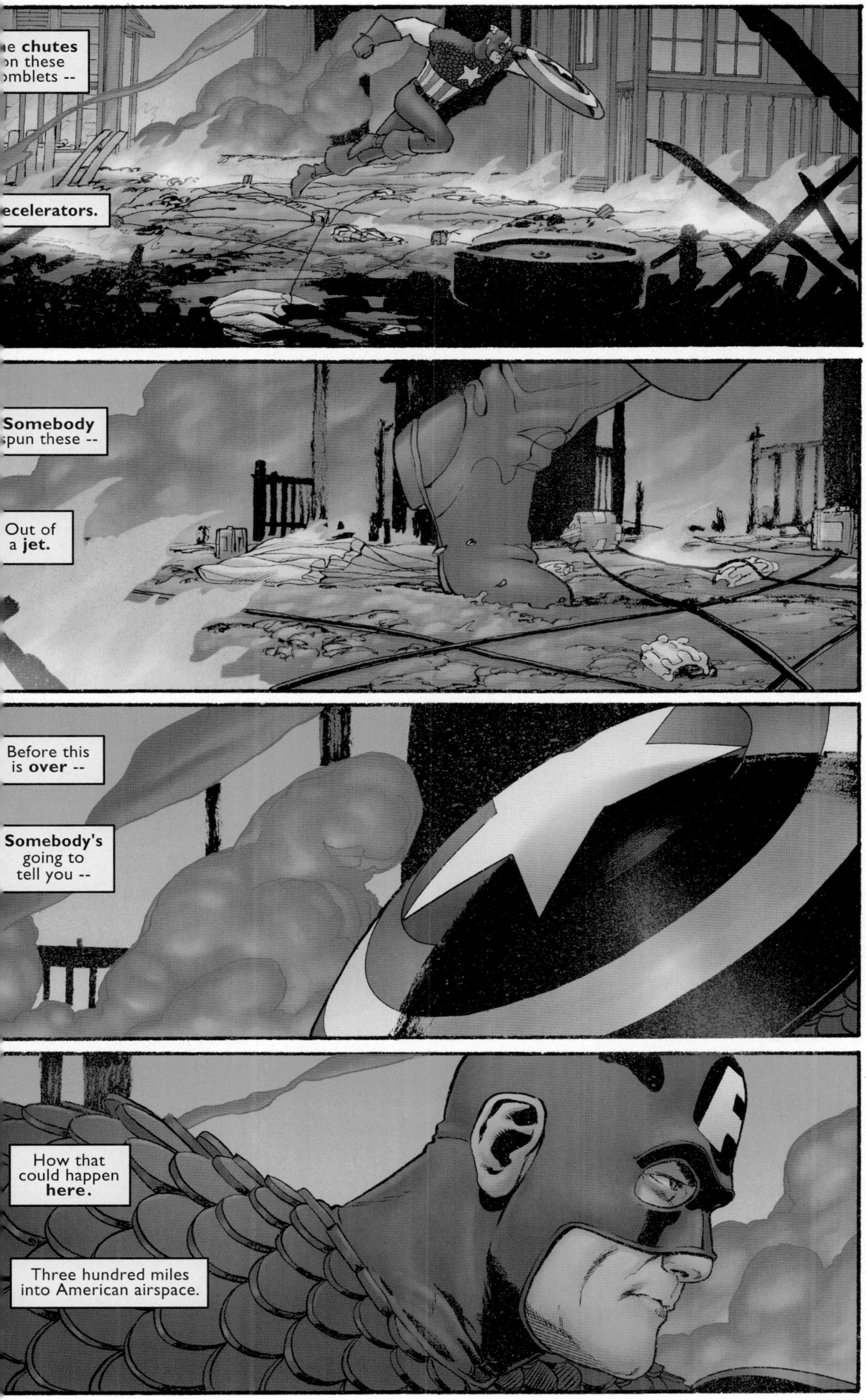
e chutes
n these
mblets --
ecelerators.
Somebody
pun these --
Out of
a jet.
Before this
is over --
Somebody's
going to
tell you --
How that
could happen
here.
Three hundred miles
into American airspace.

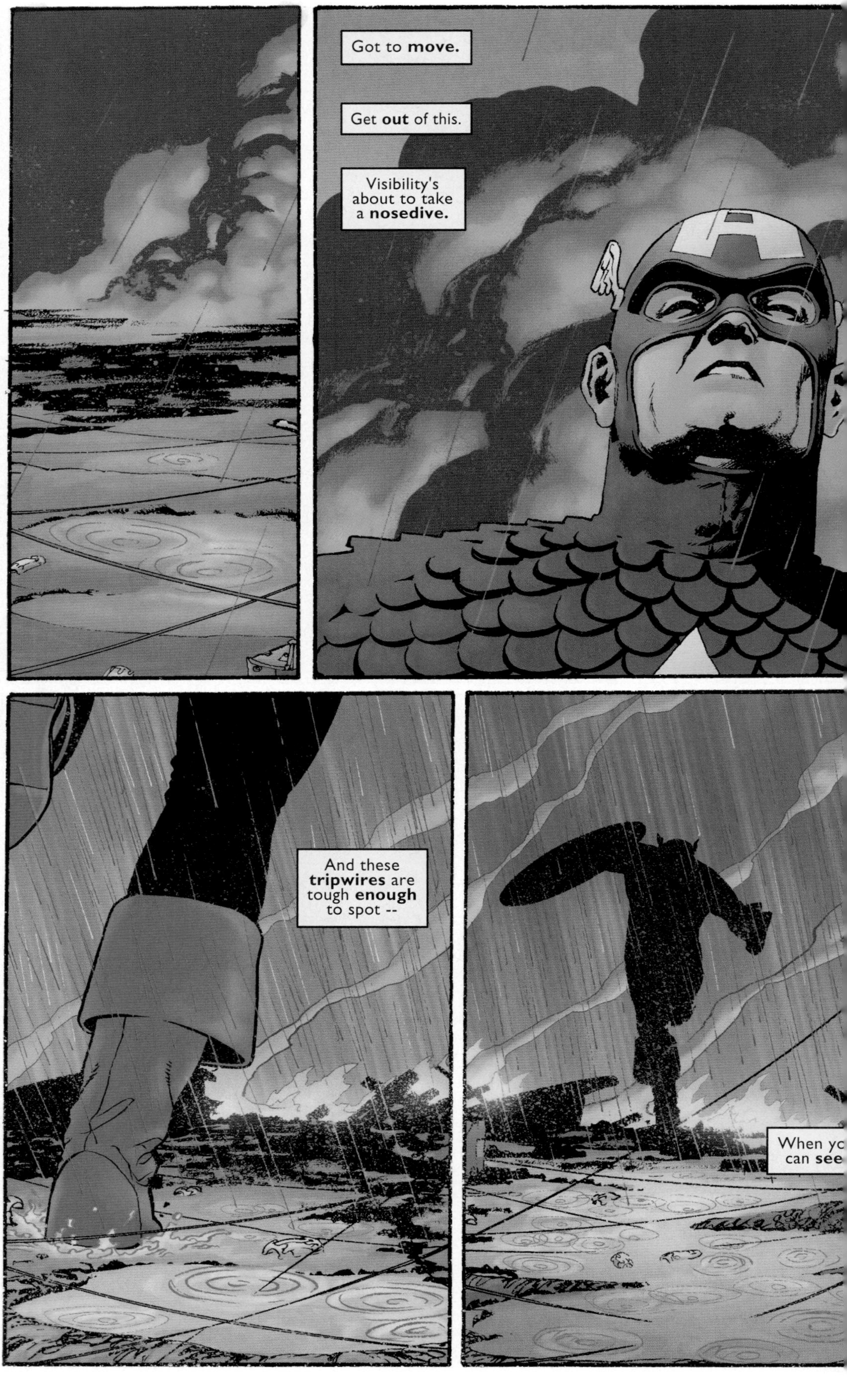
Got to **move.**
Get **out** of this.
Visibility's about to take a **nosedive.**
And these **tripwires** are tough **enough** to spot --
When yo
can see

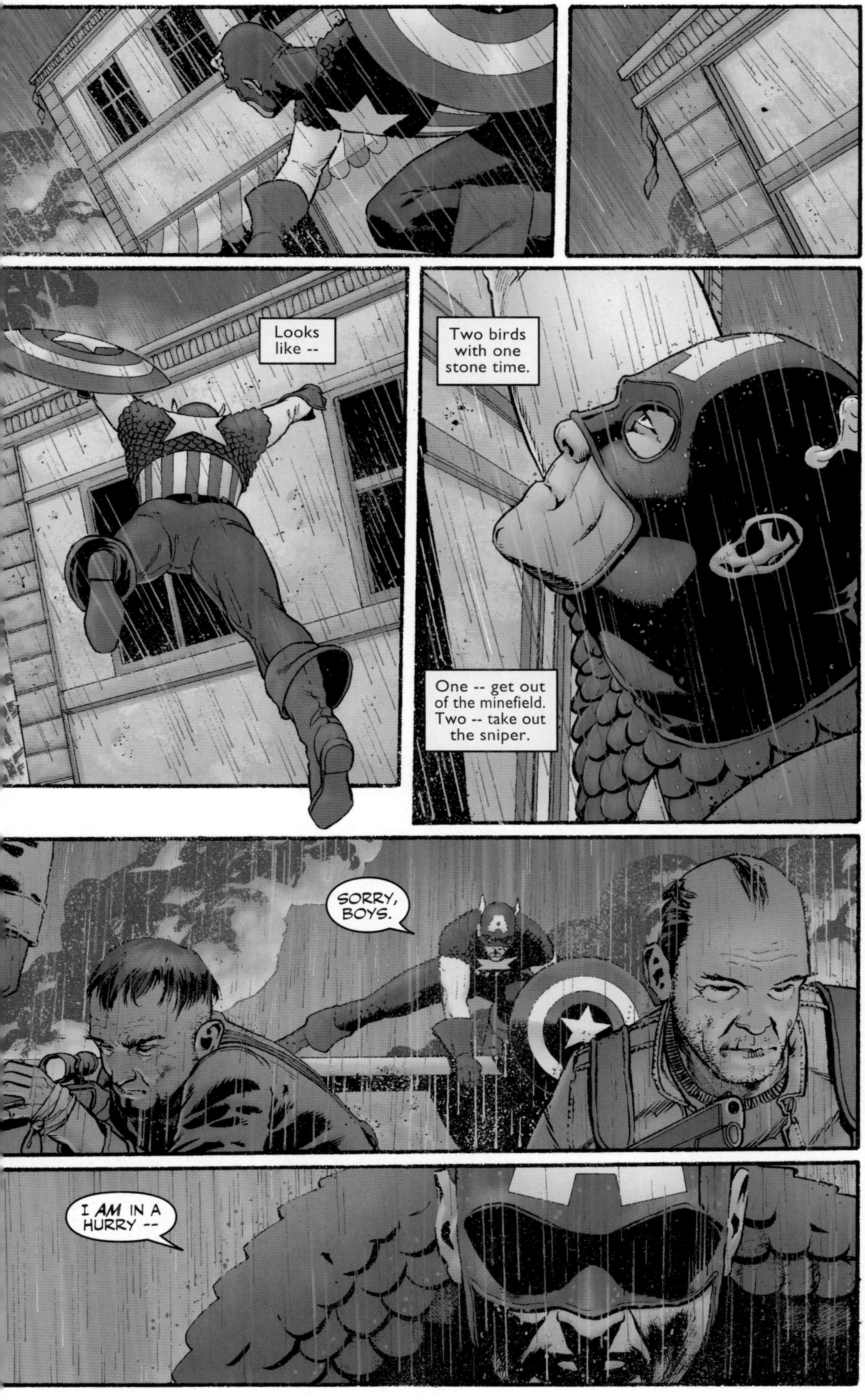
Looks like --
Two birds with one stone time.
One -- get out of the minefield. Two -- take out the sniper.
SORRY, BOYS.
I AM IN A HURRY --

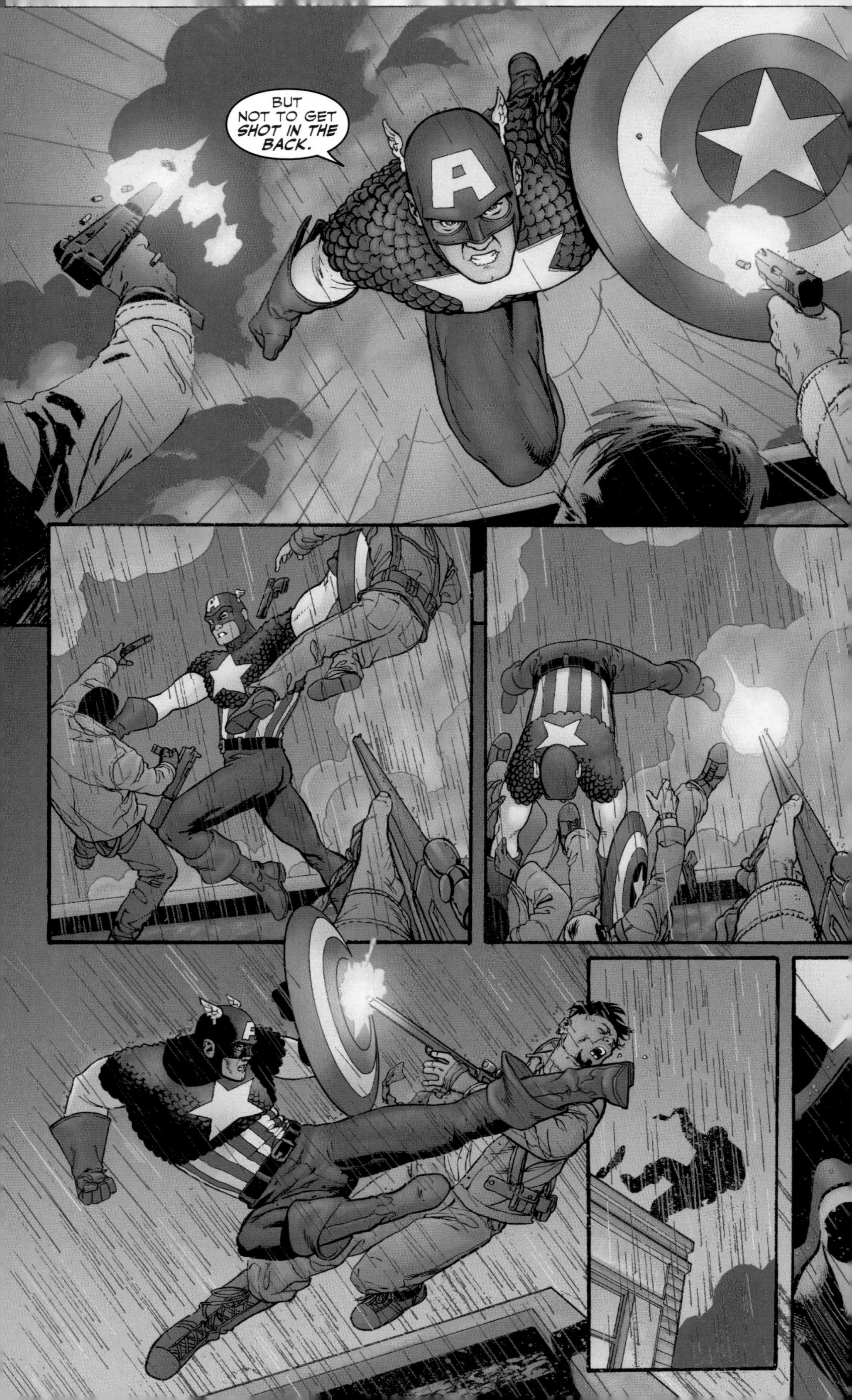
BUT NOT TO GET SHOT IN THE BACK.

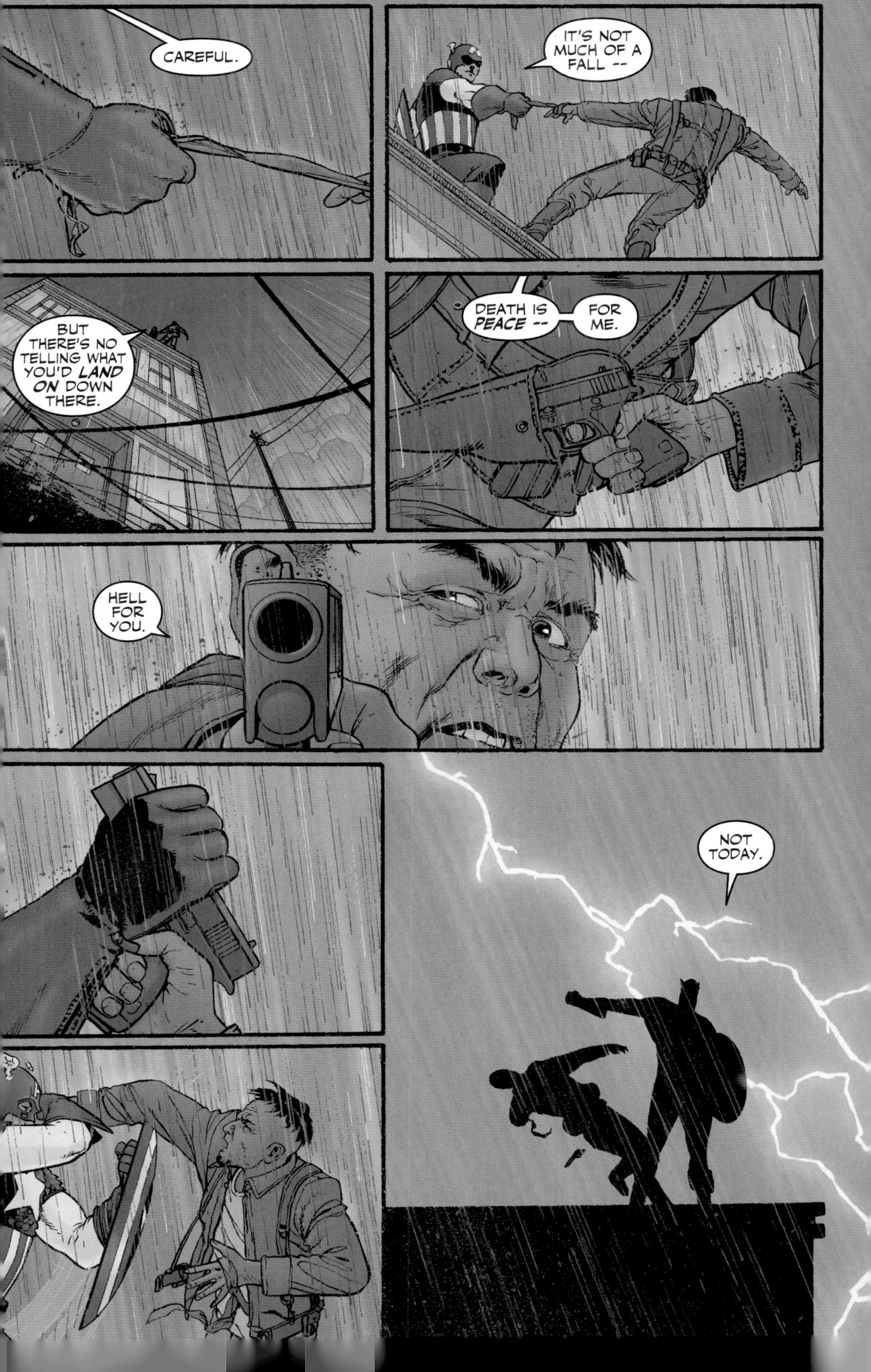
CAREFUL.
IT'S NOT MUCH OF A FALL --
BUT THERE'S NO TELLING WHAT YOU'D LAND ON DOWN THERE.
DEATH IS PEACE --
FOR ME.
HELL FOR YOU.
NOT TODAY.

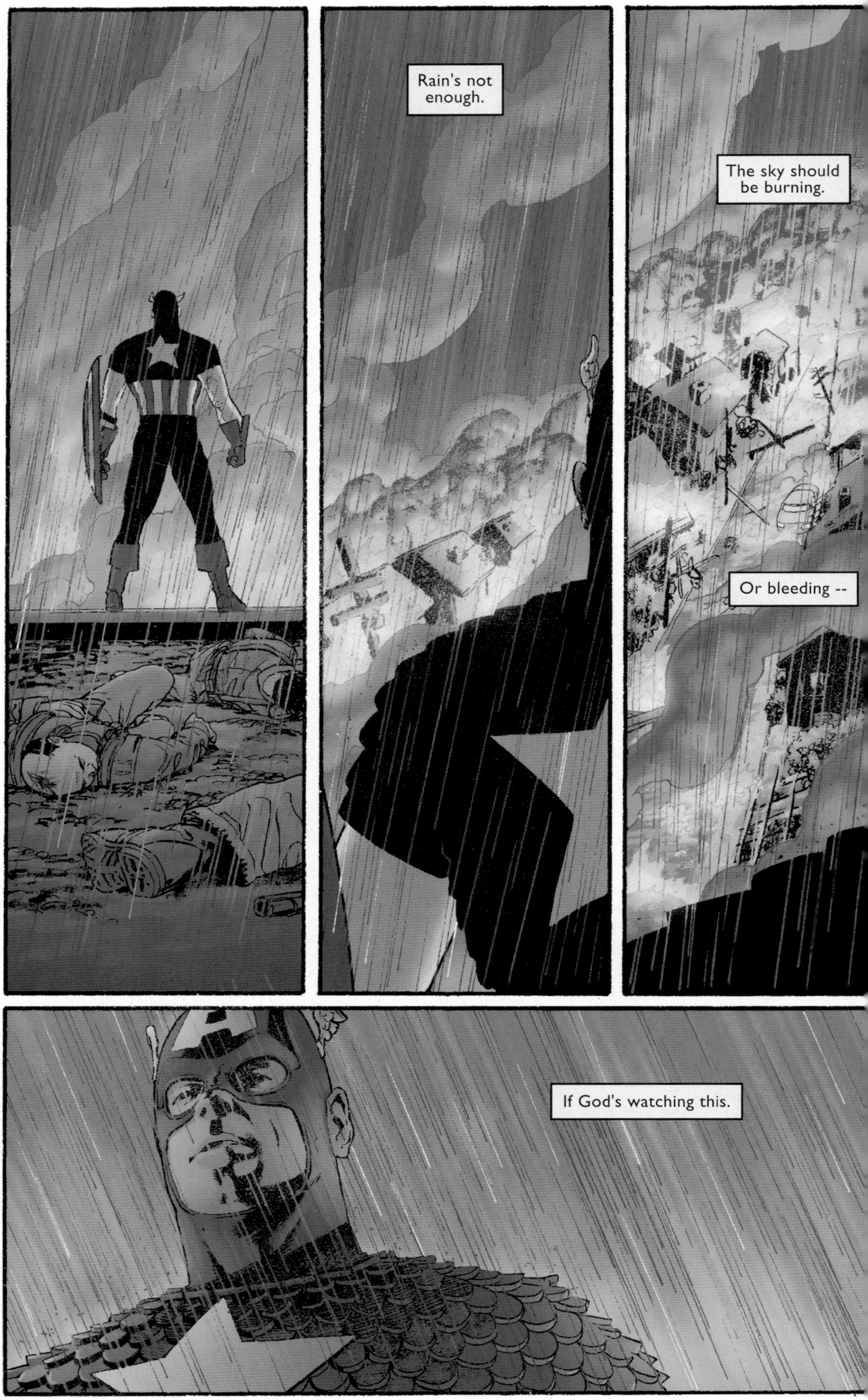
Rain's not enough.
The sky should be burning.
Or bleeding --
If God's watching this.

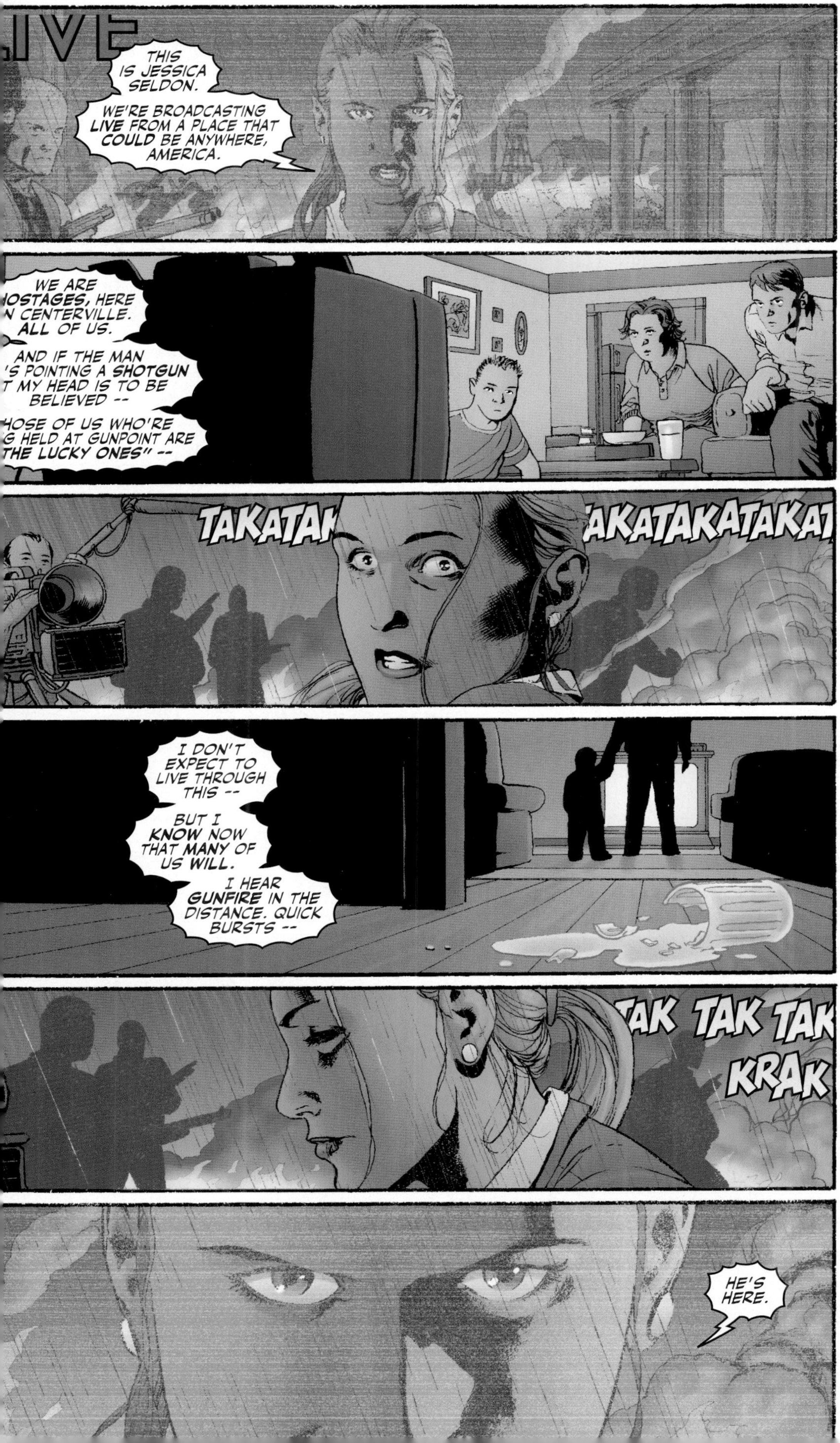
LIVE
THIS IS JESSICA SELDON.
WE'RE BROADCASTING LIVE FROM A PLACE THAT COULD BE ANYWHERE, AMERICA.
WE ARE HOSTAGES, HERE IN CENTERVILLE. ALL OF US.
AND IF THE MAN WHO'S POINTING A SHOTGUN AT MY HEAD IS TO BE BELIEVED --
THOSE OF US WHO'RE BEING HELD AT GUNPOINT ARE "THE LUCKY ONES" --
TAKATAKATAKATAKATAKAT
I DON'T EXPECT TO LIVE THROUGH THIS --
BUT I KNOW NOW THAT MANY OF US WILL.
I HEAR GUNFIRE IN THE DISTANCE. QUICK BURSTS --
TAK TAK TAK
KRAK
HE'S HERE.

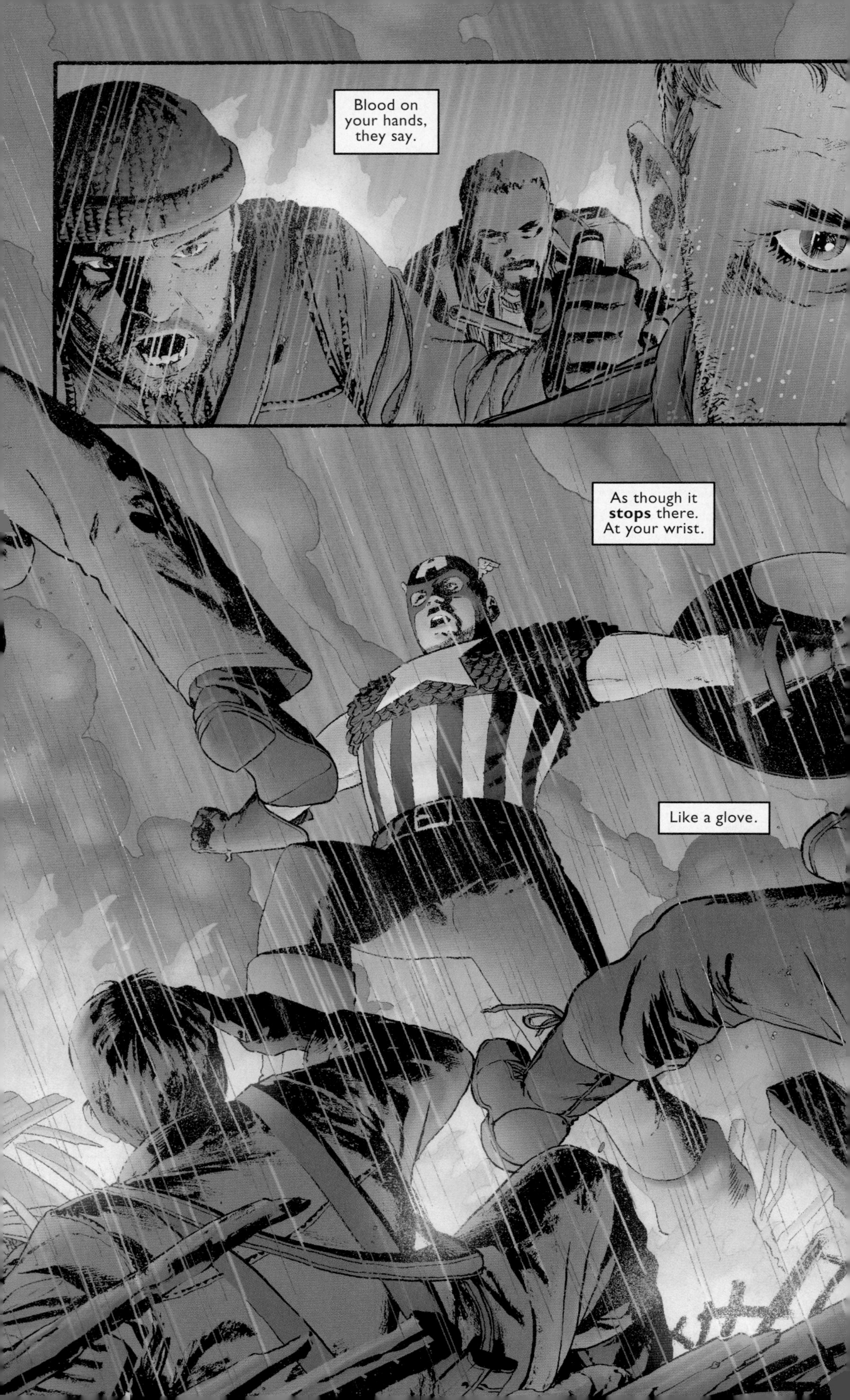
Blood on your hands, they say.
As though it **stops** there. At your wrist.
Like a glove.

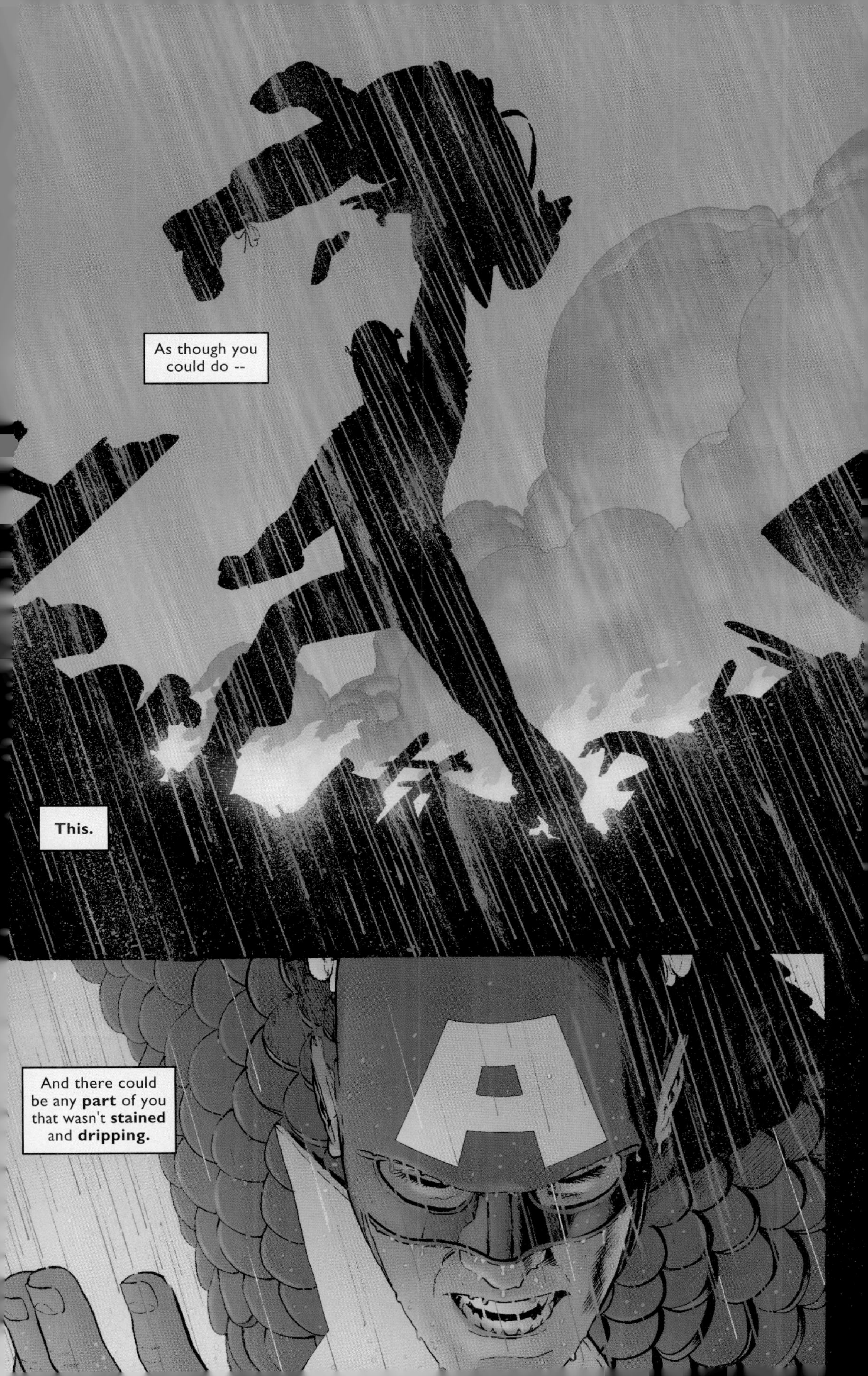
As though you could do --
This.
And there could be any part of you that wasn't stained and dripping.

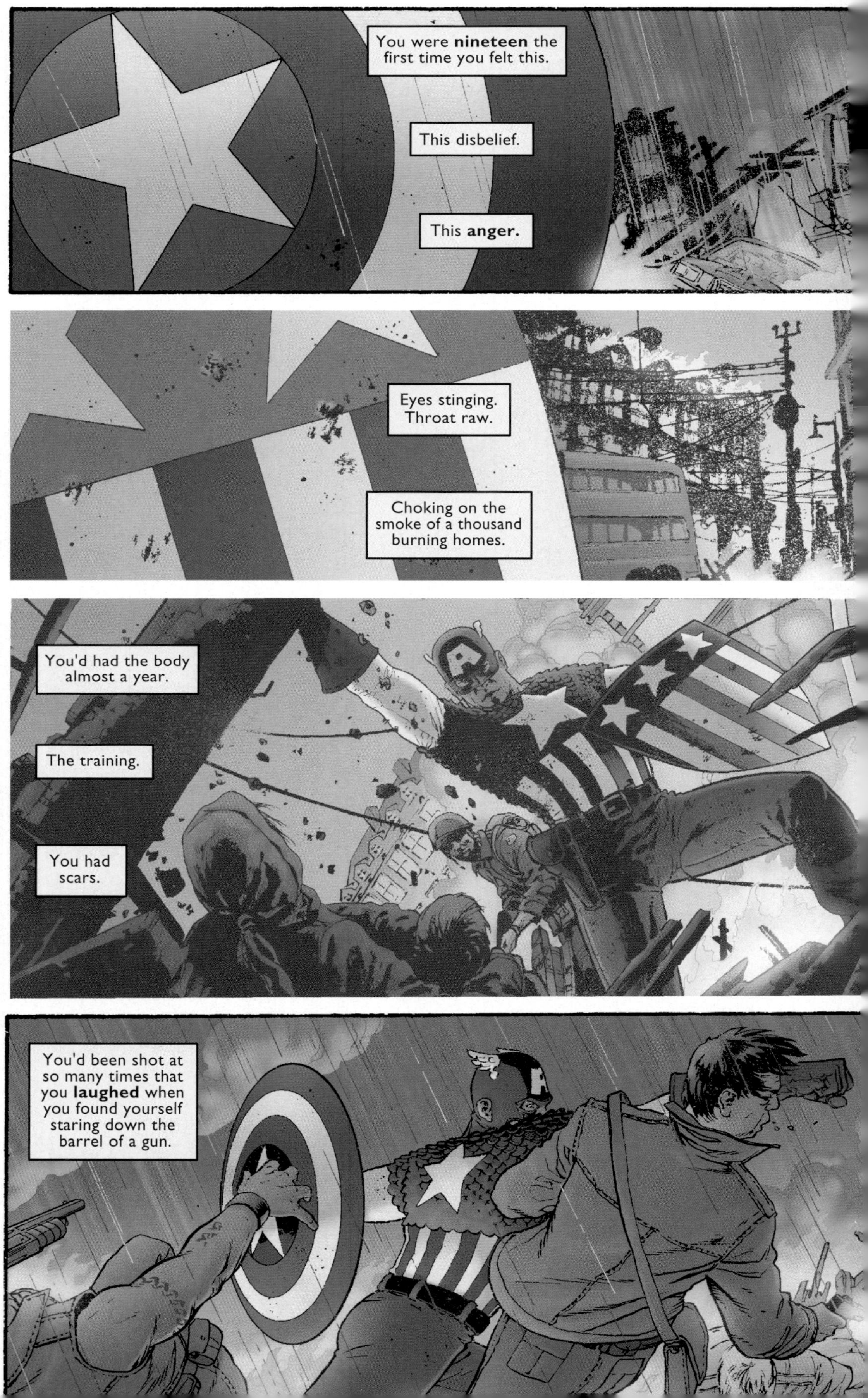
You were **nineteen** the first time you felt this.
This disbelief.
This **anger.**
Eyes stinging. Throat raw.
Choking on the smoke of a thousand burning homes.
You'd had the body almost a year.
The training.
You had scars.
You'd been shot at so many times that you **laughed** when you found yourself staring down the barrel of a gun.

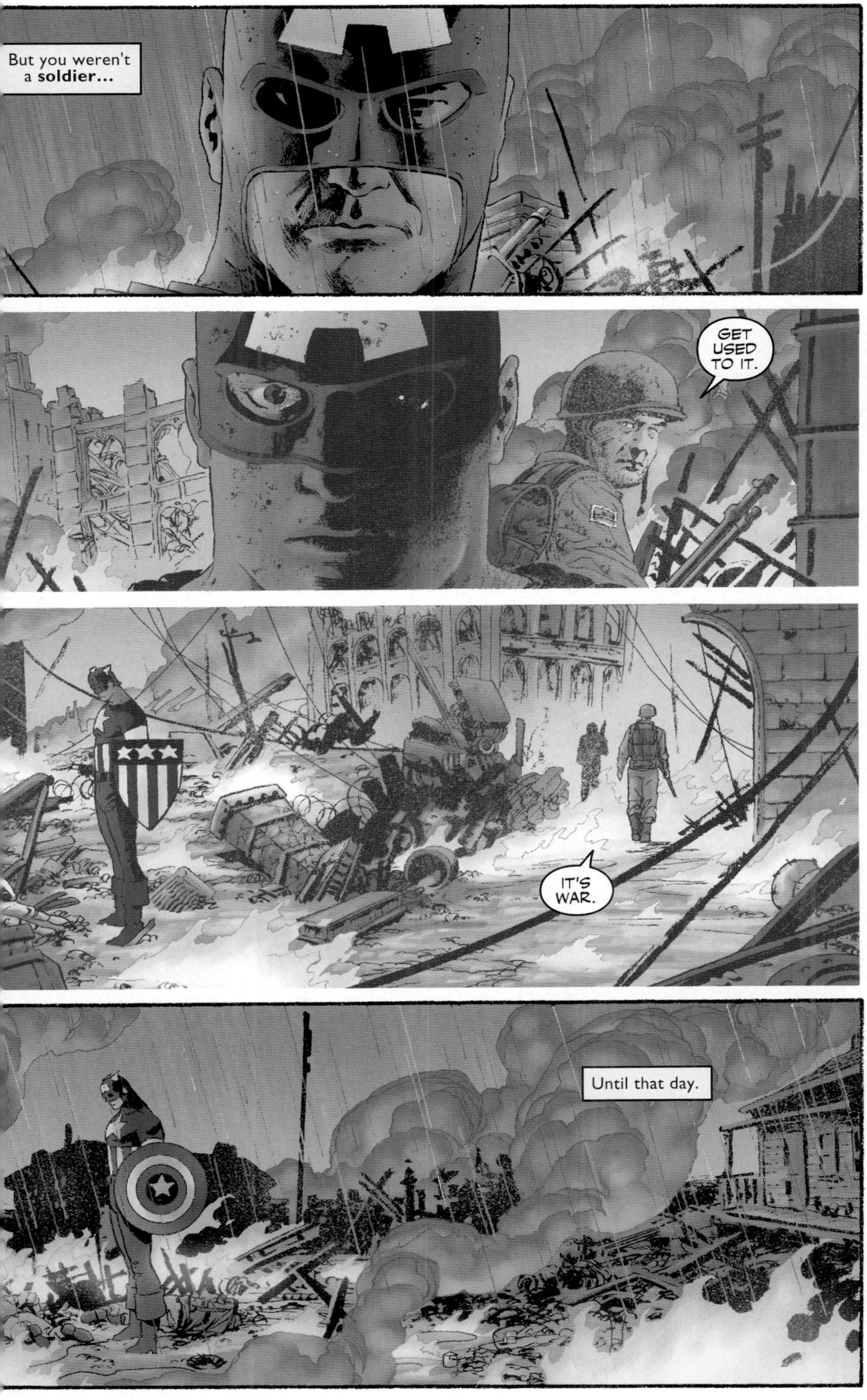
But you weren't a **soldier...**
GET USED TO IT.
IT'S WAR.
Until that day.

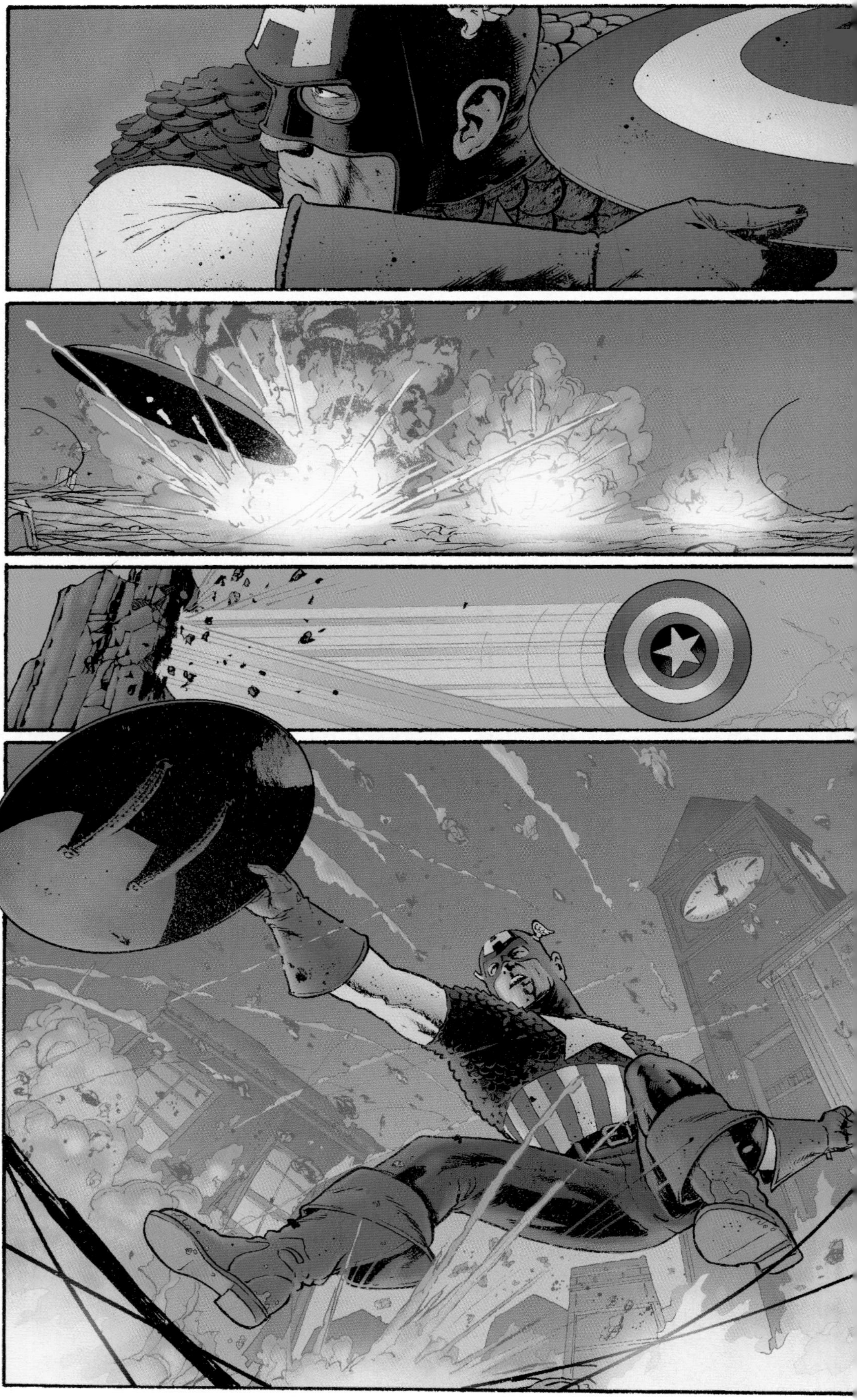

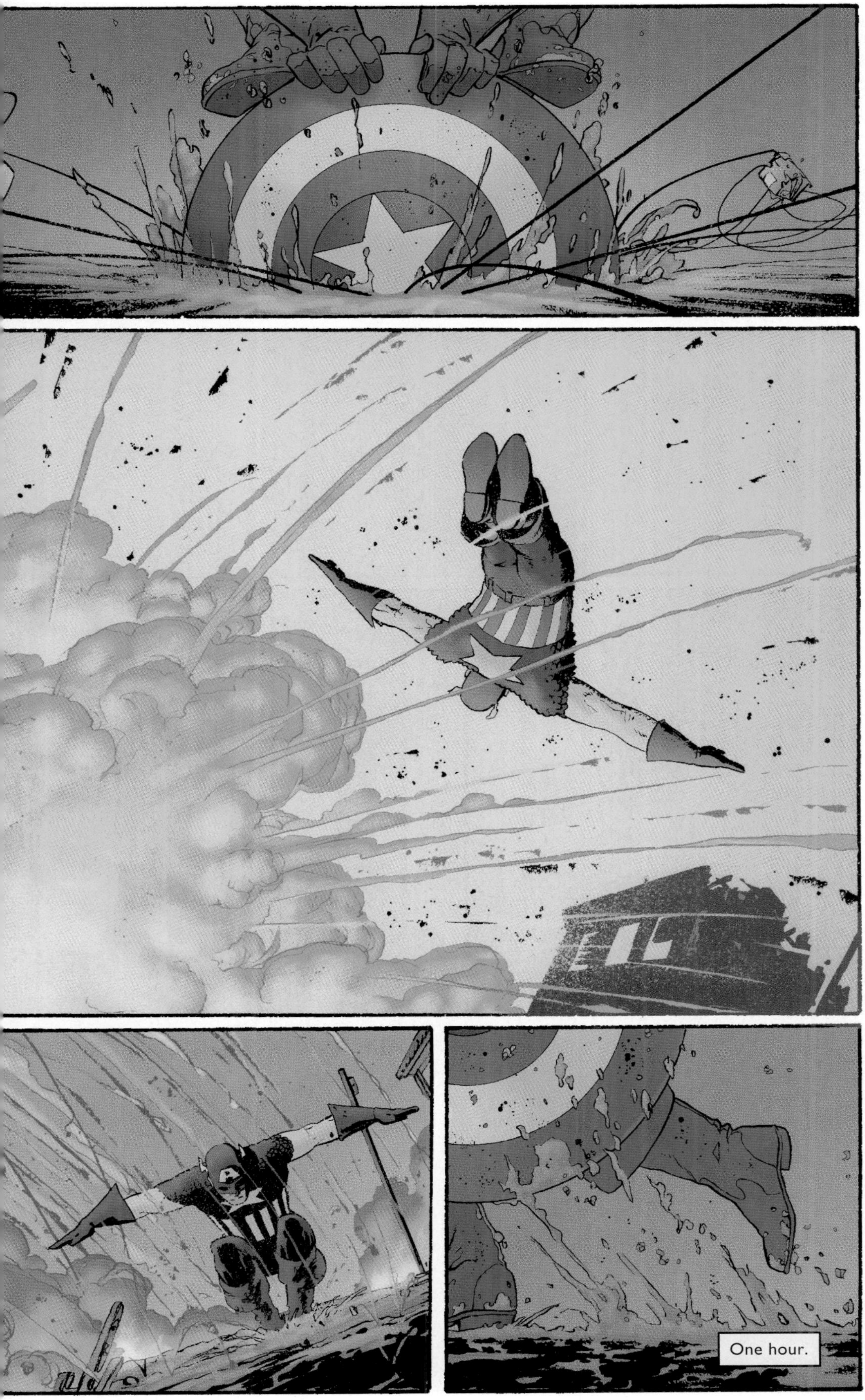
One hour.

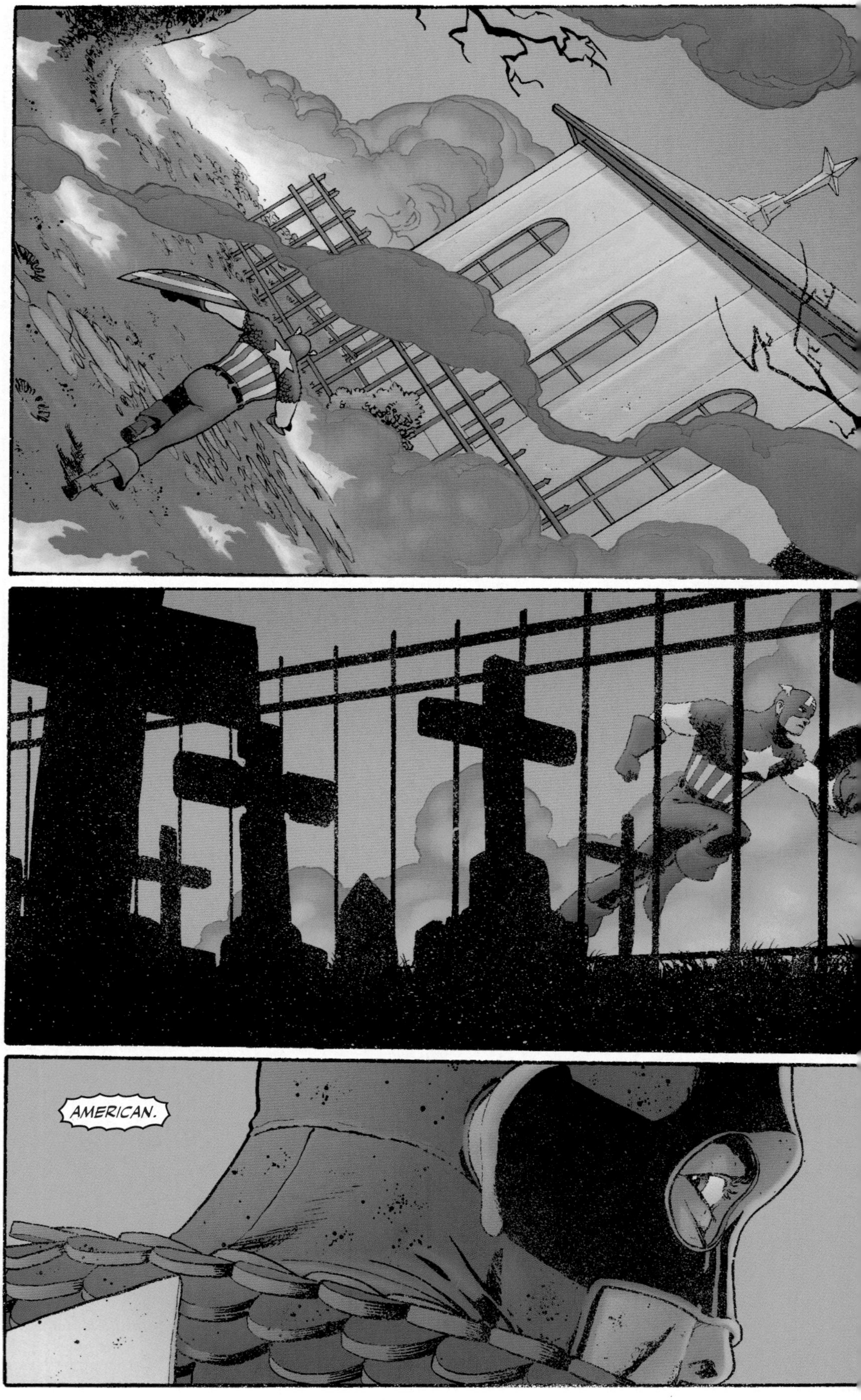
AMERICAN.

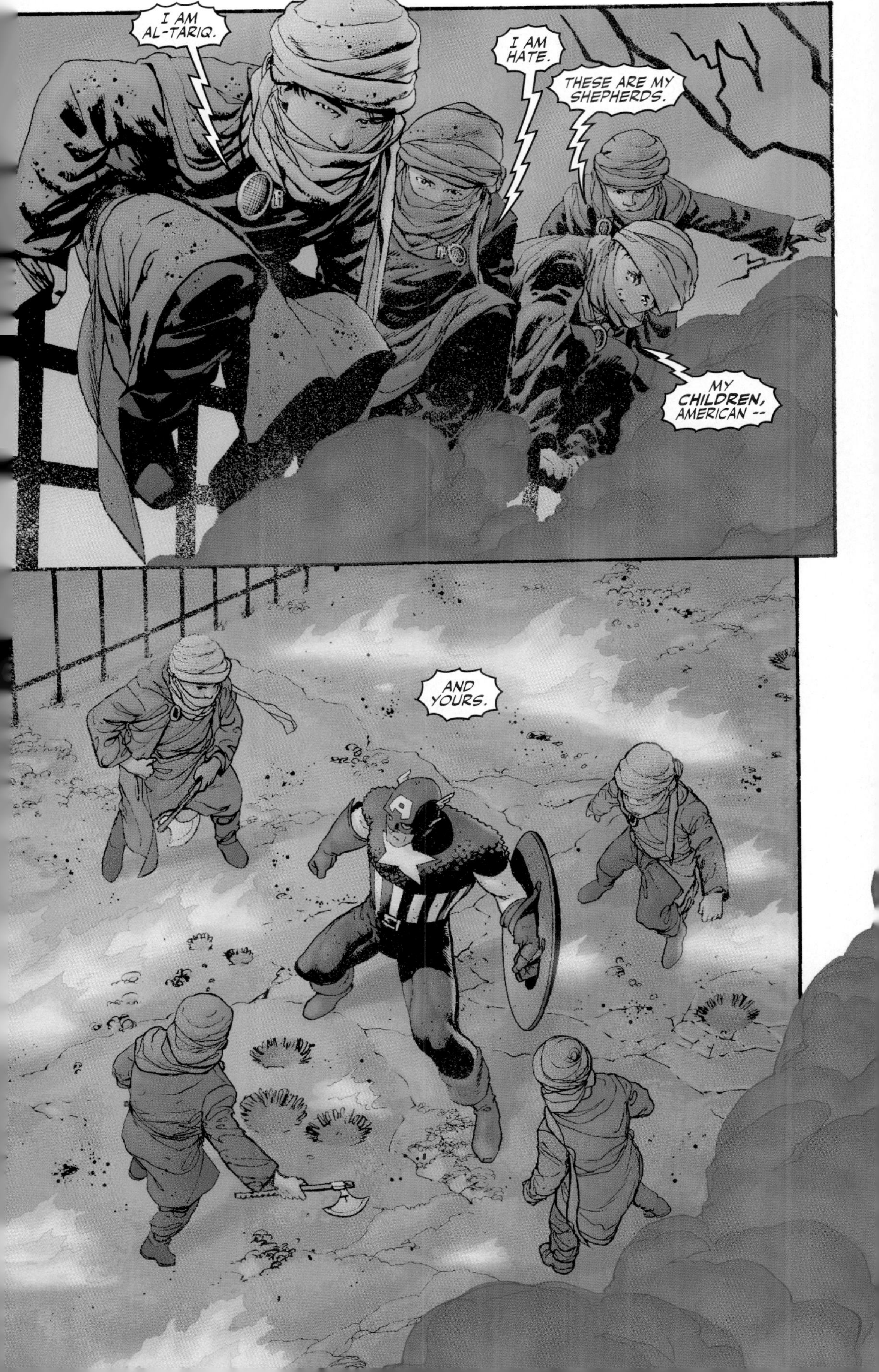
I AM AL-TARIQ.
I AM HATE.
THESE ARE MY SHEPHERDS.
MY CHILDREN, AMERICAN --
AND YOURS.

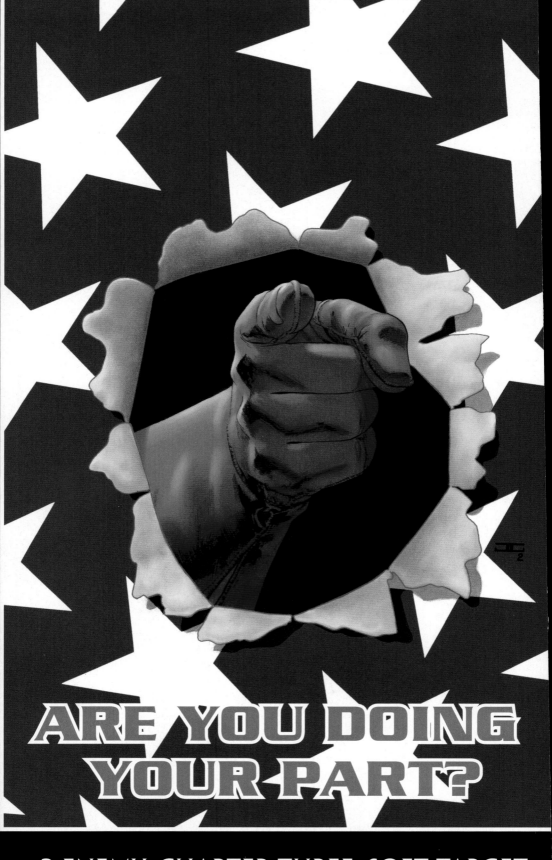

3 ENEMY, CHAPTER THREE: SOFT TARGET

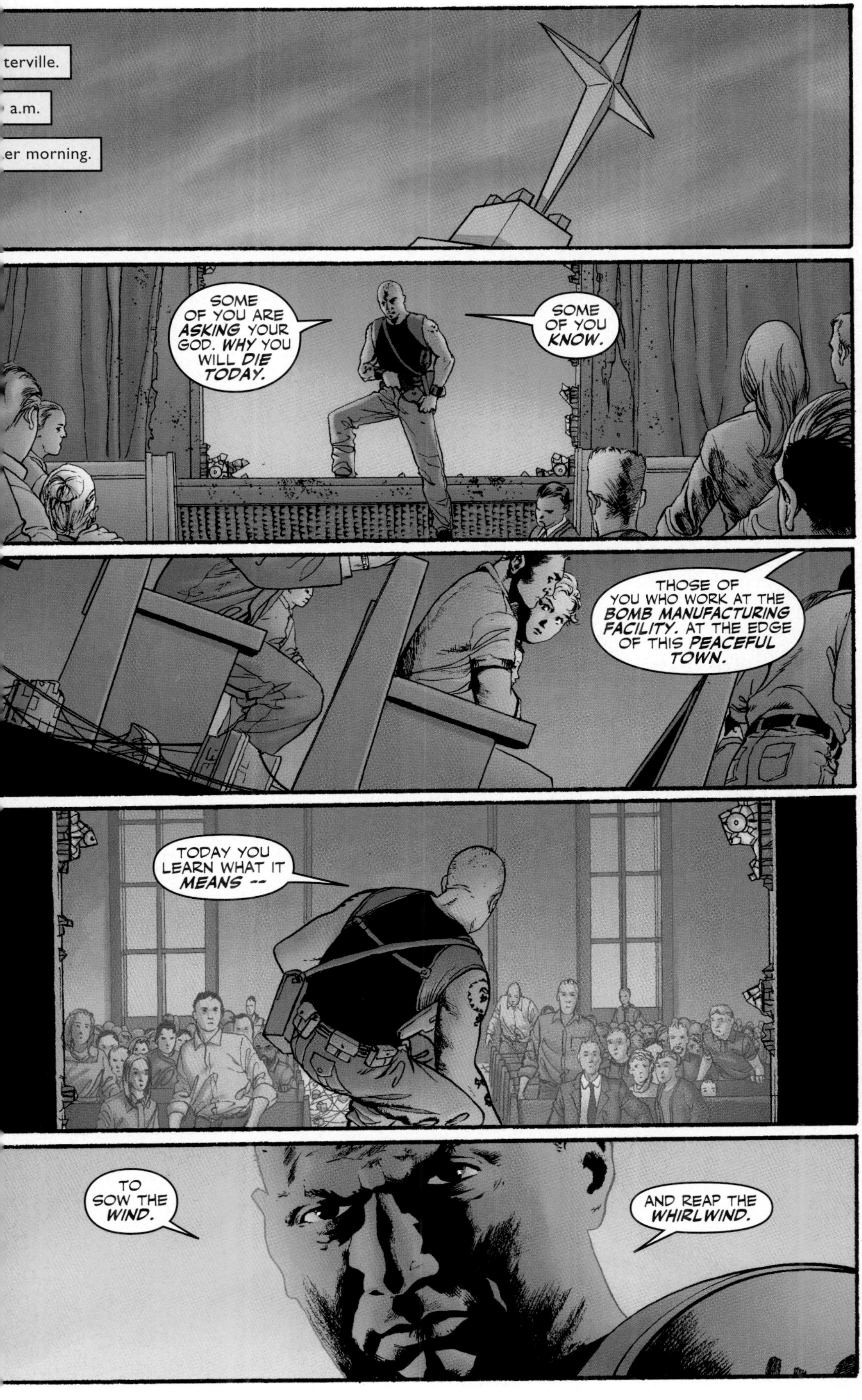
terville.
a.m.
er morning.
SOME OF YOU ARE ASKING YOUR GOD. WHY YOU WILL DIE TODAY.
SOME OF YOU KNOW.
THOSE OF YOU WHO WORK AT THE BOMB MANUFACTURING FACILITY. AT THE EDGE OF THIS PEACEFUL TOWN.
TODAY YOU LEARN WHAT IT MEANS --
TO SOW THE WIND.
AND REAP THE WHIRLWIND.

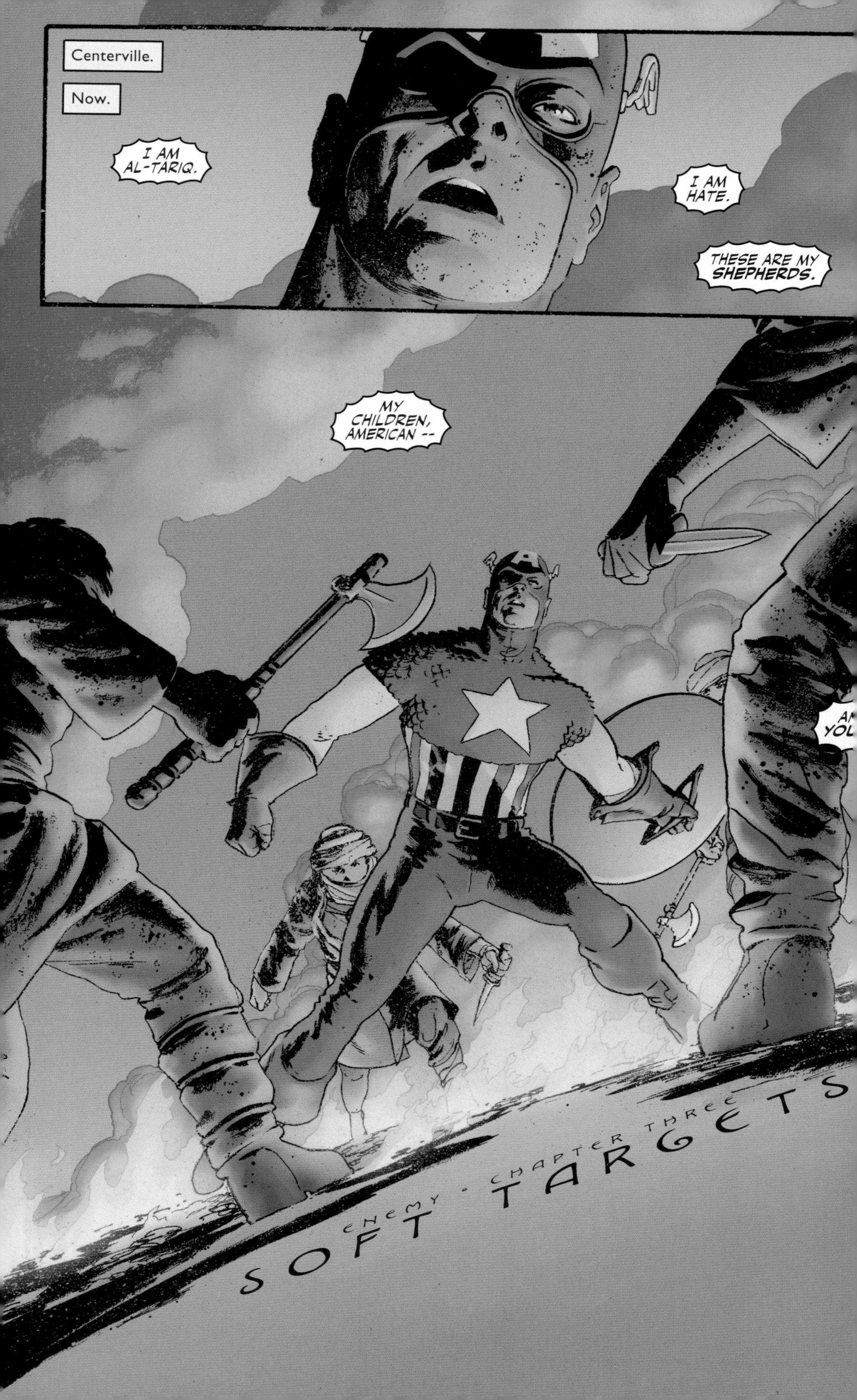
Centerville.
Now.
I AM AL-TARIQ.
I AM HATE.
THESE ARE MY SHEPHERDS.
MY CHILDREN, AMERICAN --
ENEMY • CHAPTER THREE
SOFT TARGETS

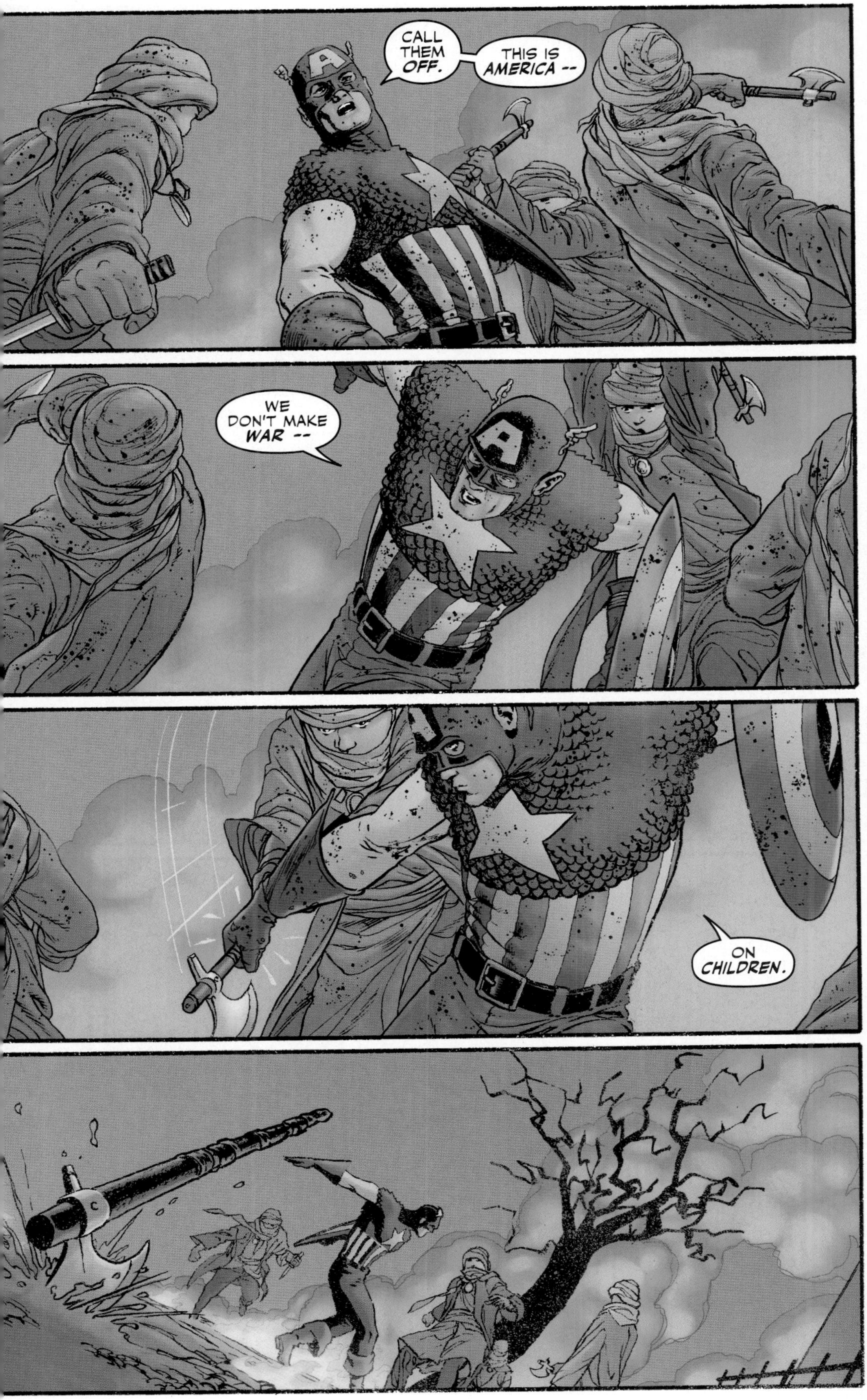
CALL THEM OFF.
THIS IS AMERICA --
WE DON'T MAKE WAR --
ON CHILDREN.

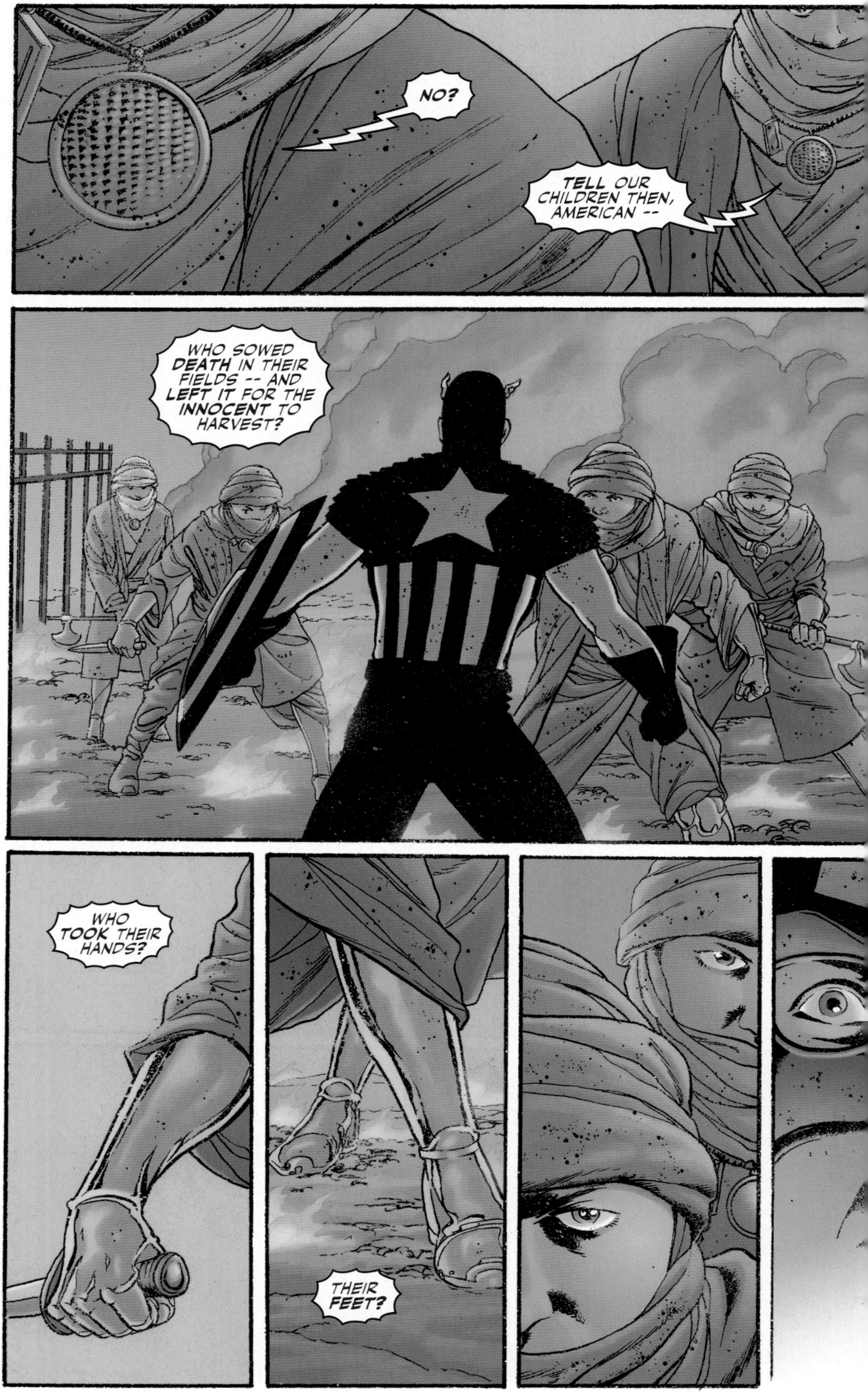
NO?
TELL OUR CHILDREN THEN, AMERICAN --
WHO SOWED DEATH IN THEIR FIELDS -- AND LEFT IT FOR THE INNOCENT TO HARVEST?
WHO TOOK THEIR HANDS?
THEIR FEET?

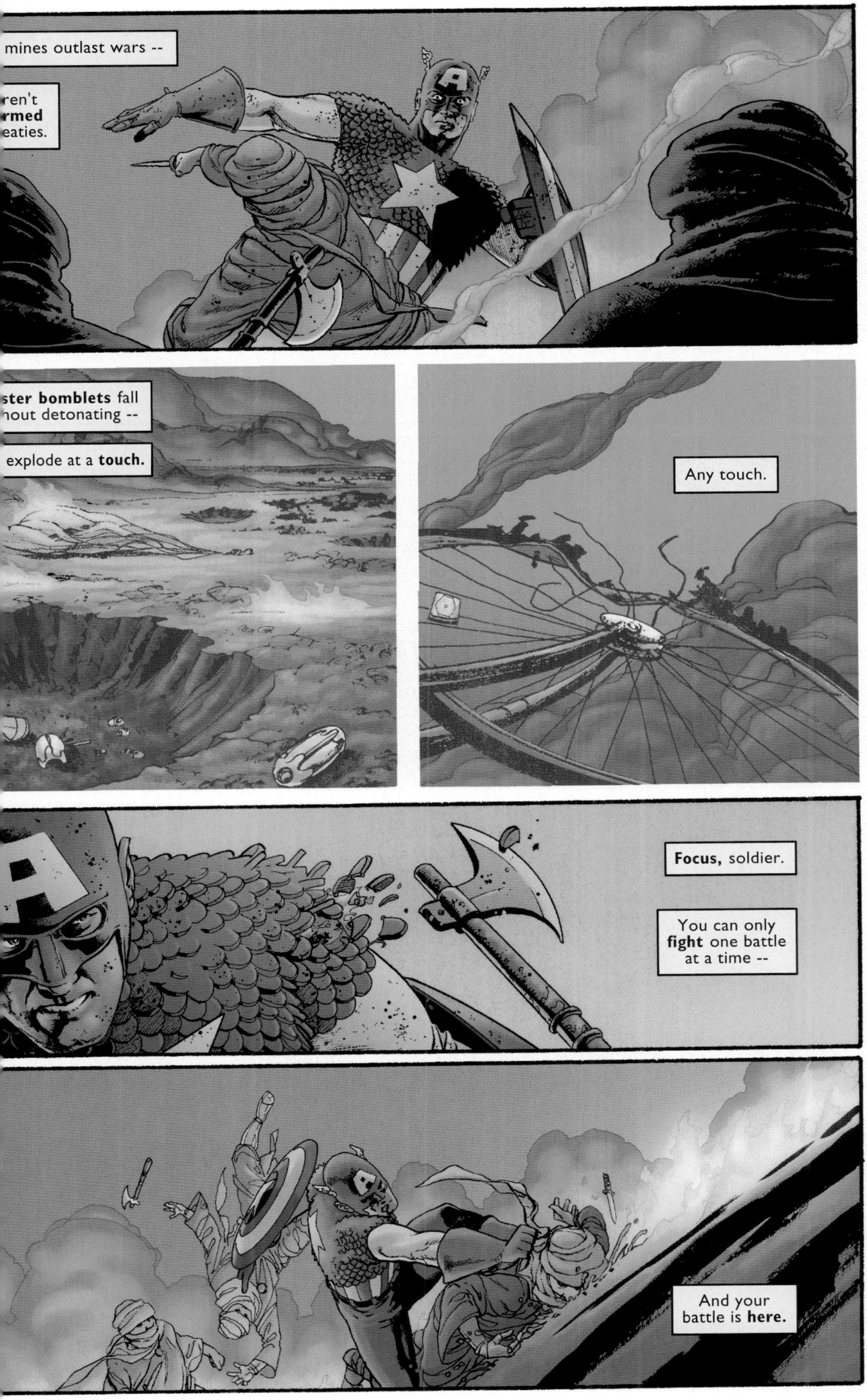
mines outlast wars --
ren't **rmed** eaties.
ster bomblets fall hout detonating --
explode at a **touch.**
Any touch.
Focus, soldier.
You can only **fight** one battle at a time --
And your battle is **here.**

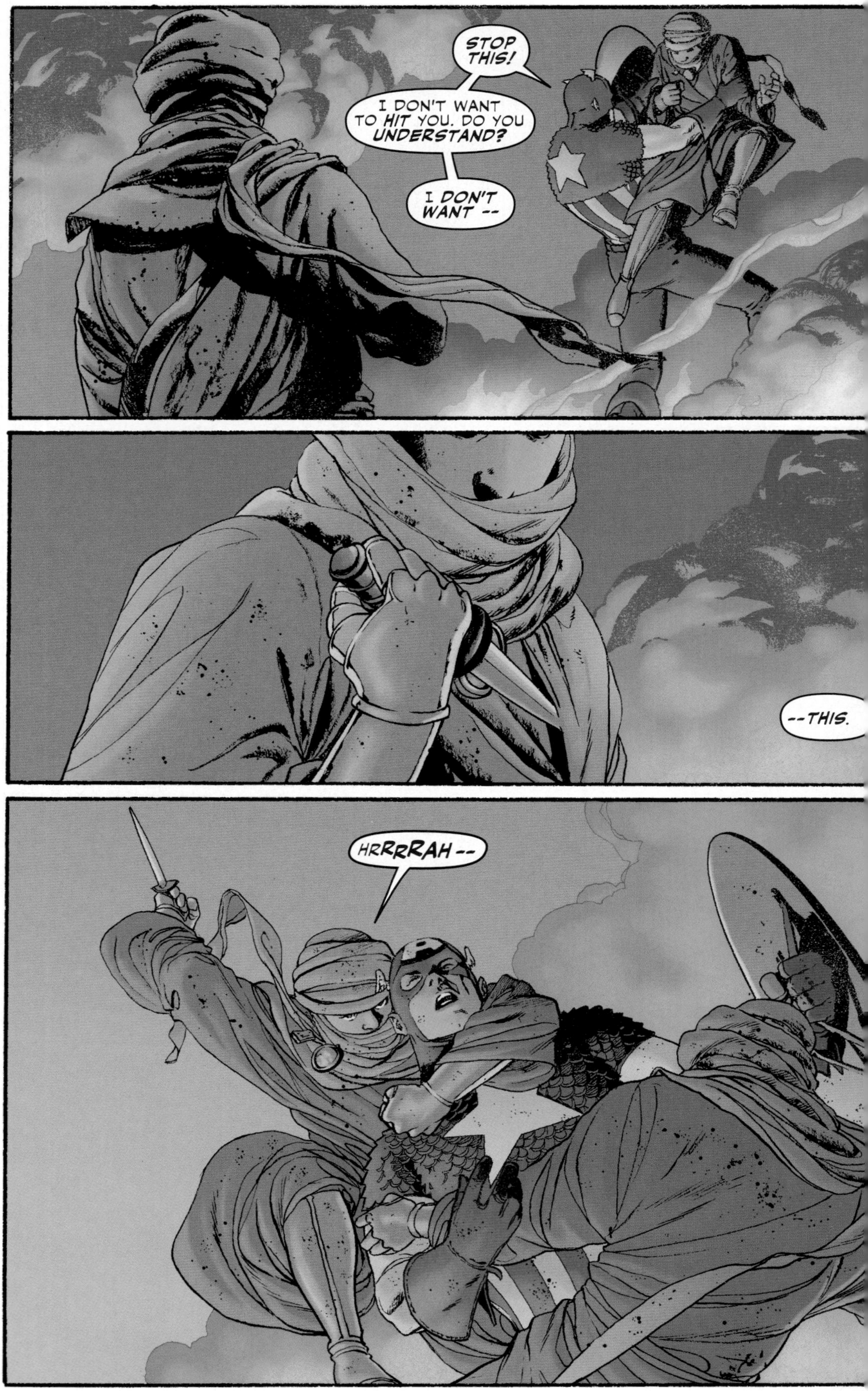
STOP THIS!
I DON'T WANT TO HIT YOU. DO YOU UNDERSTAND?
I DON'T WANT --
--THIS.
HRRRRAH --

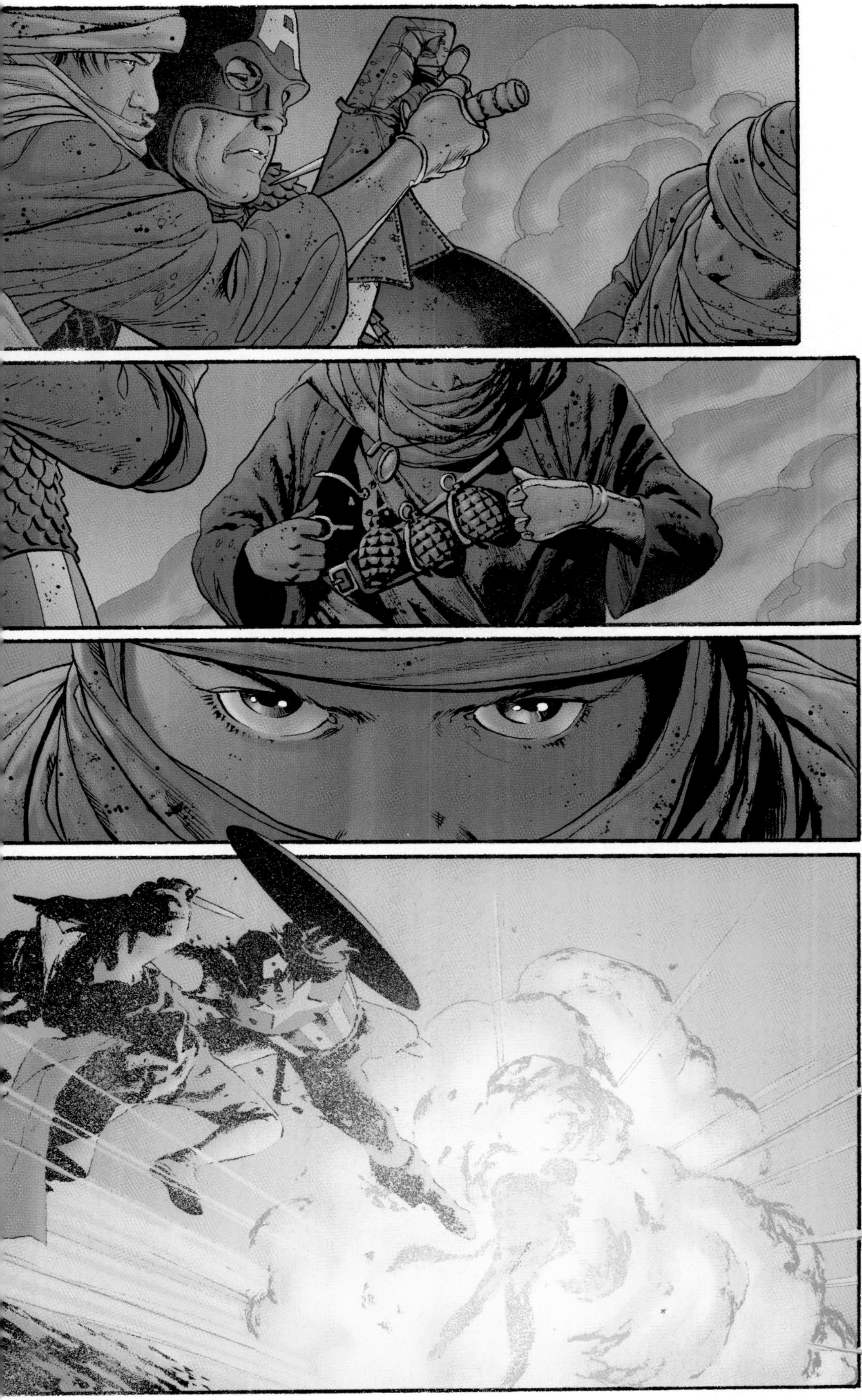

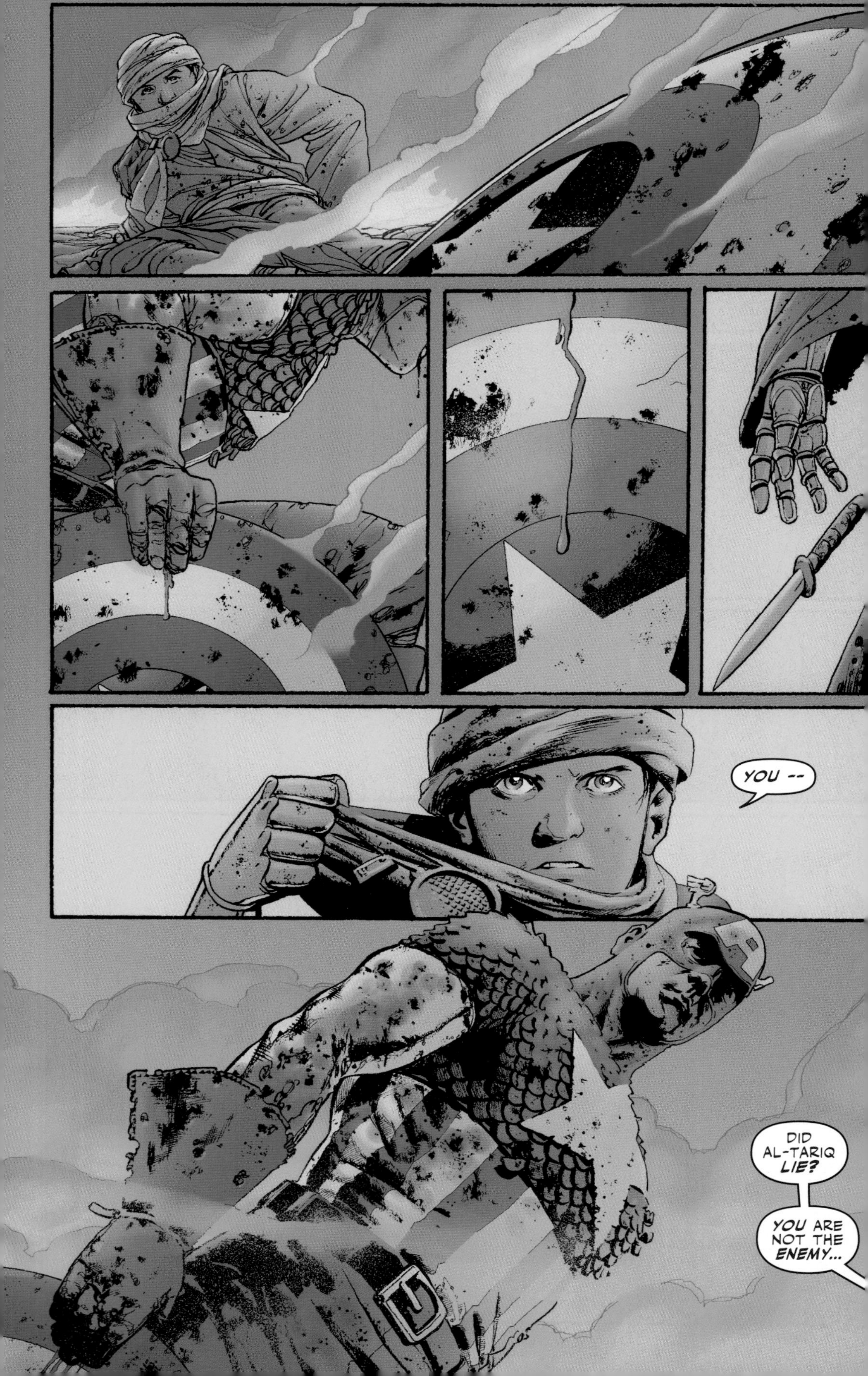
YOU --
DID AL-TARIQ LIE?
YOU ARE NOT THE ENEMY...

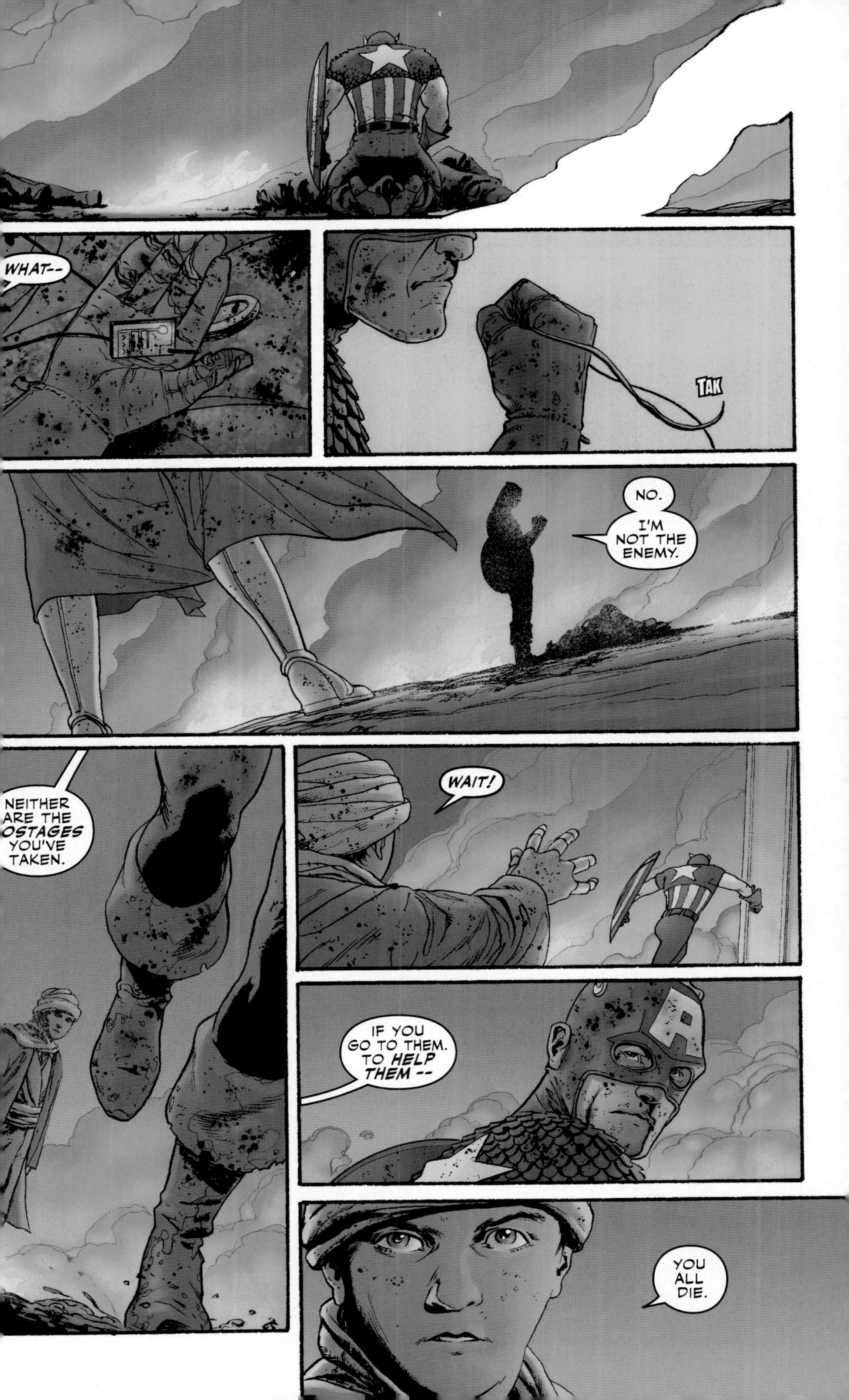
WHAT--
TAK
NO.
I'M NOT THE ENEMY.
NEITHER ARE THE OSTAGES YOU'VE TAKEN.
WAIT!
IF YOU GO TO THEM. TO HELP THEM --
YOU ALL DIE.

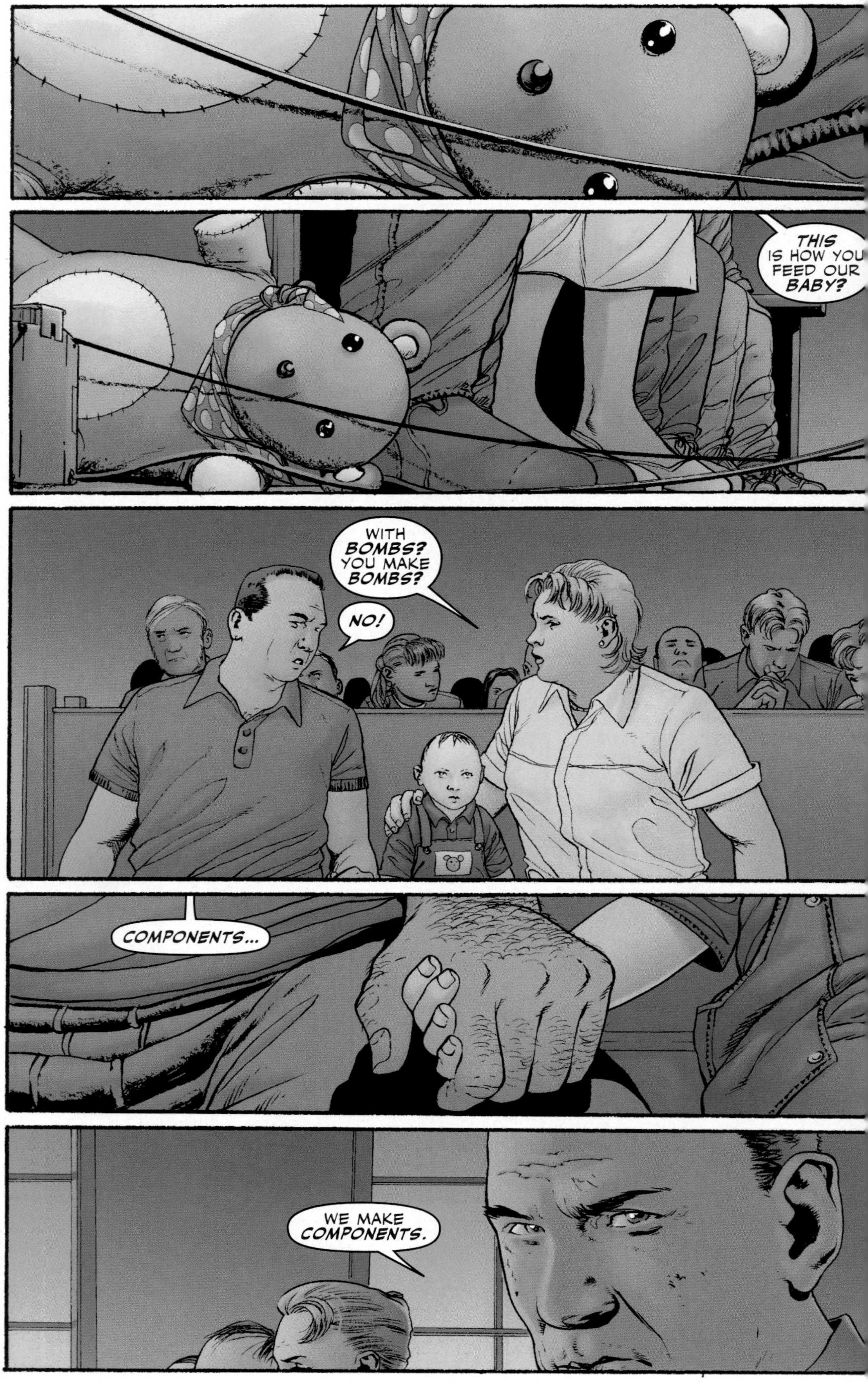
THIS IS HOW YOU FEED OUR BABY?
WITH BOMBS? YOU MAKE BOMBS?
NO!
COMPONENTS...
WE MAKE COMPONENTS.

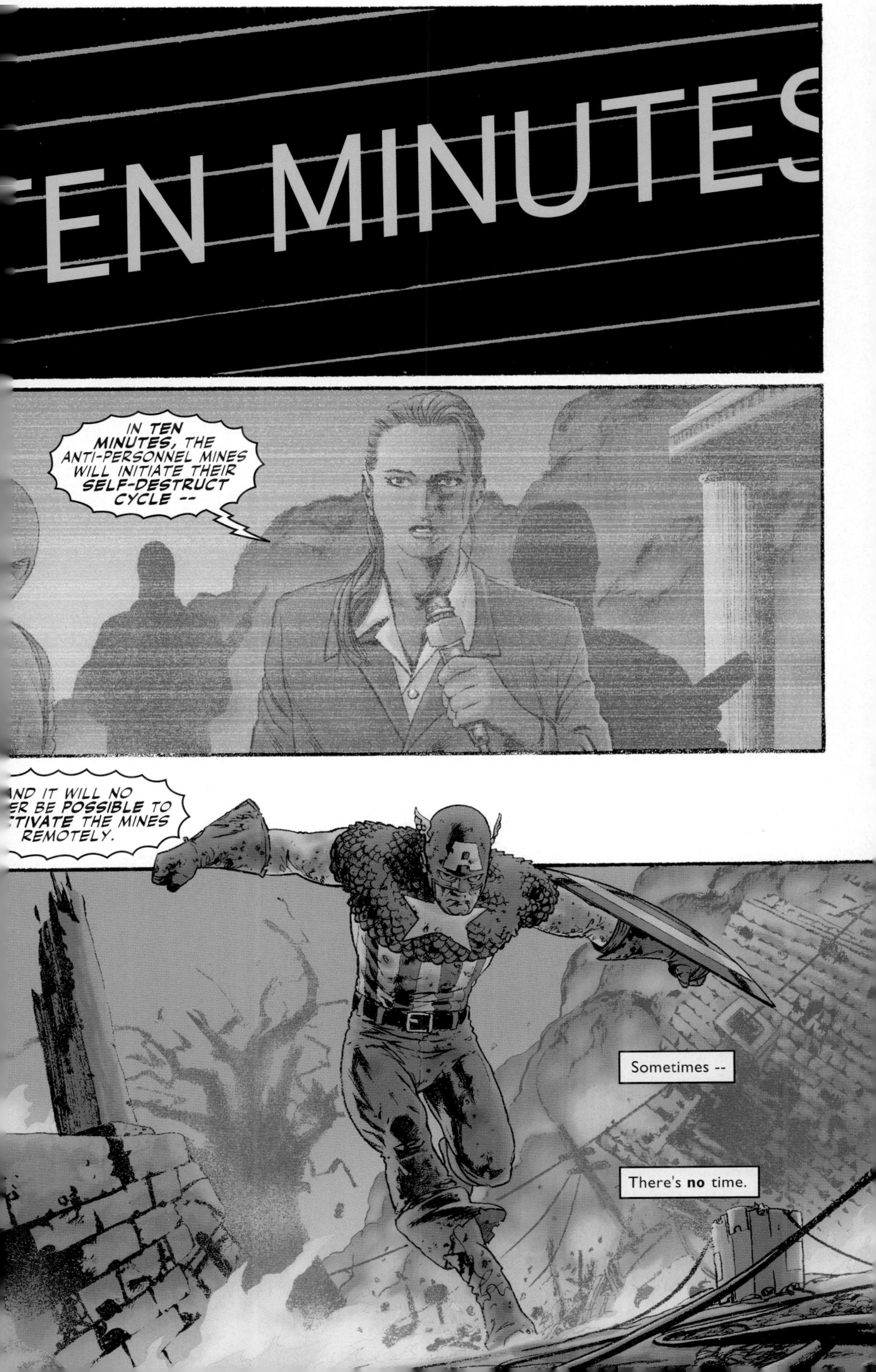
TEN MINUTES
IN TEN MINUTES, THE ANTI-PERSONNEL MINES WILL INITIATE THEIR SELF-DESTRUCT CYCLE --
AND IT WILL NO ER BE POSSIBLE TO TIVATE THE MINES REMOTELY.
Sometimes --
There's no time.

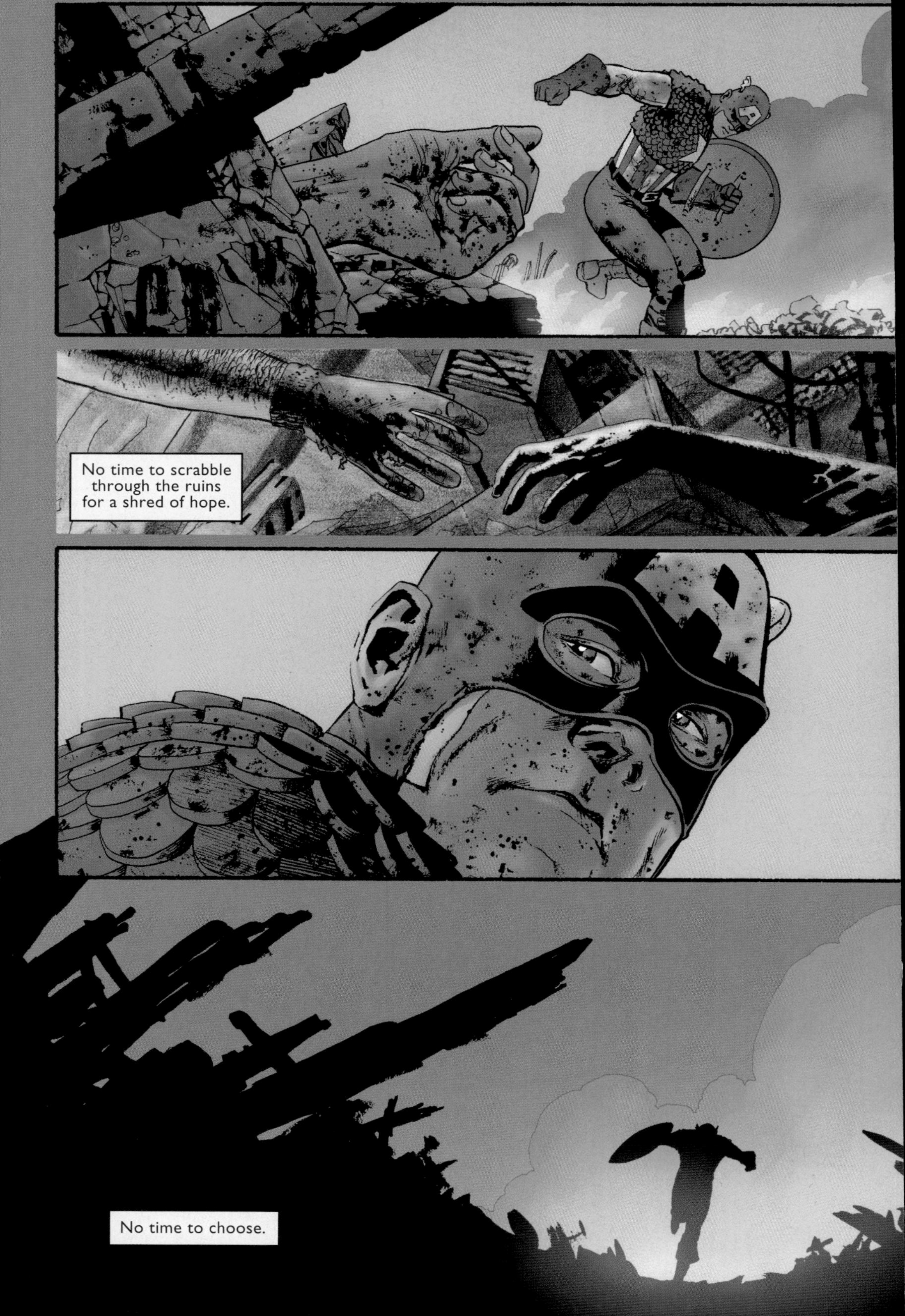
No time to scrabble through the ruins for a shred of hope.
No time to choose.

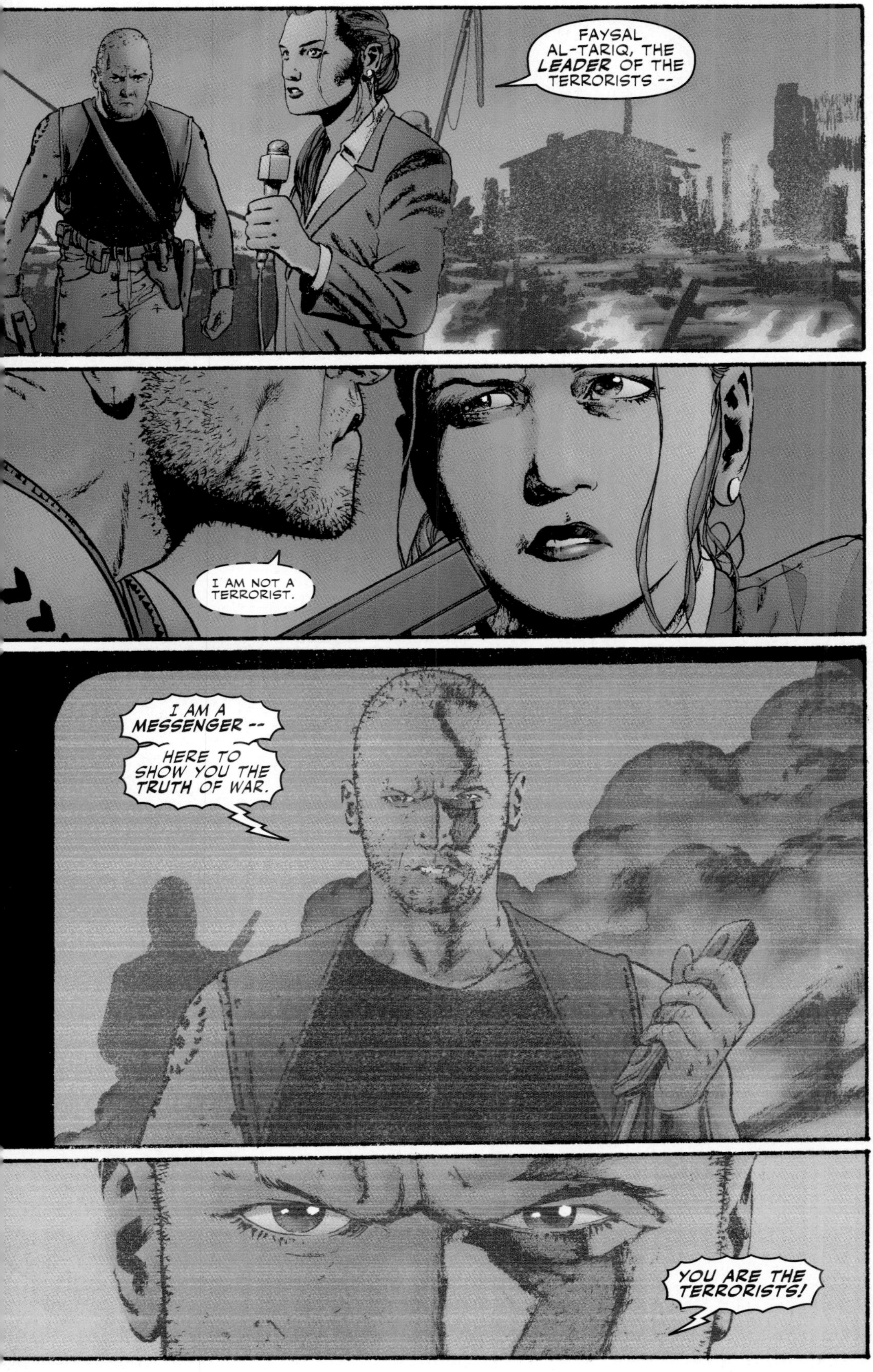
FAYSAL AL-TARIQ, THE LEADER OF THE TERRORISTS --
I AM NOT A TERRORIST.
I AM A MESSENGER --
HERE TO SHOW YOU THE TRUTH OF WAR.
YOU ARE THE TERRORISTS!

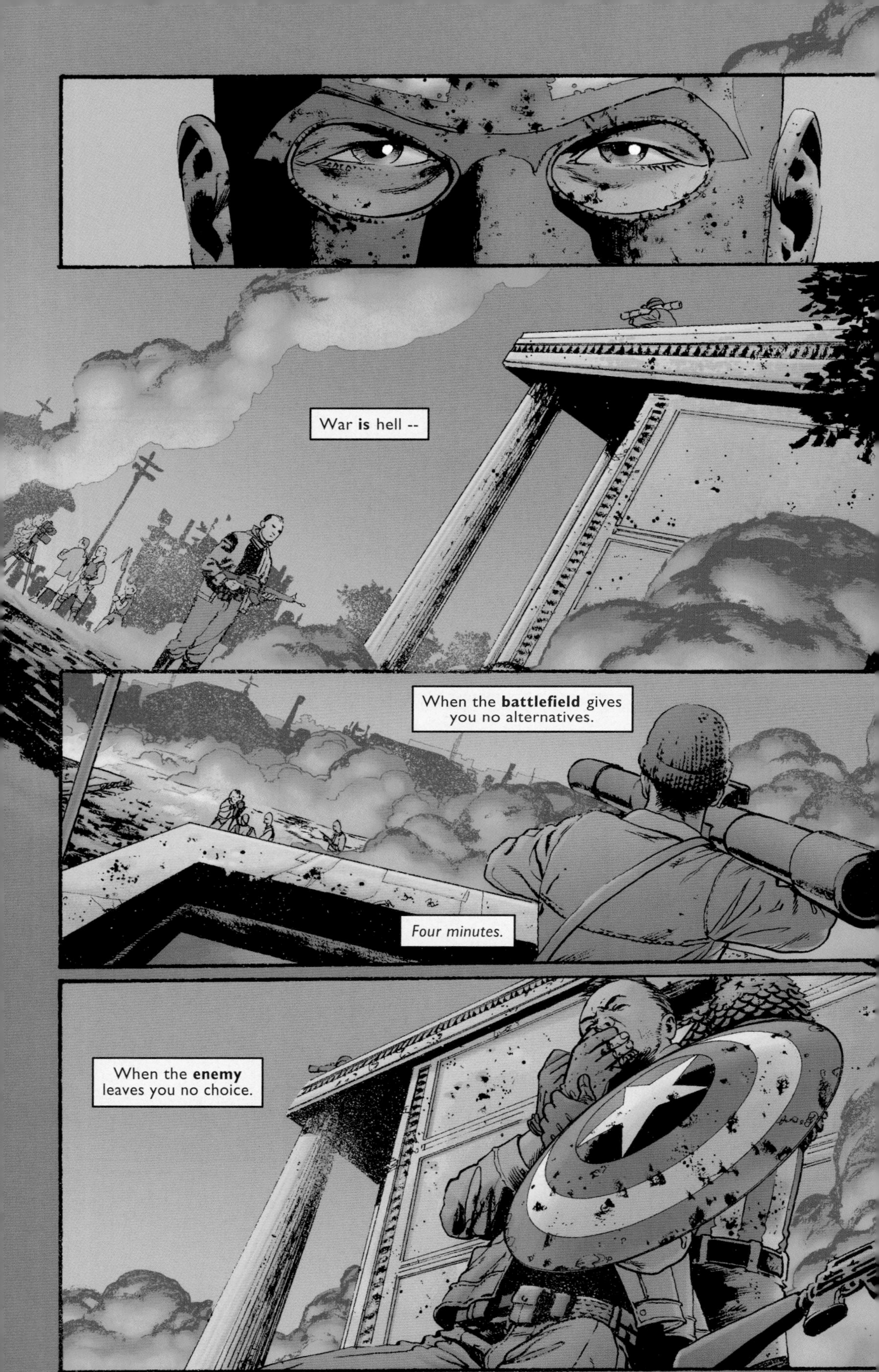
War **is** hell --
When the **battlefield** gives you no alternatives.
Four minutes.
When the **enemy** leaves you no choice.

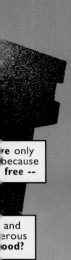

e only
because
free --

and
erous
ood?

does the light
e cast shadows
we don't --

e monsters like
-Tariq can plant
seeds of hate?

WHEN INNOCENT *AMERICANS* DIE -- IT'S AN *ATROCITY.*

BUT WHEN *WE* DIE --

WE ARE "*COLLATERAL DAMAGE.*"

The questions don't **matter.**

Not **here.**
Not **now.**

Three minutes.

Nothing matters --

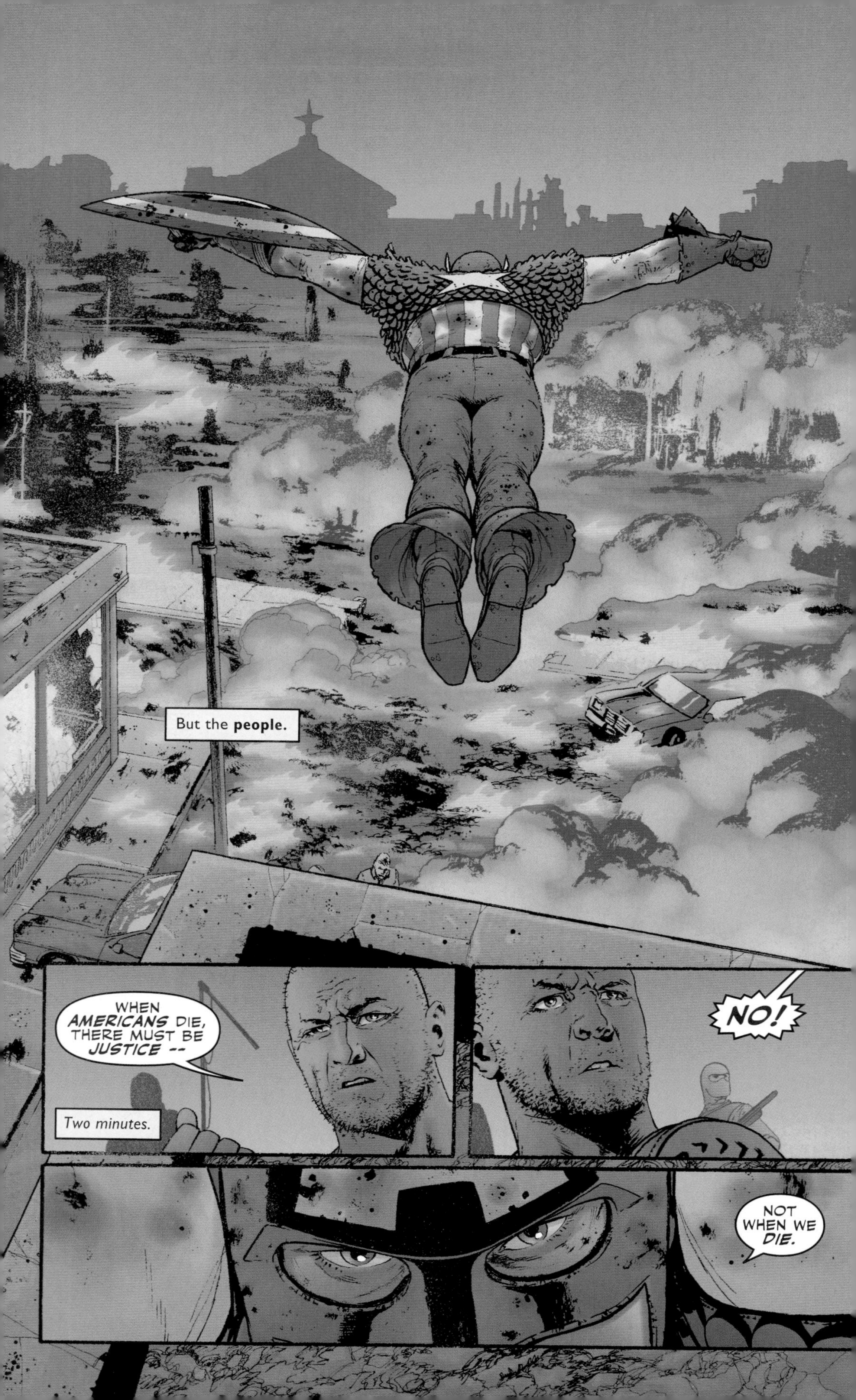
But the people.
WHEN AMERICANS DIE, THERE MUST BE JUSTICE --
Two minutes.
NO!
NOT WHEN WE DIE.

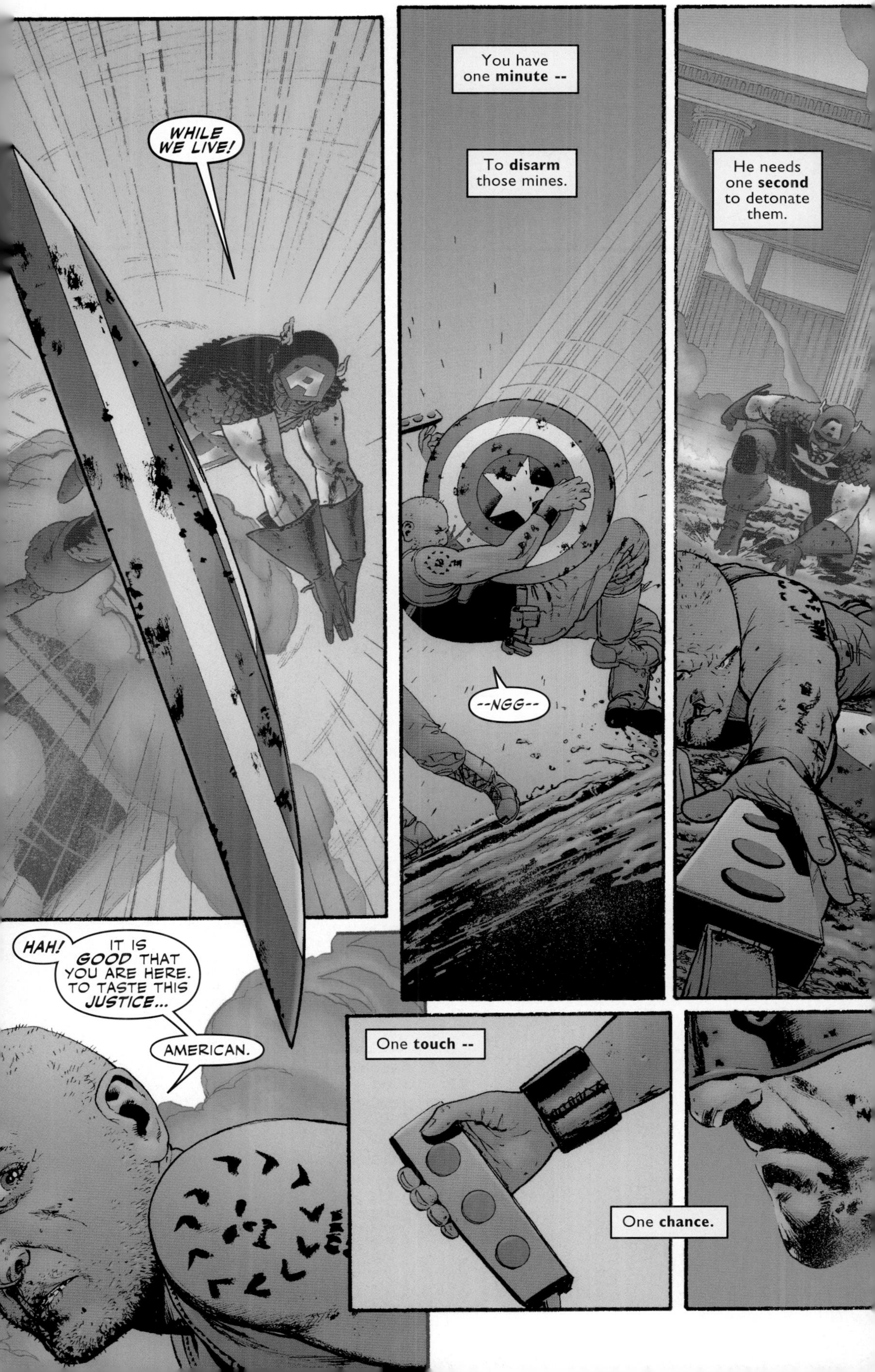
WHILE WE LIVE!
You have one **minute** --
To **disarm** those mines.
--NGG--
He needs one **second** to detonate them.
HAH!
IT IS *GOOD* THAT YOU ARE HERE. TO TASTE THIS *JUSTICE...*
AMERICAN.
One **touch** --
One **chance.**

To turn two hundred **lives** into clouds of **blood** and **fire** and **shrapnel**.

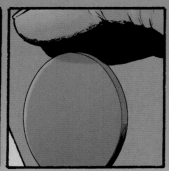

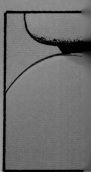

THOKK

The man you are can only **pray** --

As the soldier **strikes** --

To **end** the battle.

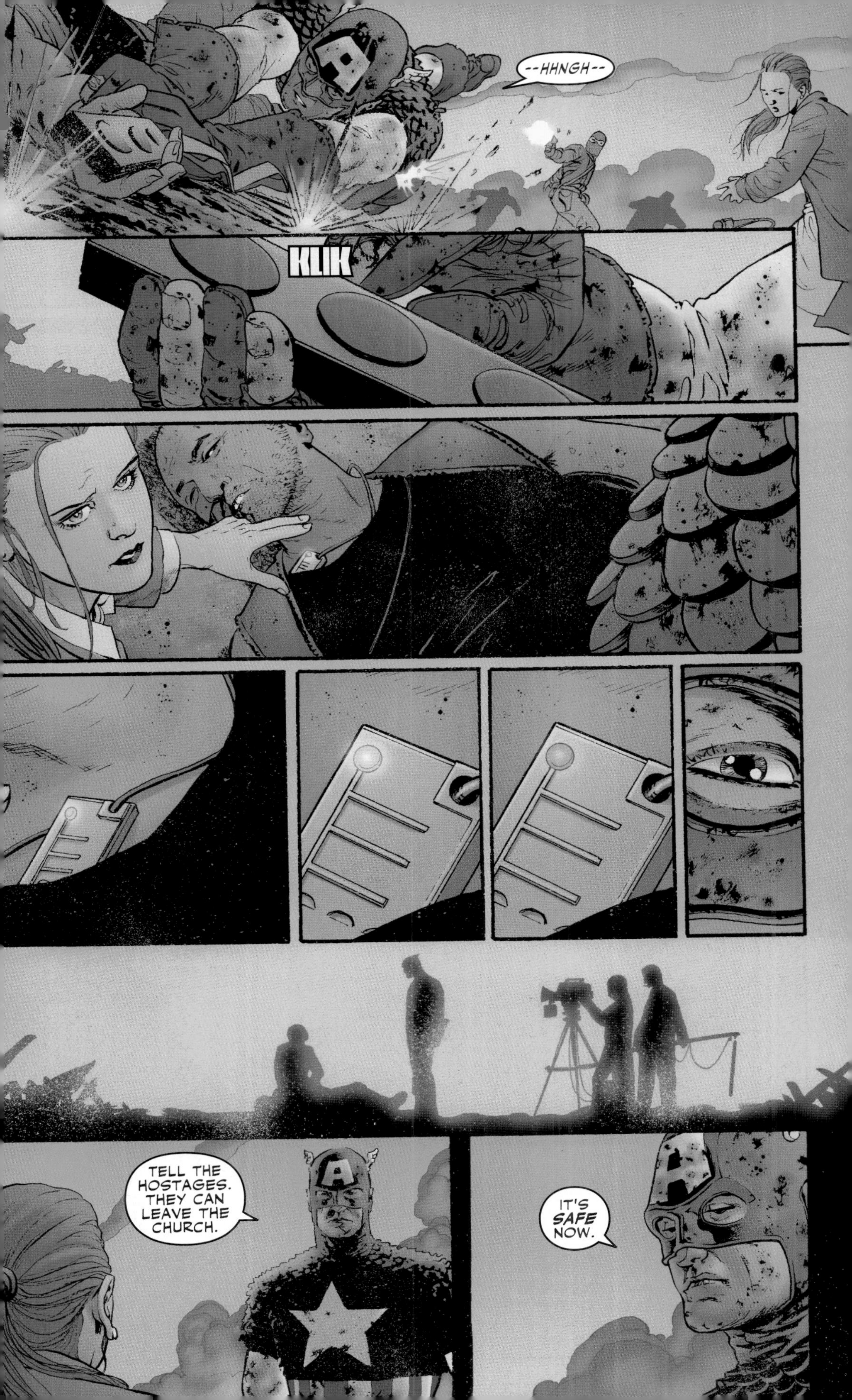
--HHNGH--
KLIK
TELL THE HOSTAGES. THEY CAN LEAVE THE CHURCH.
IT'S SAFE NOW.

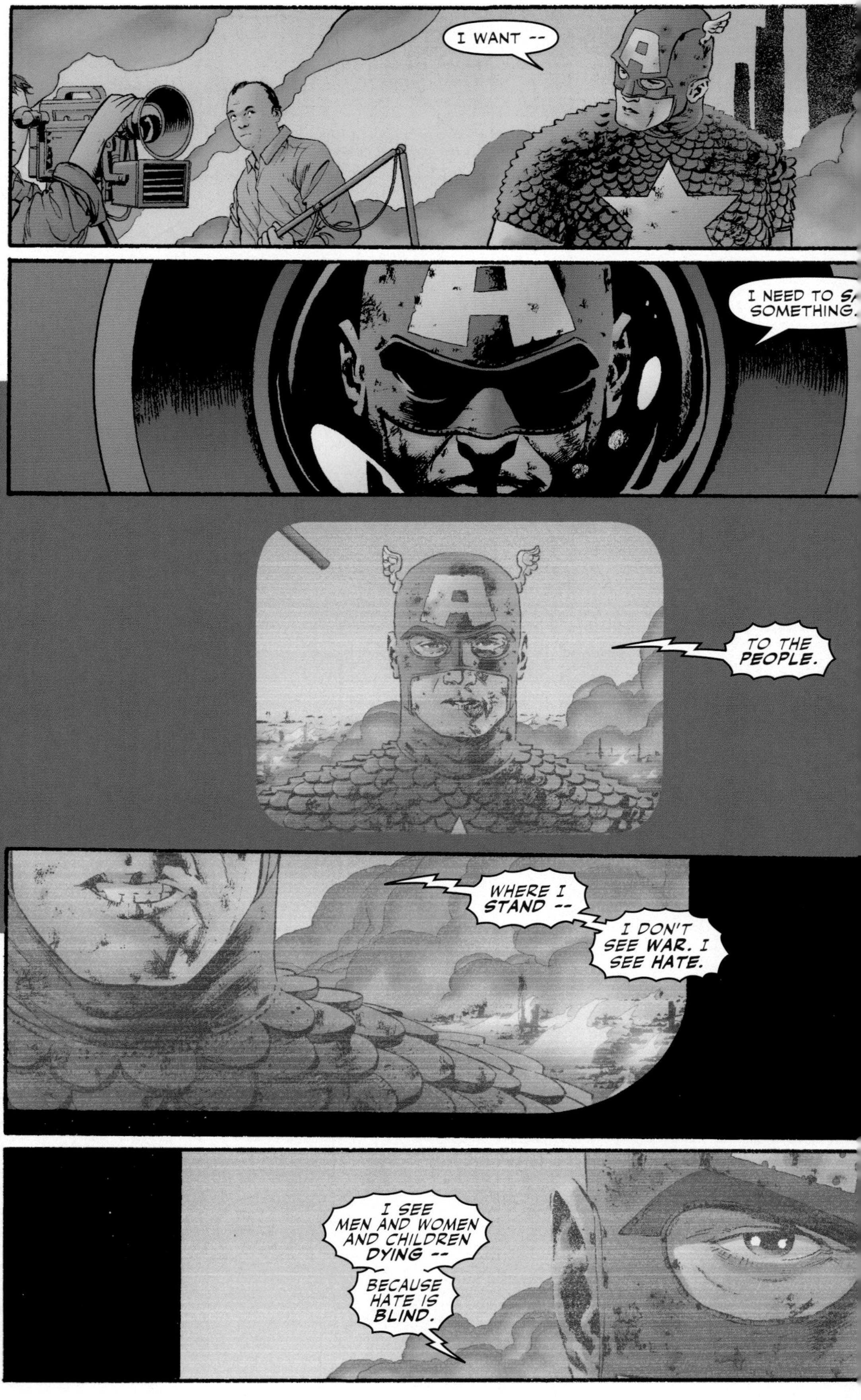
I WANT --
I NEED TO S
SOMETHING.
TO THE PEOPLE.
WHERE I STAND --
I DON'T SEE WAR. I SEE HATE.
I SEE MEN AND WOMEN AND CHILDREN DYING --
BECAUSE HATE IS BLIND.

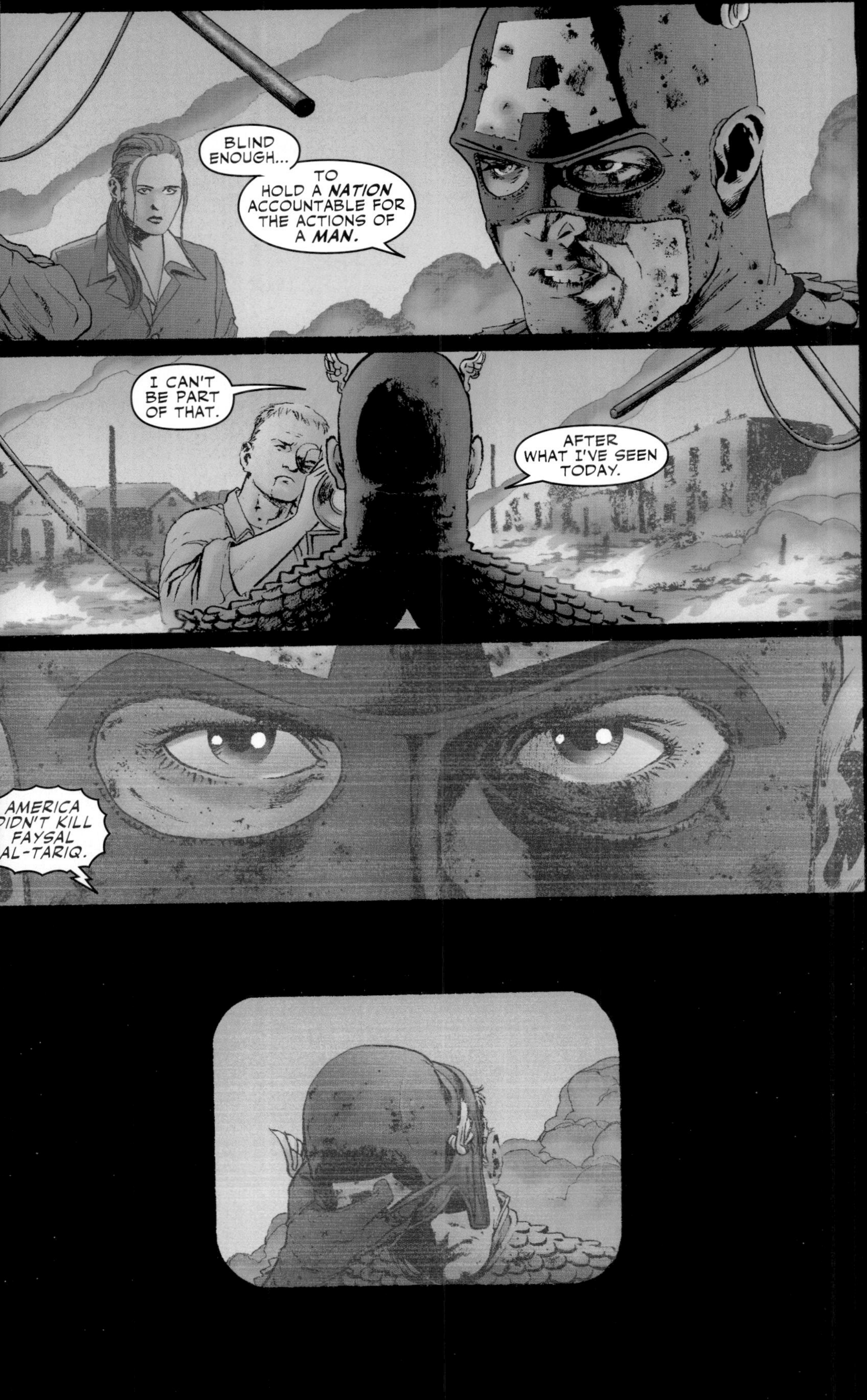
BLIND ENOUGH...
TO HOLD A NATION ACCOUNTABLE FOR THE ACTIONS OF A MAN.
I CAN'T BE PART OF THAT.
AFTER WHAT I'VE SEEN TODAY.
AMERICA DIDN'T KILL FAYSAL AL-TARIQ.

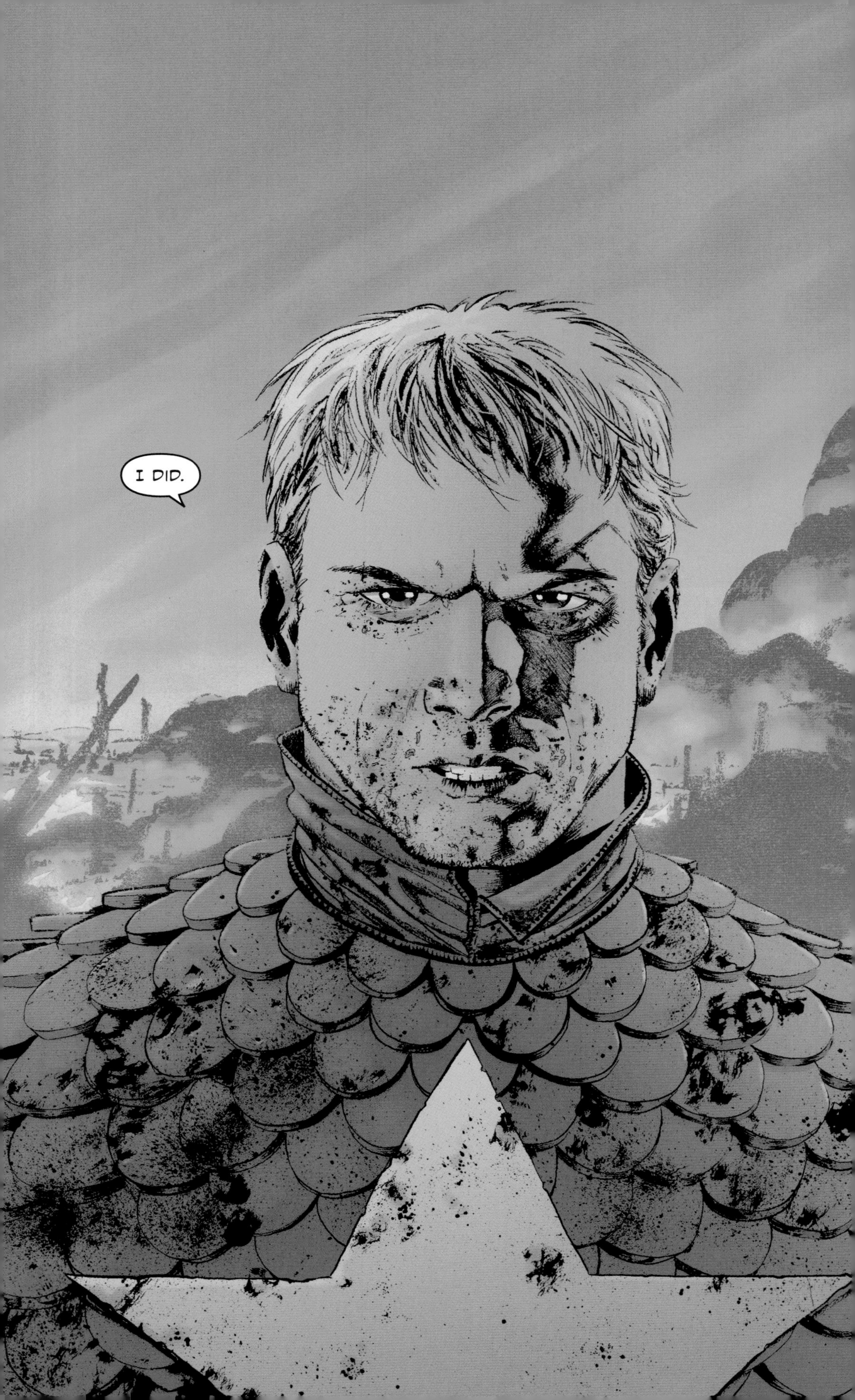
I DID.

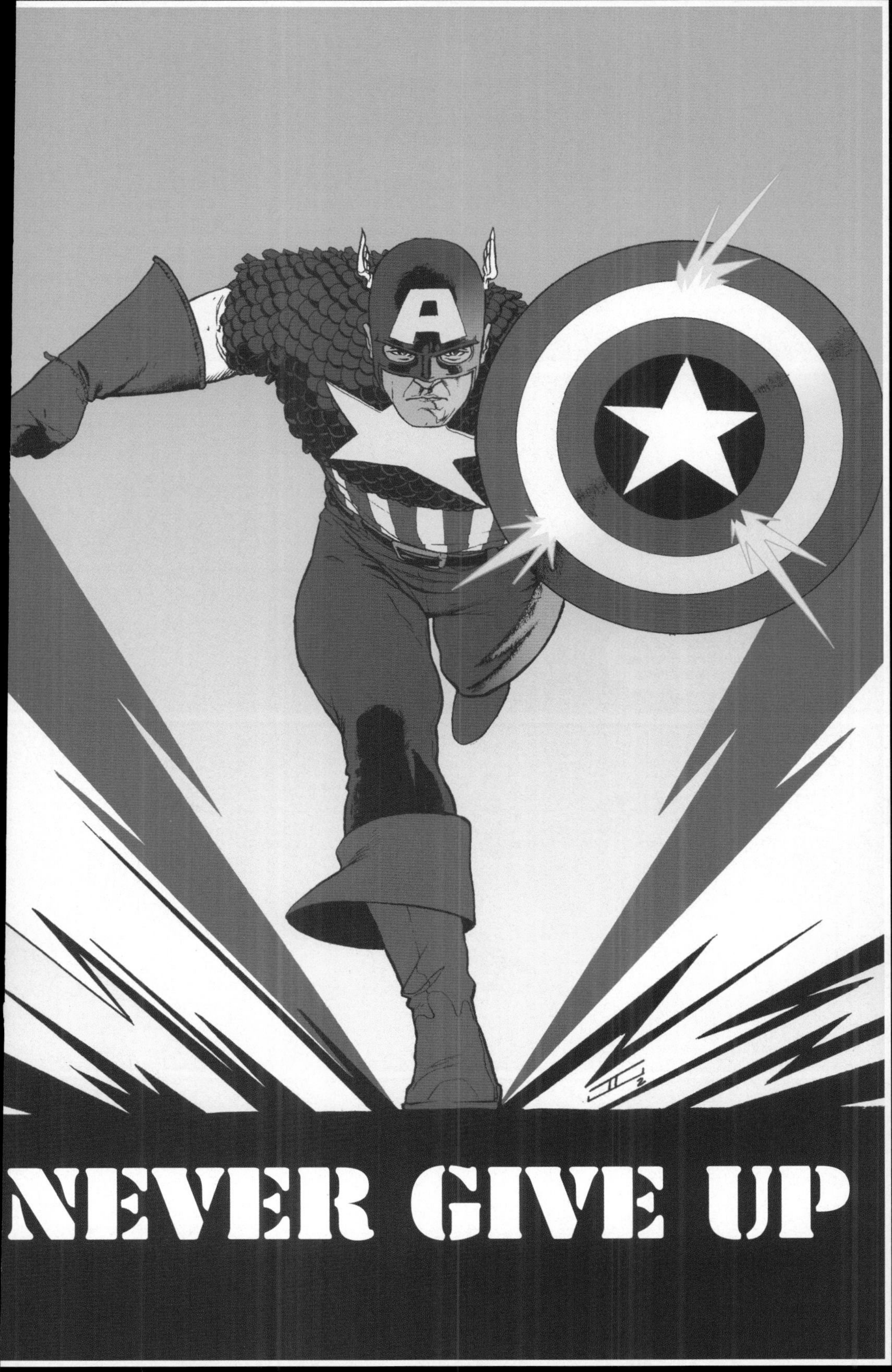
NEVER GIVE UP

4 WARLORDS, PART 1

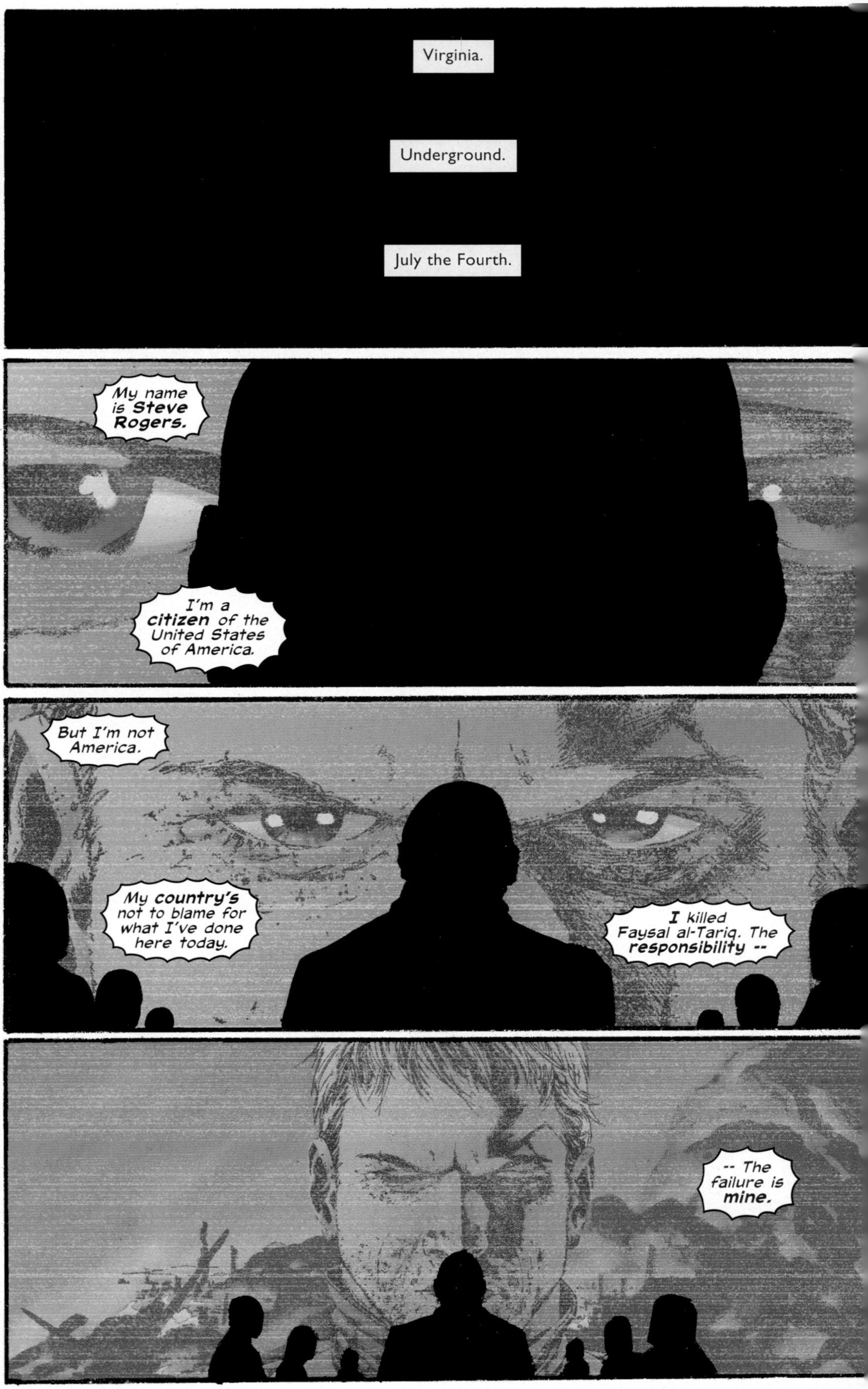

Virginia.
Underground.
July the Fourth.
My name is Steve Rogers.
I'm a citizen of the United States of America.
But I'm not America.
My country's not to blame for what I've done here today.
I killed Faysal al-Tariq. The responsibility --
-- The failure is mine.

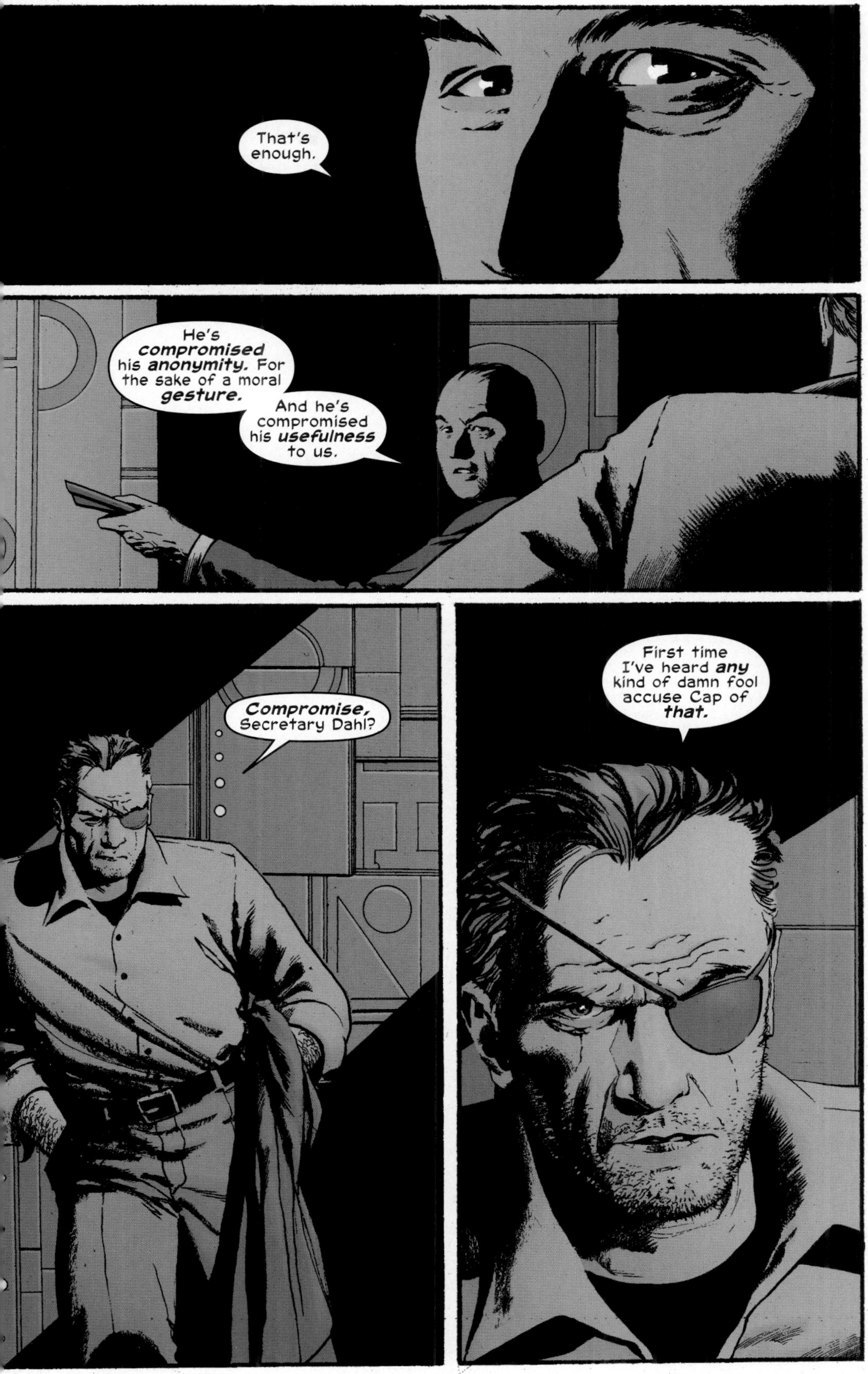
That's enough.
He's **compromised** his **anonymity.** For the sake of a moral **gesture.**
And he's compromised his **usefulness** to us.
Compromise, Secretary Dahl?
First time I've heard **any** kind of damn fool accuse Cap of **that.**

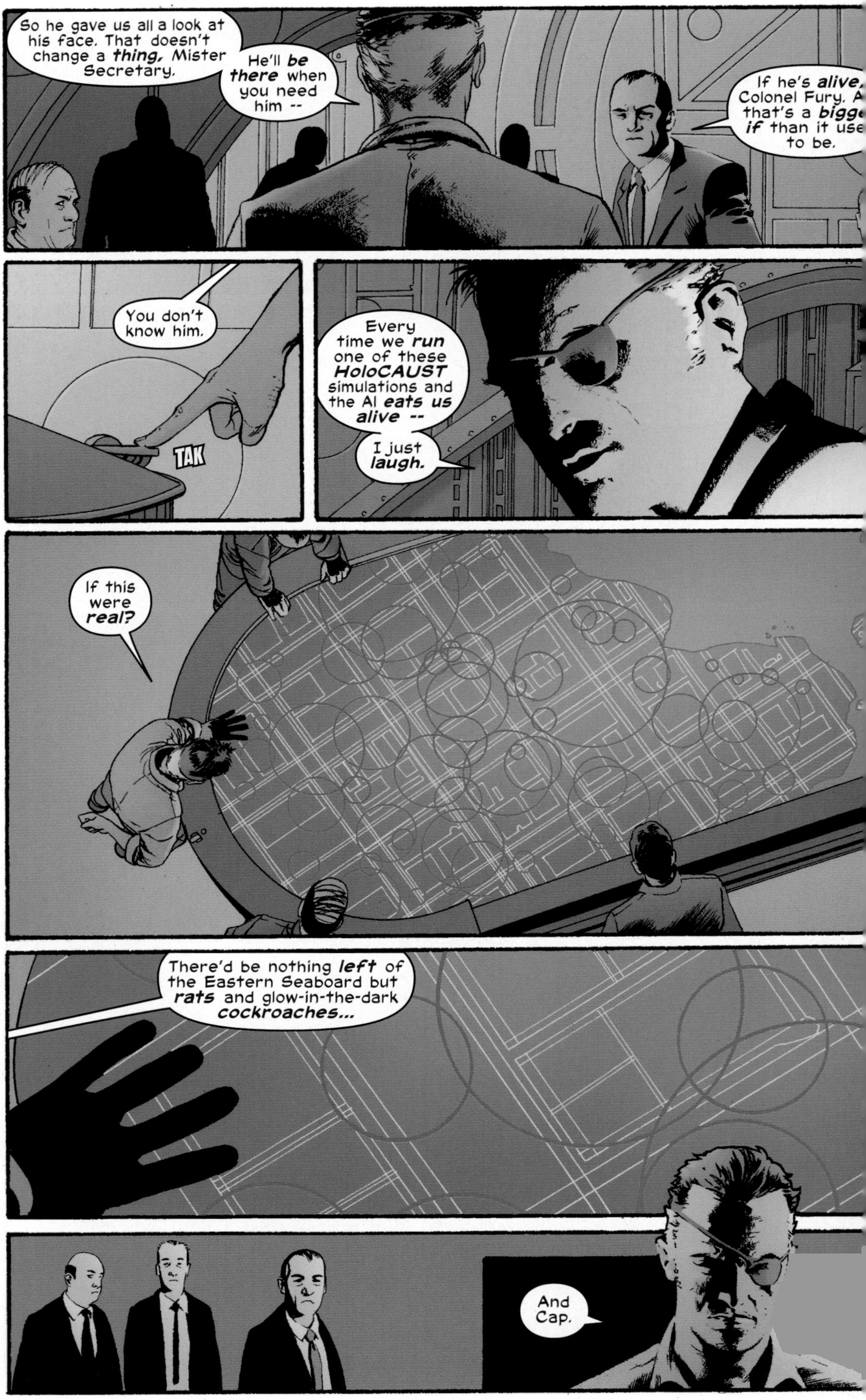
So he gave us all a look at his face. That doesn't change a thing, Mister Secretary.
He'll be there when you need him --
If he's alive, Colonel Fury. A that's a bigg if than it use to be.
You don't know him.
TAK
Every time we run one of these HoloCAUST simulations and the AI eats us alive --
I just laugh.
If this were real?
There'd be nothing left of the Eastern Seaboard but rats and glow-in-the-dark cockroaches...
And Cap.

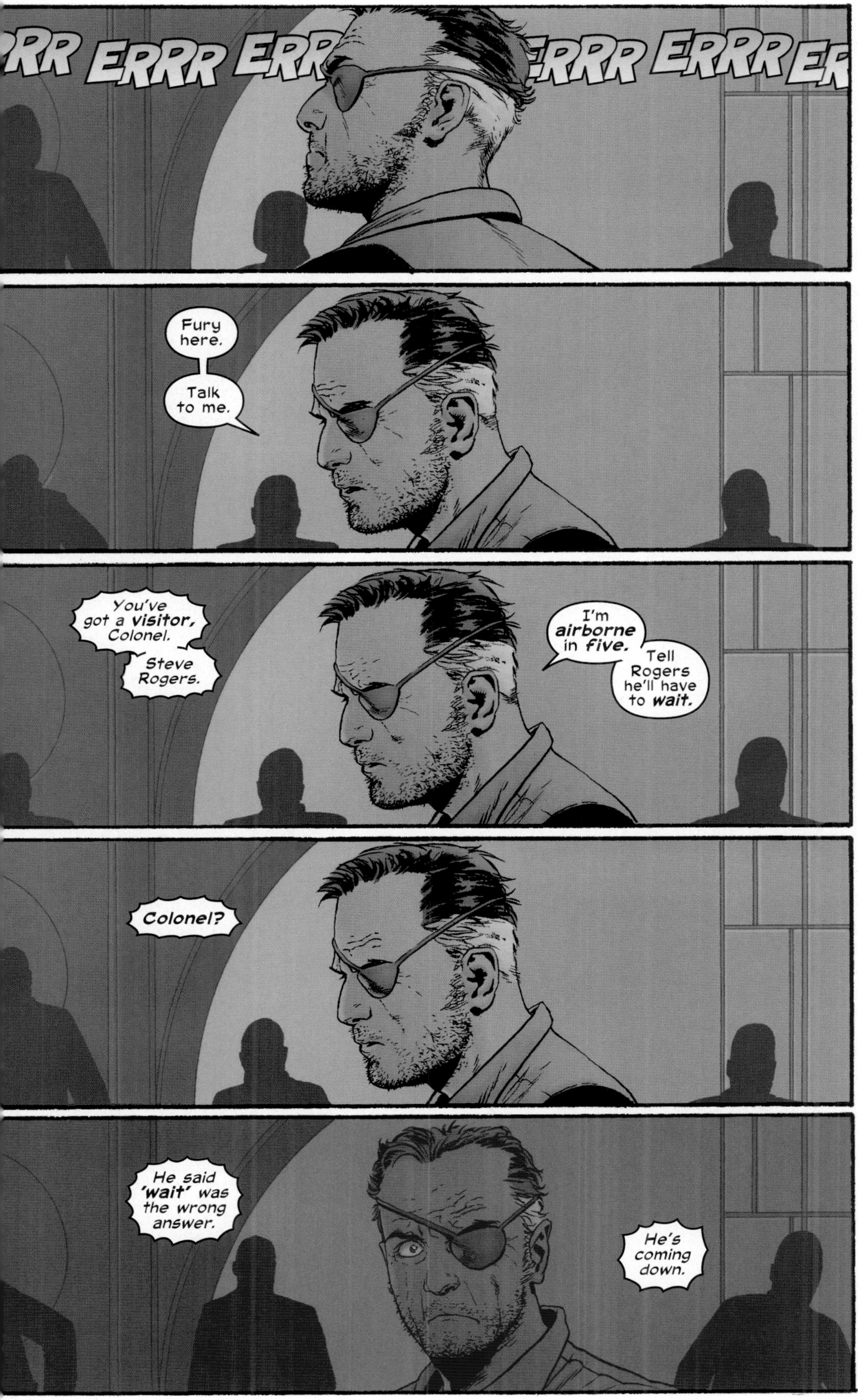
RRR ERRR ERR ERRR ERRR ER
Fury here.
Talk to me.
You've got a visitor, Colonel.
Steve Rogers.
I'm airborne in five.
Tell Rogers he'll have to wait.
Colonel?
He said 'wait' was the wrong answer.
He's coming down.

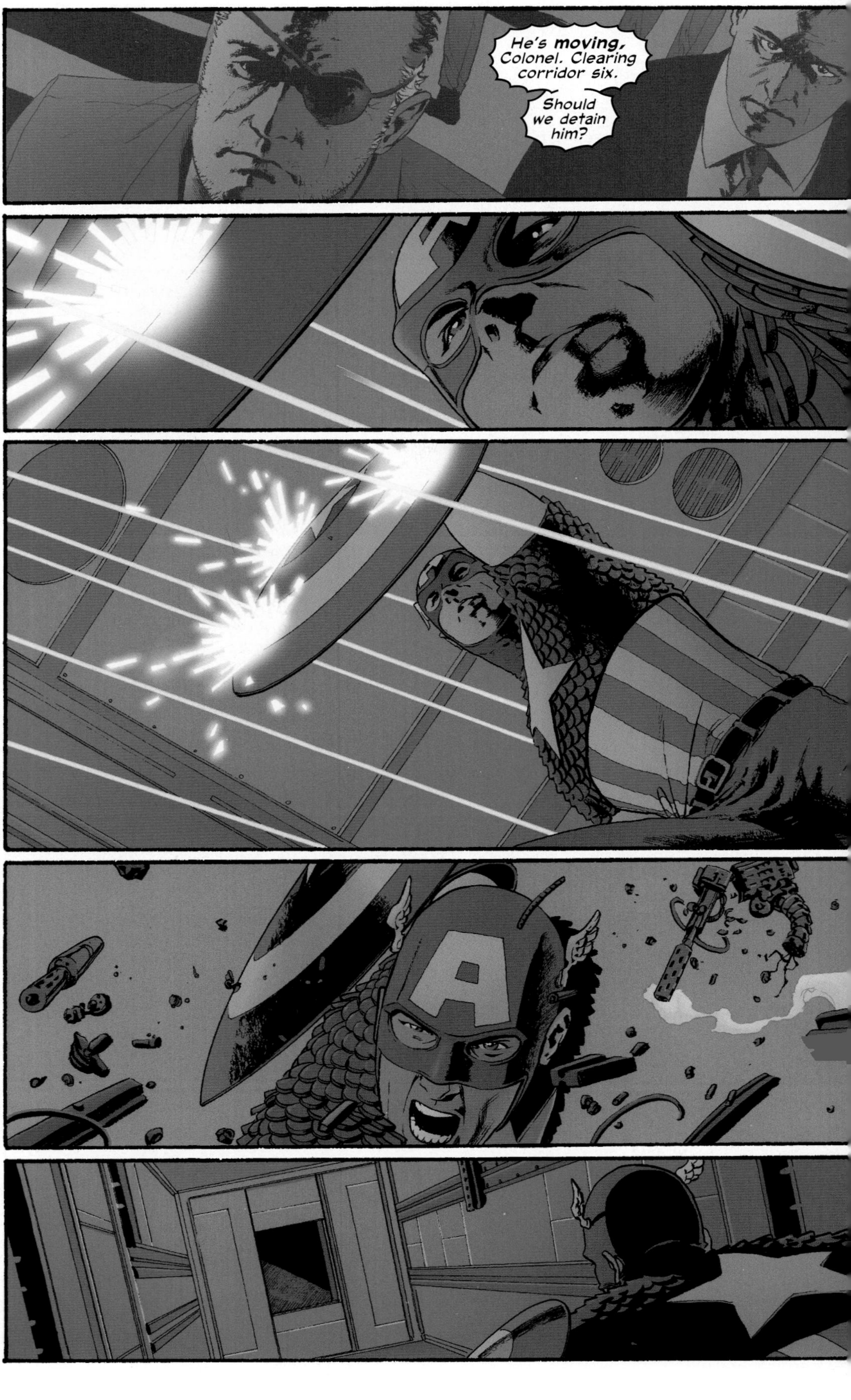
He's moving, Colonel. Clearing corridor six.
Should we detain him?

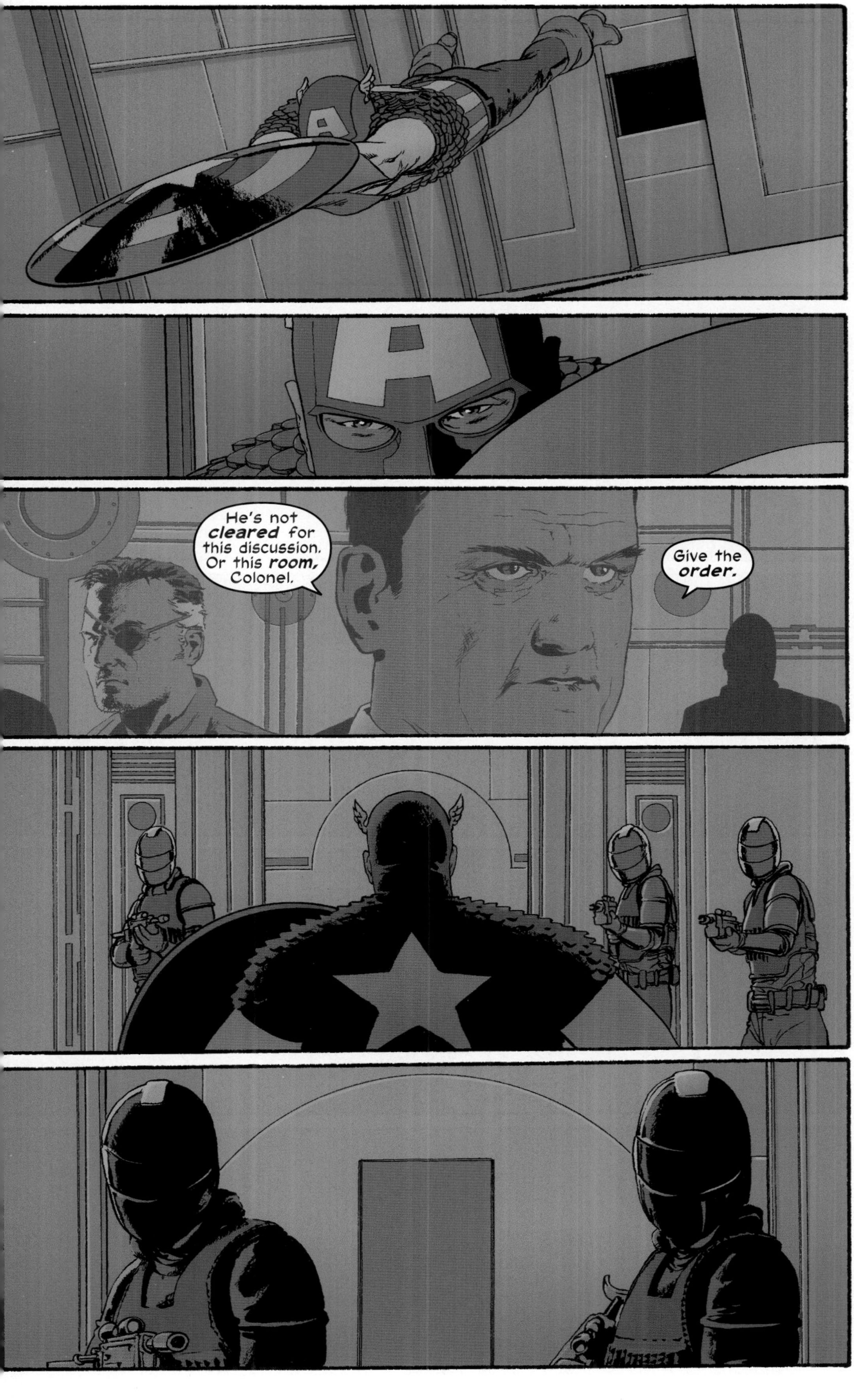
He's not **cleared** for this discussion. Or this ***room,*** Colonel.
Give the ***order.***

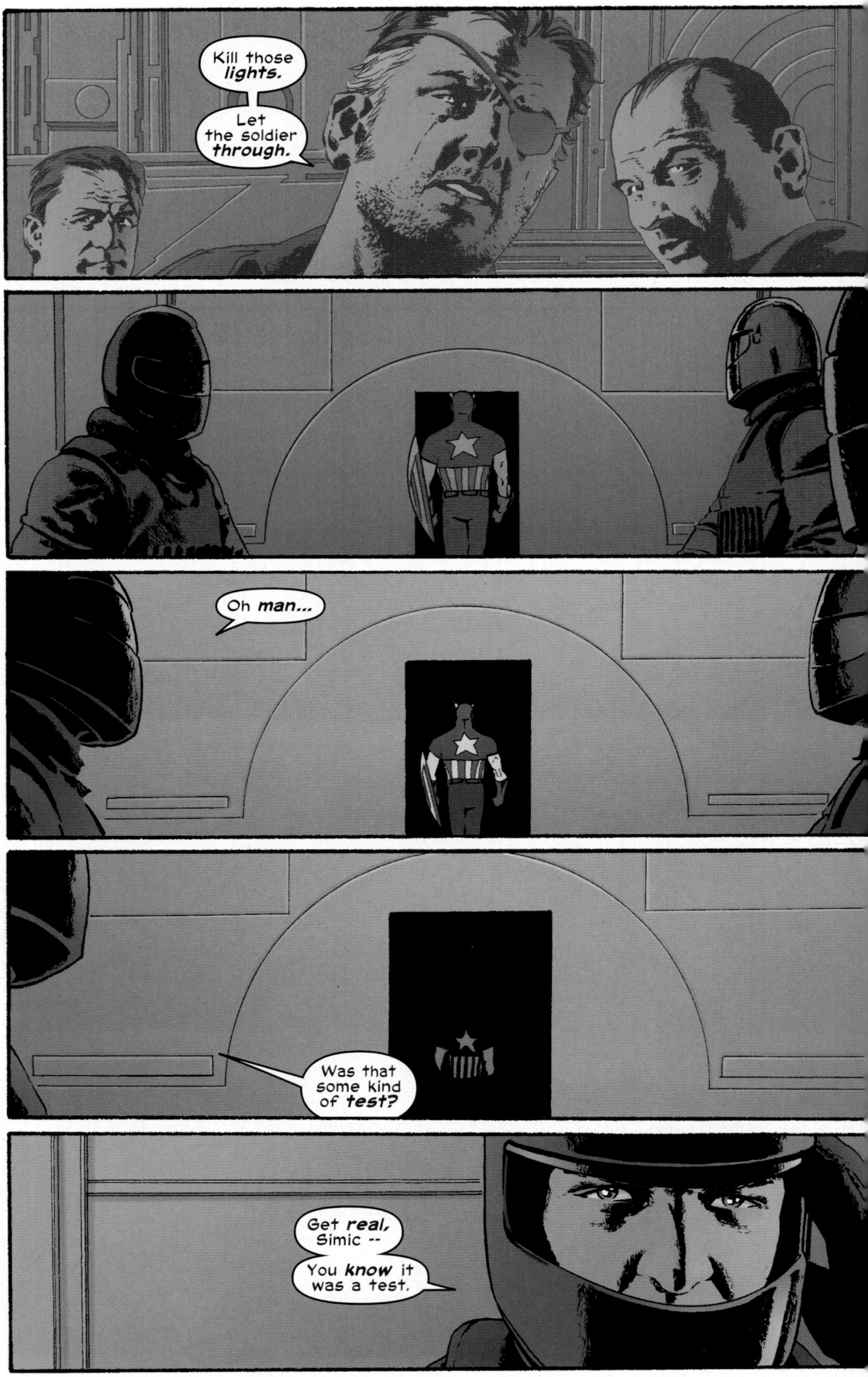

Kill those lights.
Let the soldier through.
Oh man...
Was that some kind of test?
Get real, Simic --
You know it was a test.

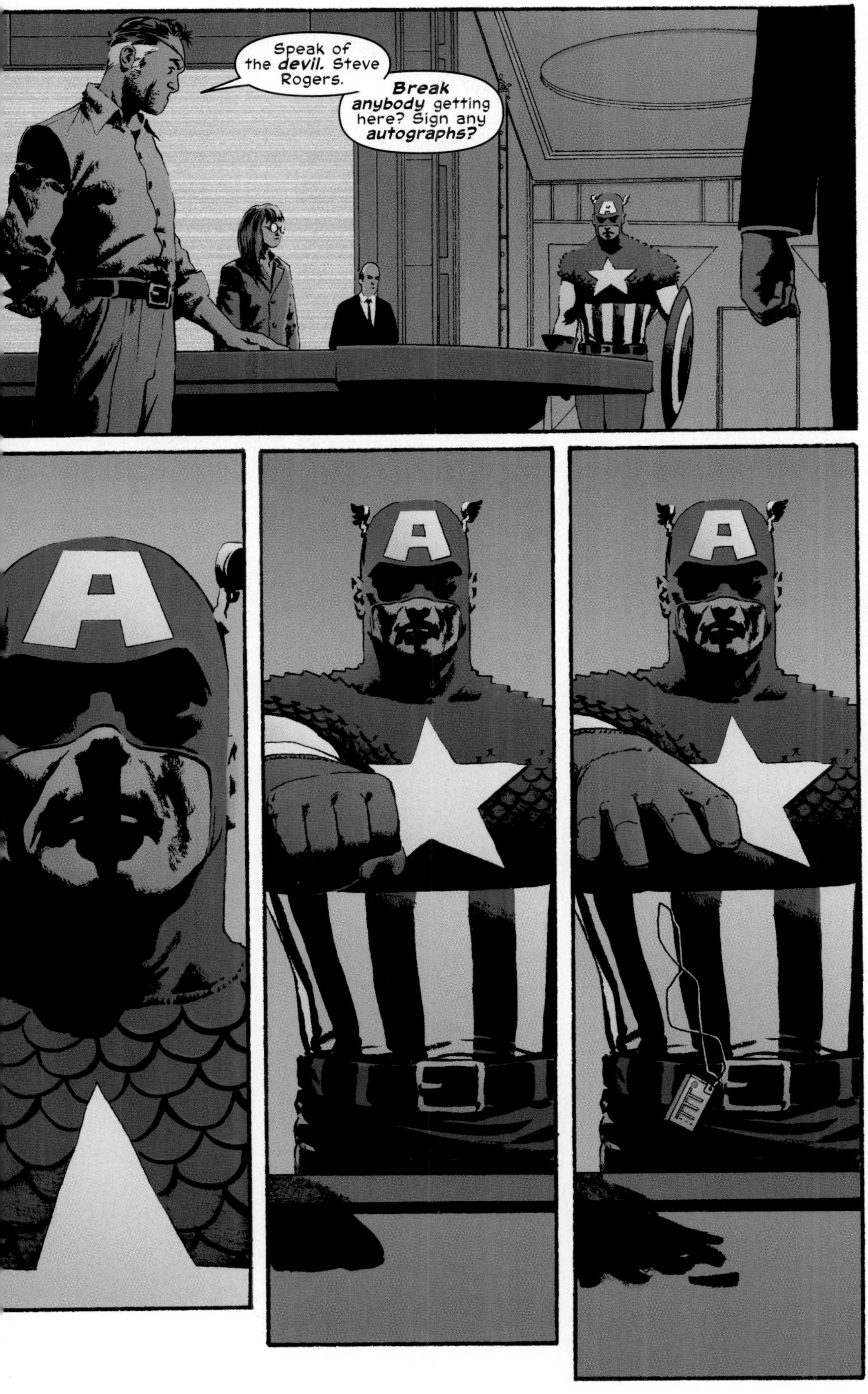
Speak of the **devil.** Steve Rogers.
Break anybody getting here? Sign any ***autographs?***

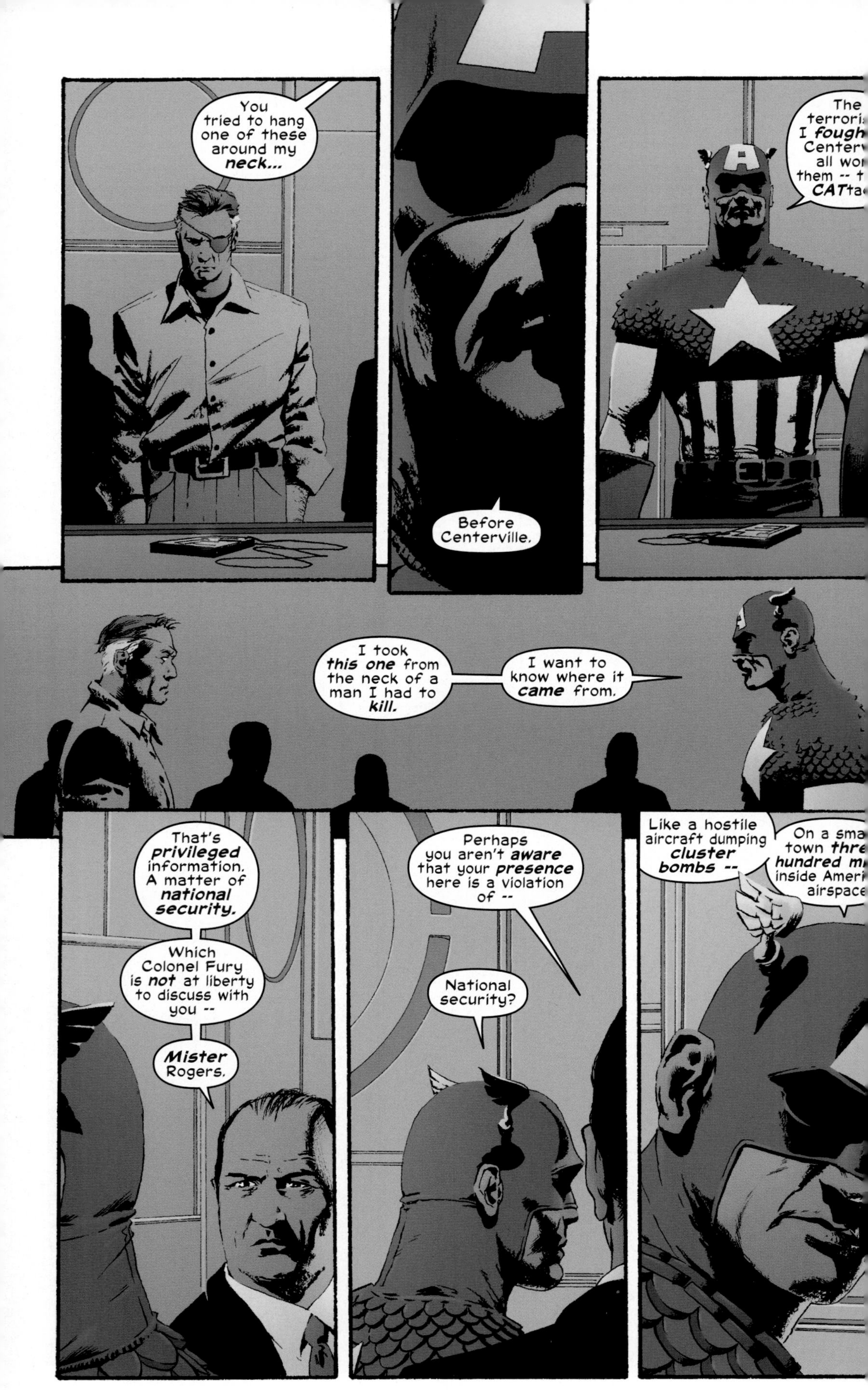
You tried to hang one of these around my neck...
Before Centerville.
The
I took this one from the neck of a man I had to kill.
I want to know where it came from.
That's privileged information. A matter of national security.
Which Colonel Fury is not at liberty to discuss with you --
Mister Rogers.
Perhaps you aren't aware that your presence here is a violation of --
National security?
Like a hostile aircraft dumping cluster bombs --
On a
town
hundred
inside
airspace

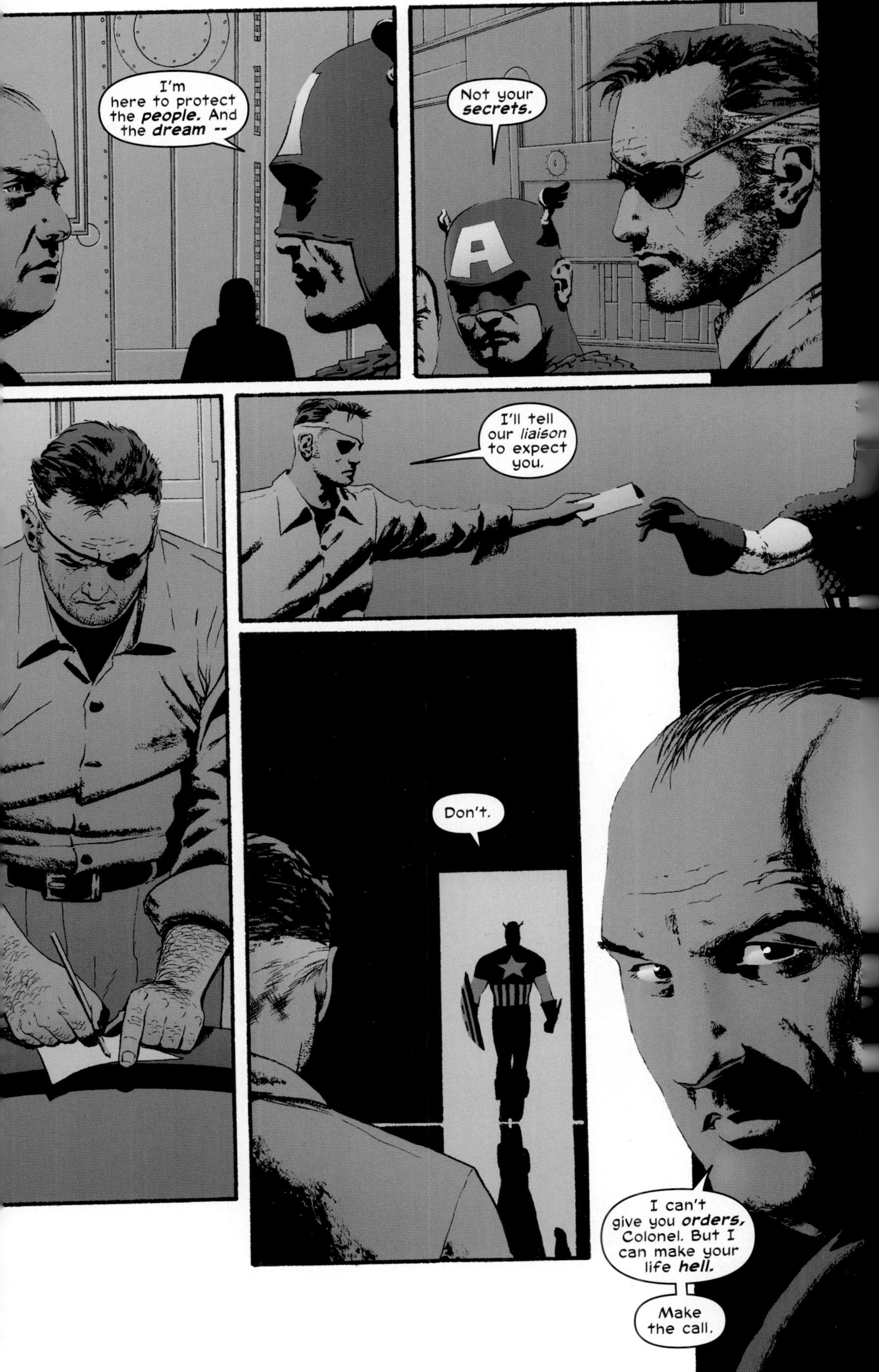
I'm here to protect the *people.* And the *dream* --
Not your *secrets.*
I'll tell our *liaison* to expect you.
Don't.
I can't give you *orders,* Colonel. But I can make your life *hell.*
Make the call.

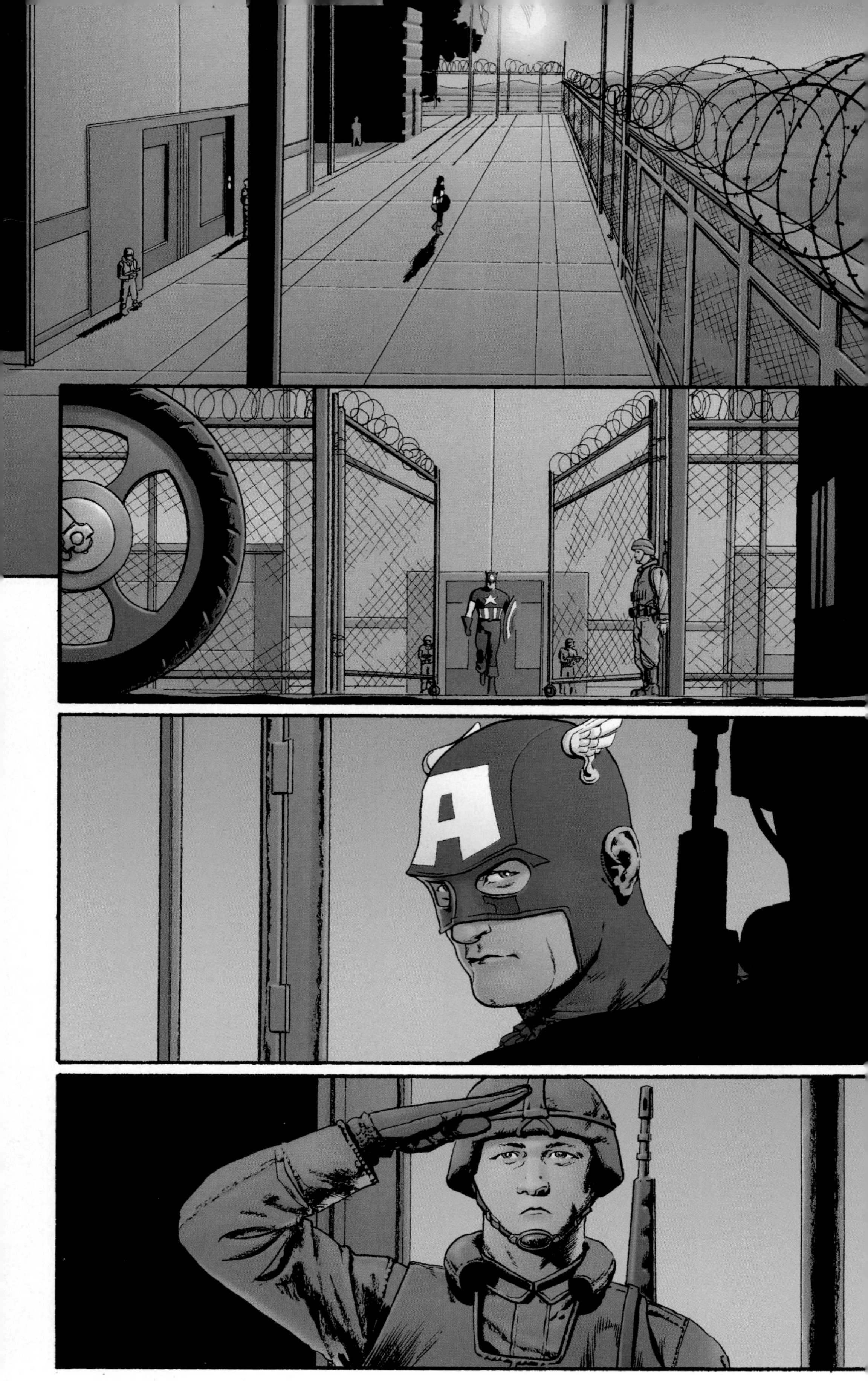

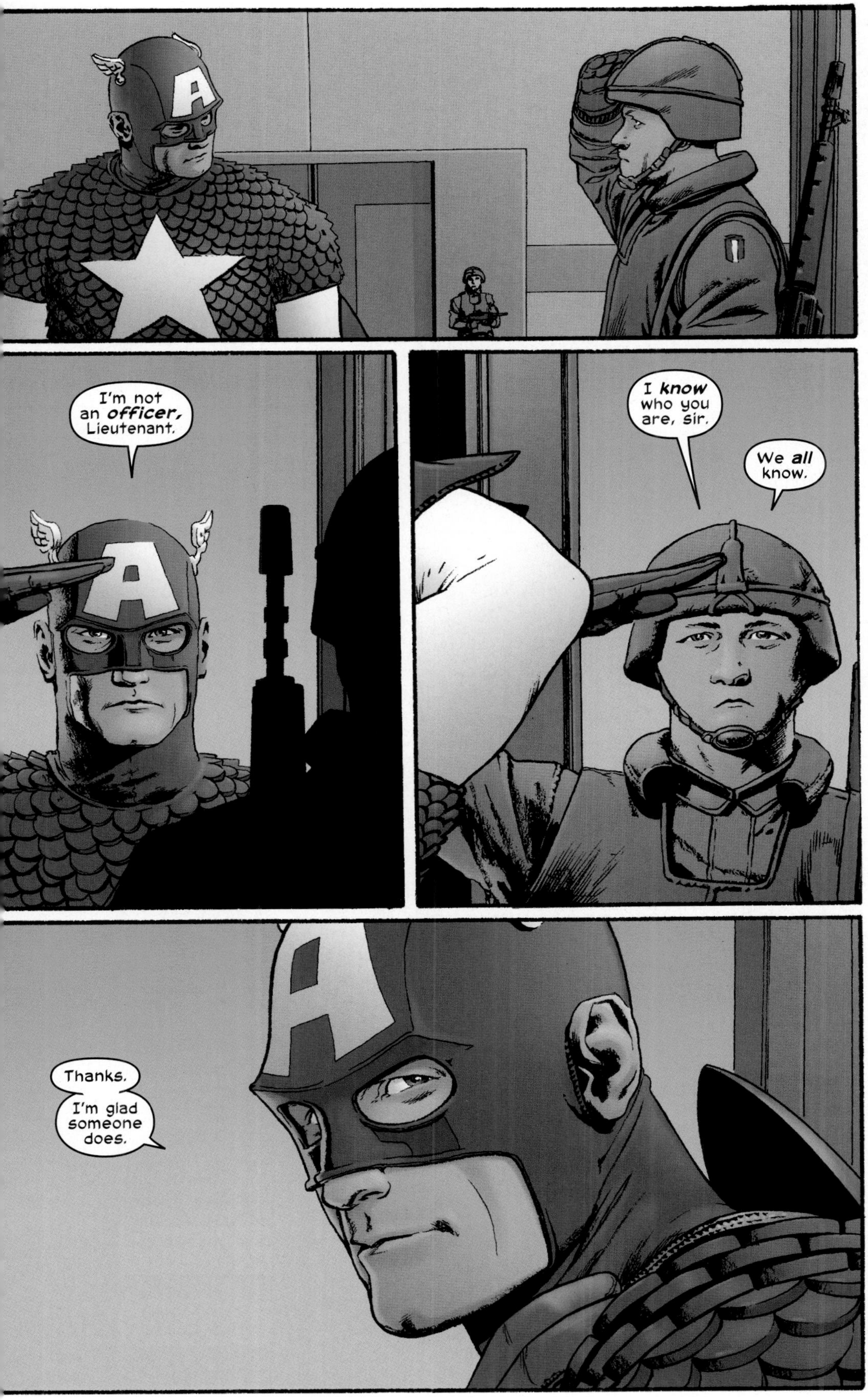
I'm not an officer, Lieutenant.
I know who you are, sir.
We all know.
Thanks.
I'm glad someone does.

Looks like Fury's going to take some **heat...**

And for **what?**

Trusting you?

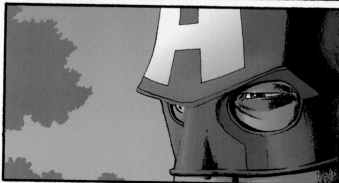

You haven't made his life any **easier** today.

His life **or** yours.

Now you have a **destination.** One you prayed you'd never see **again.**

You'd rather go to **hell.**

But as soon as you can find a **plane** --

You're flying back to **Dresden.**

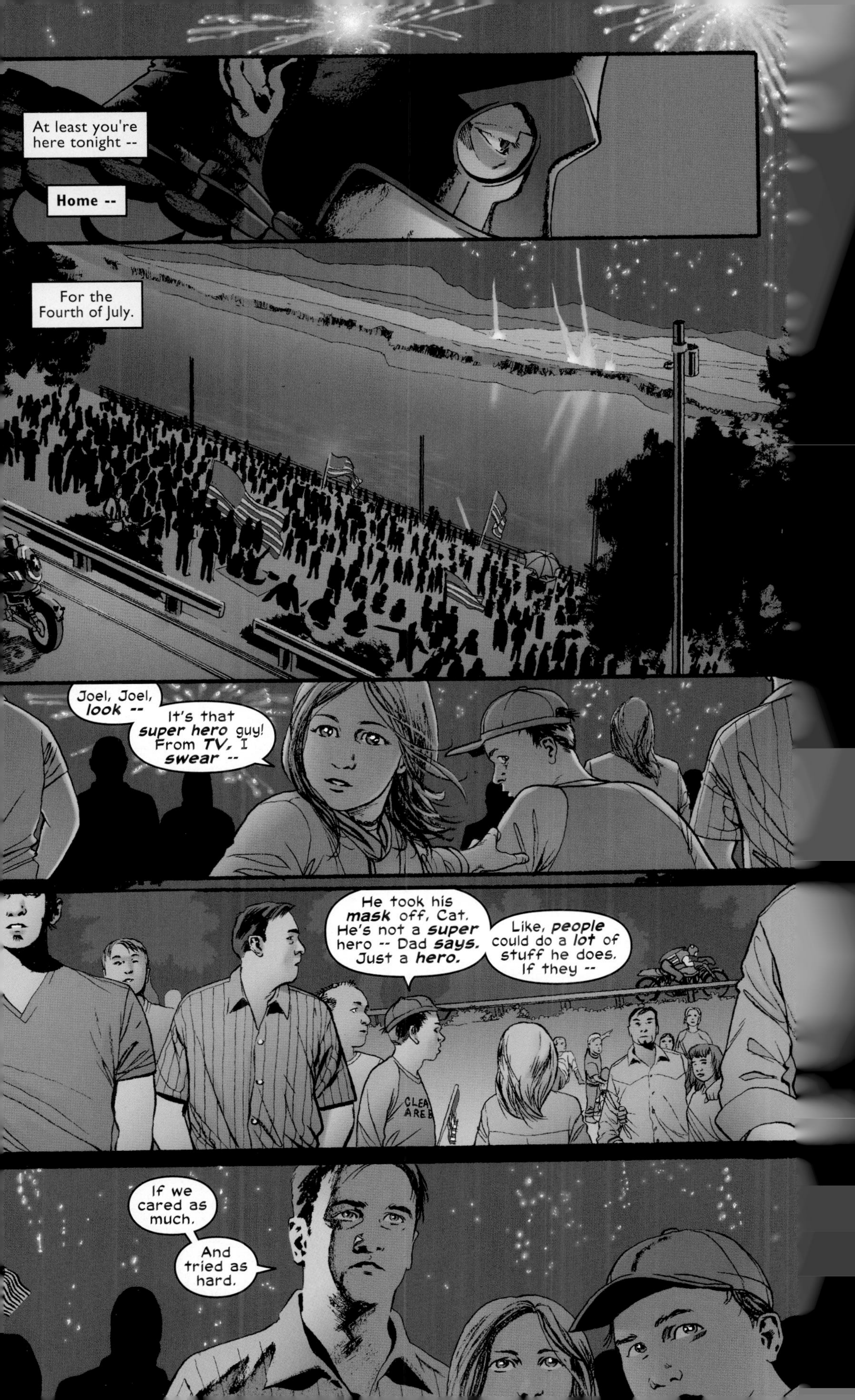

At least you're here tonight --
Home --
For the Fourth of July.
Joel, Joel, look --
It's that super hero guy! From TV, I swear --
He took his mask off, Cat. He's not a super hero -- Dad says. Just a hero.
Like, people could do a lot of stuff he does. If they --
If we cared as much.
And tried as hard.

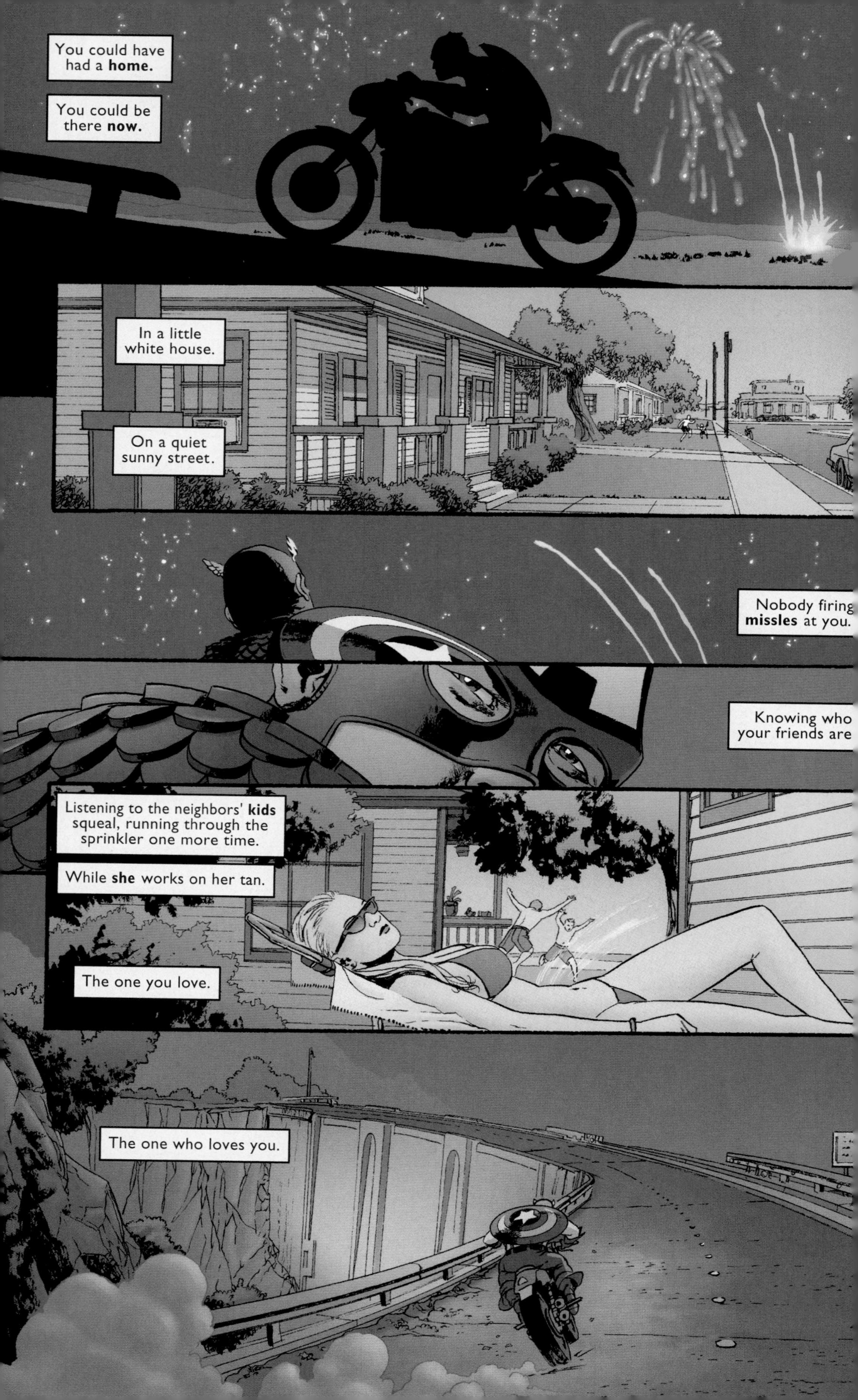
You could have had a **home.**
You could be there **now.**
In a little white house.
On a quiet sunny street.
Nobody firing **missles** at you.
Knowing who your friends are
Listening to the neighbors' **kids** squeal, running through the sprinkler one more time.
While **she** works on her tan.
The one you love.
The one who loves you.

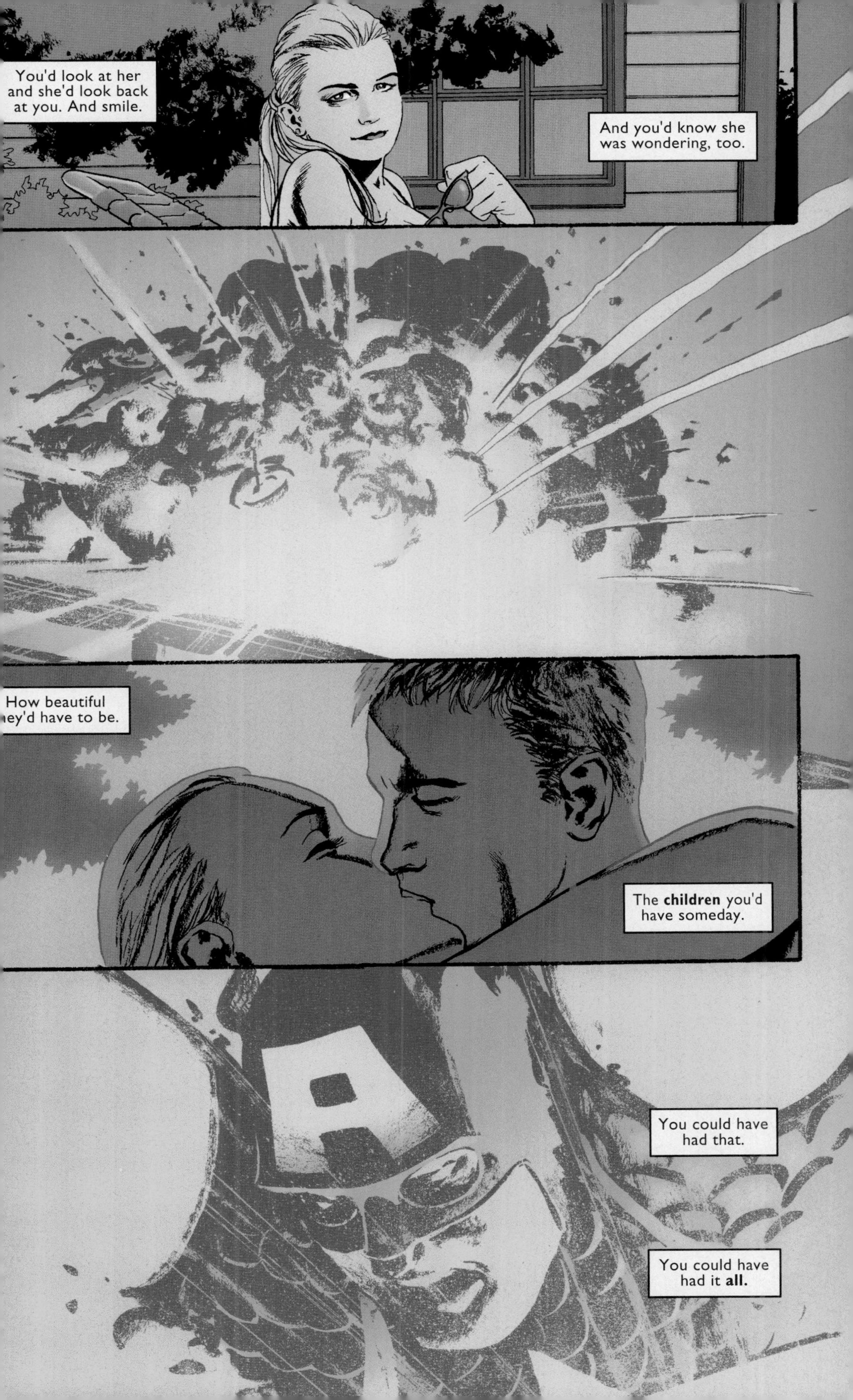
You'd look at her and she'd look back at you. And smile.
And you'd know she was wondering, too.
How beautiful
ey'd have to be.
The **children** you'd have someday.
You could have had that.
You could have had it **all.**

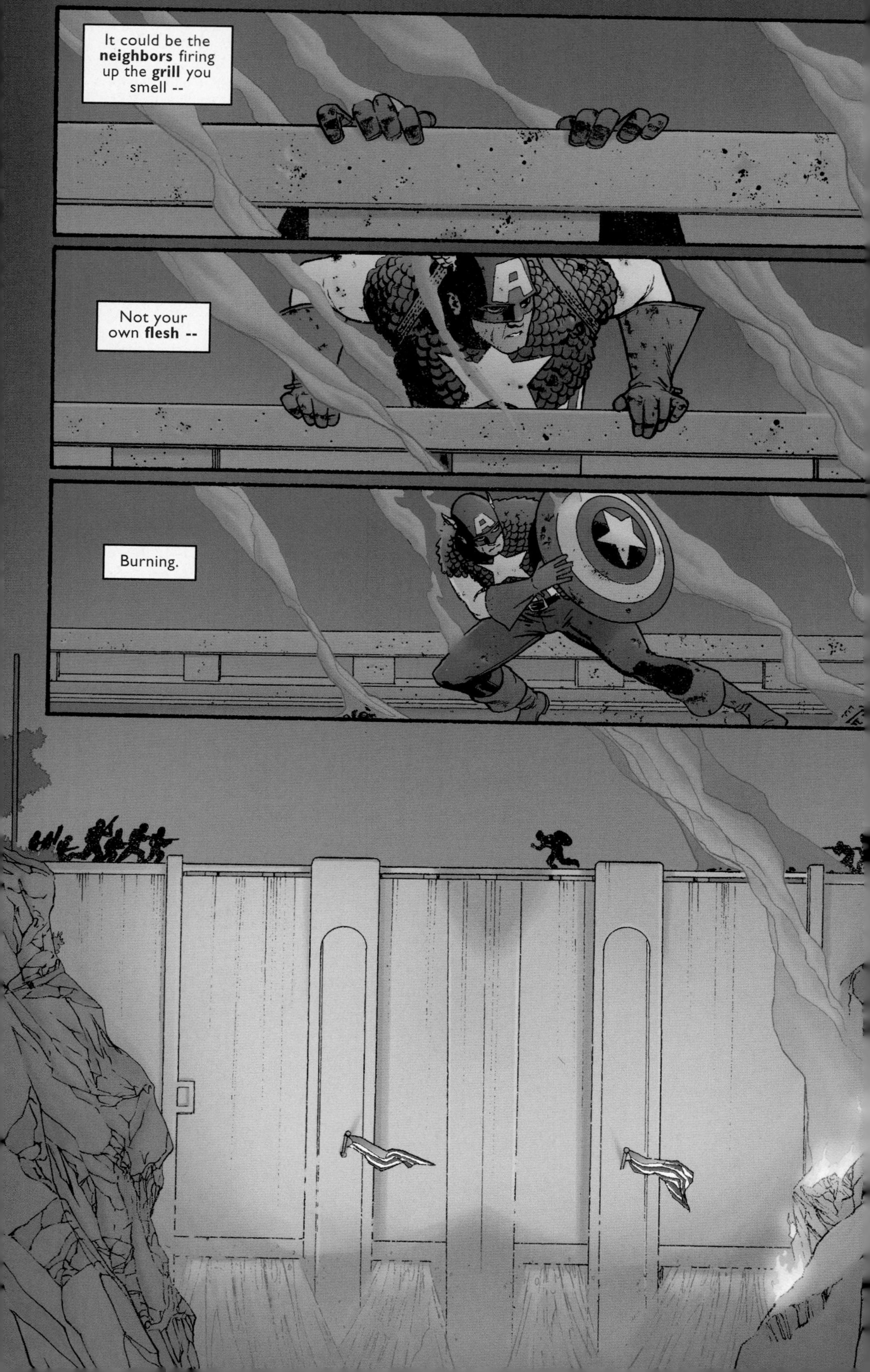
It could be the **neighbors** firing up the **grill** you smell --
Not your own **flesh** --
Burning.

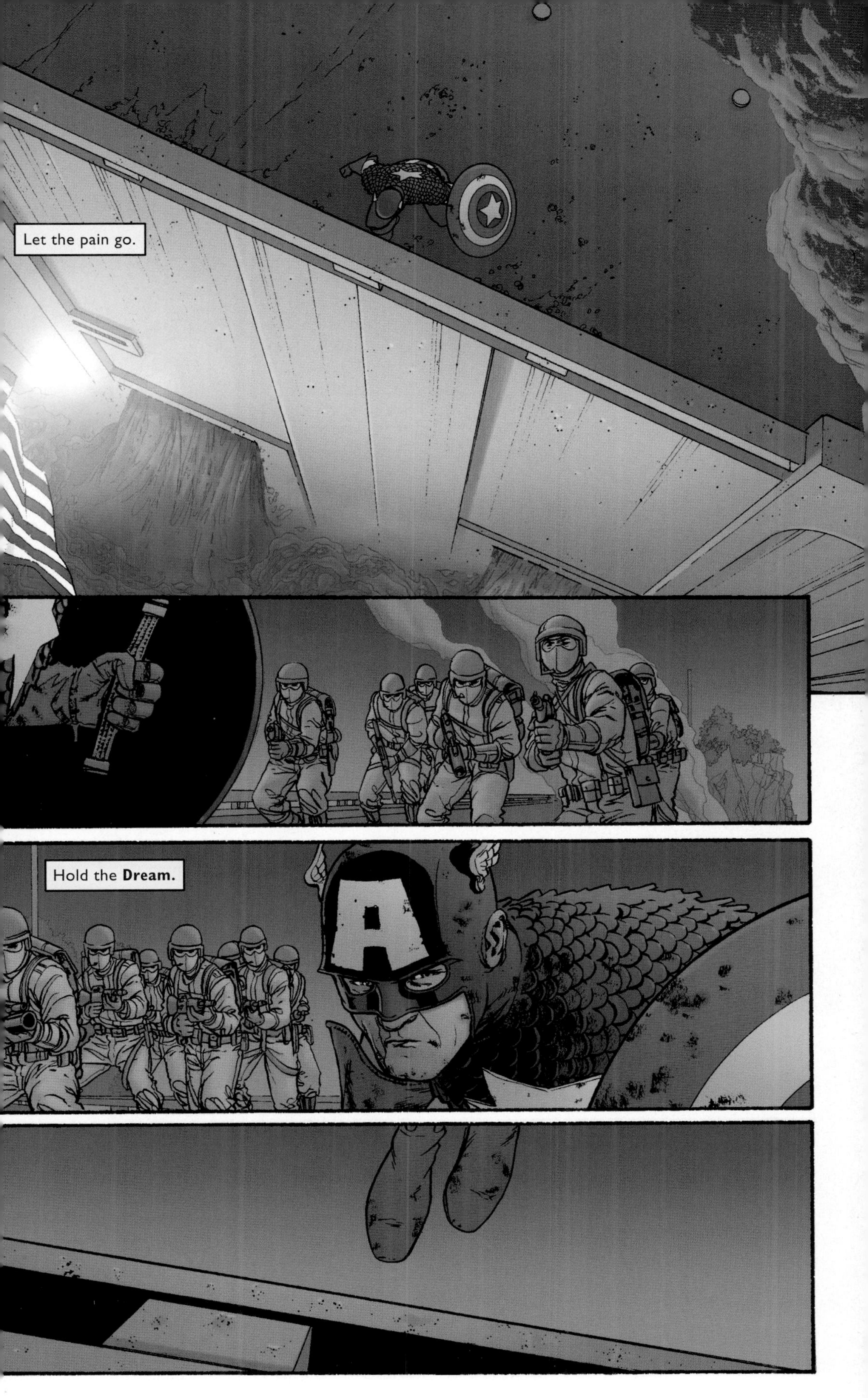
Let the pain go.
Hold the **Dream.**

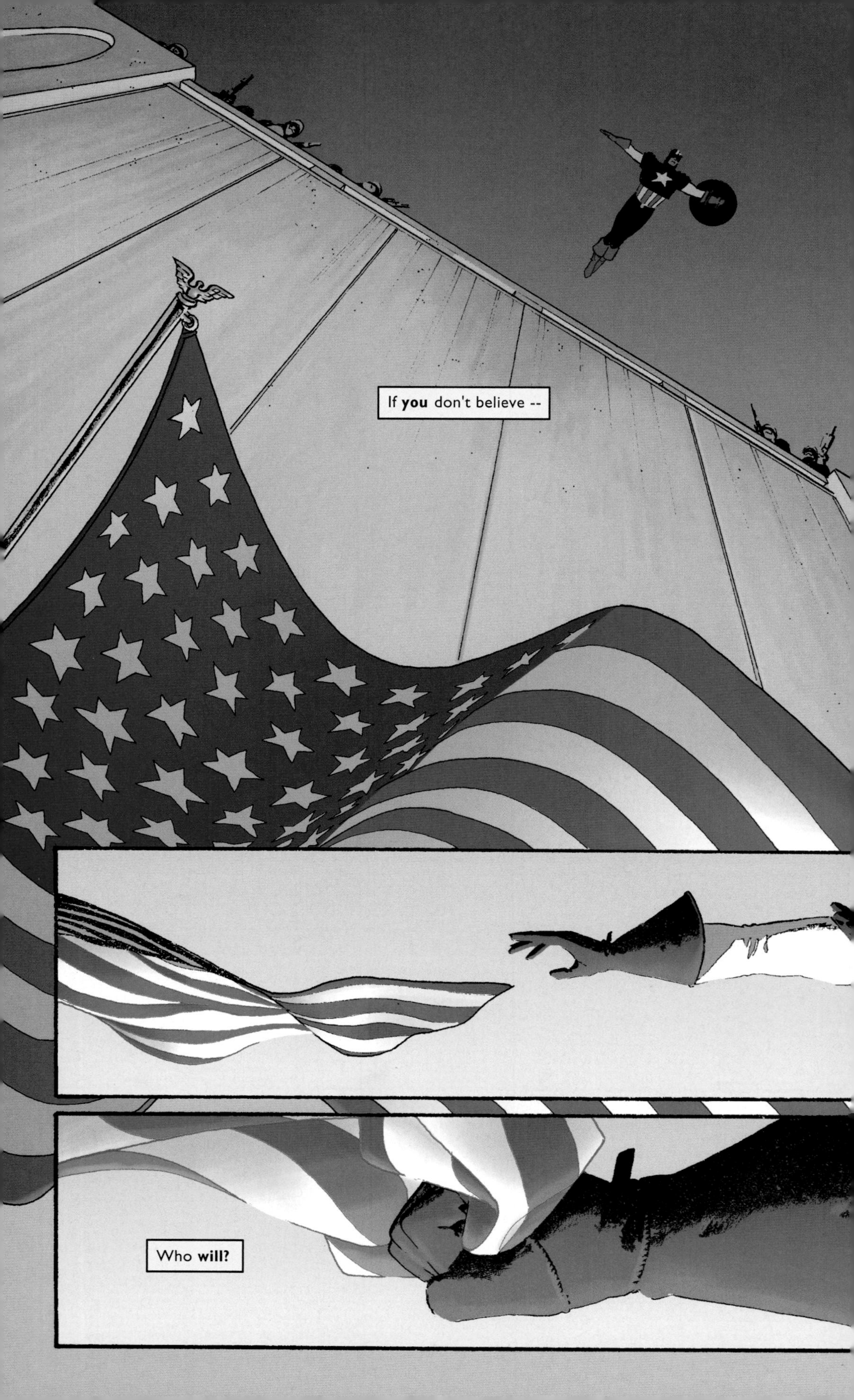
If **you** don't believe --
Who **will?**

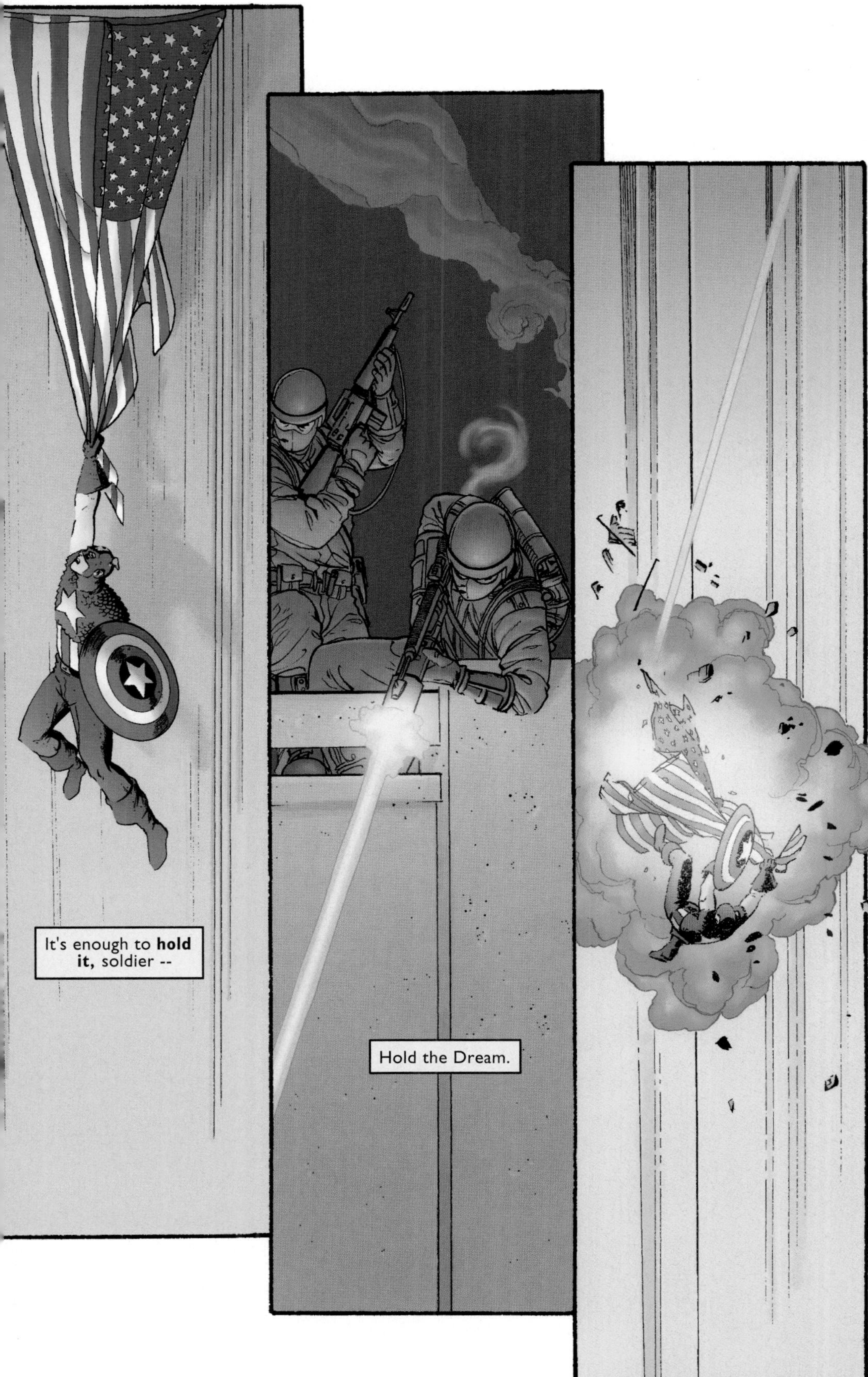
It's enough to **hold it,** soldier --
Hold the Dream.

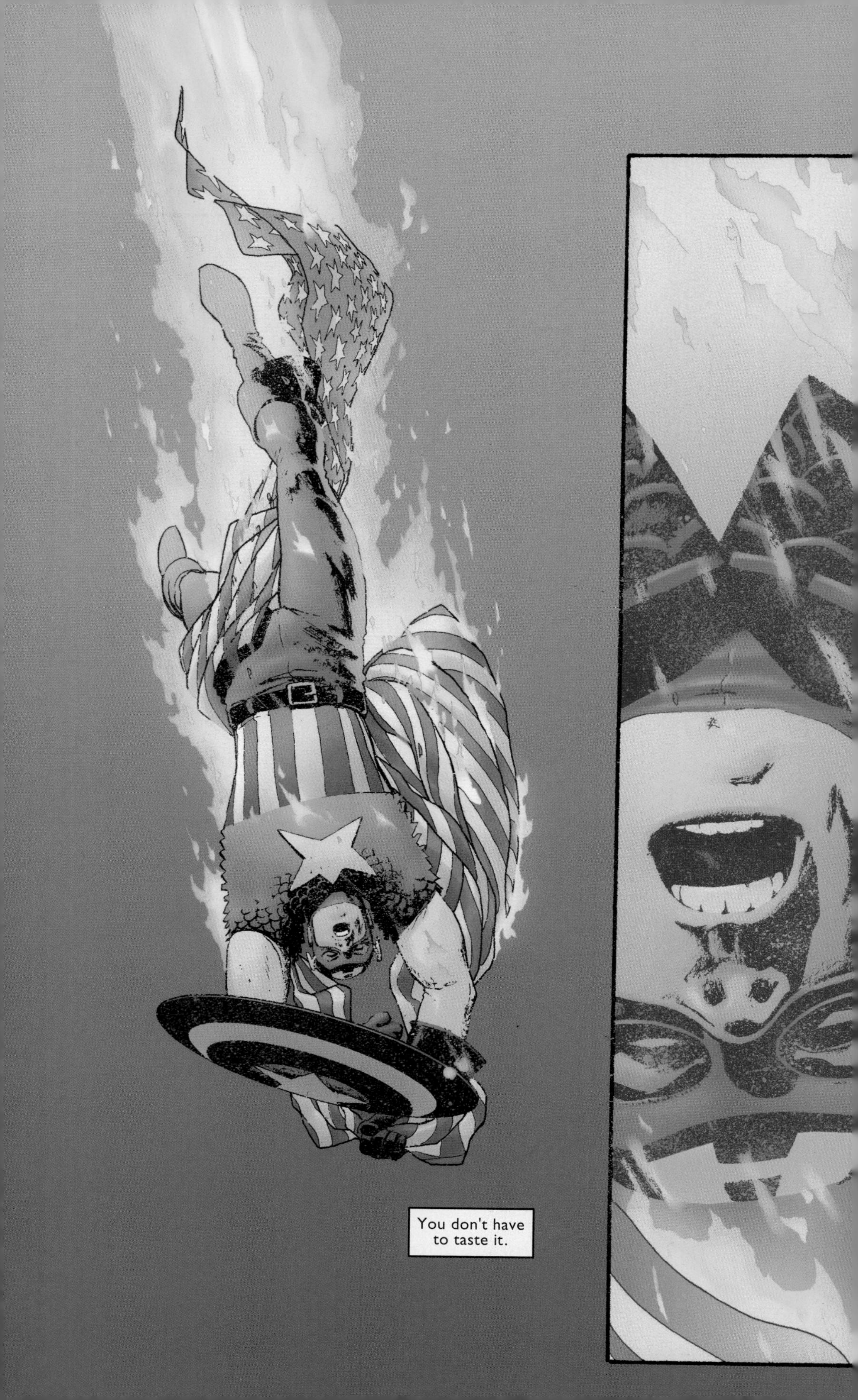
You don't have to taste it.

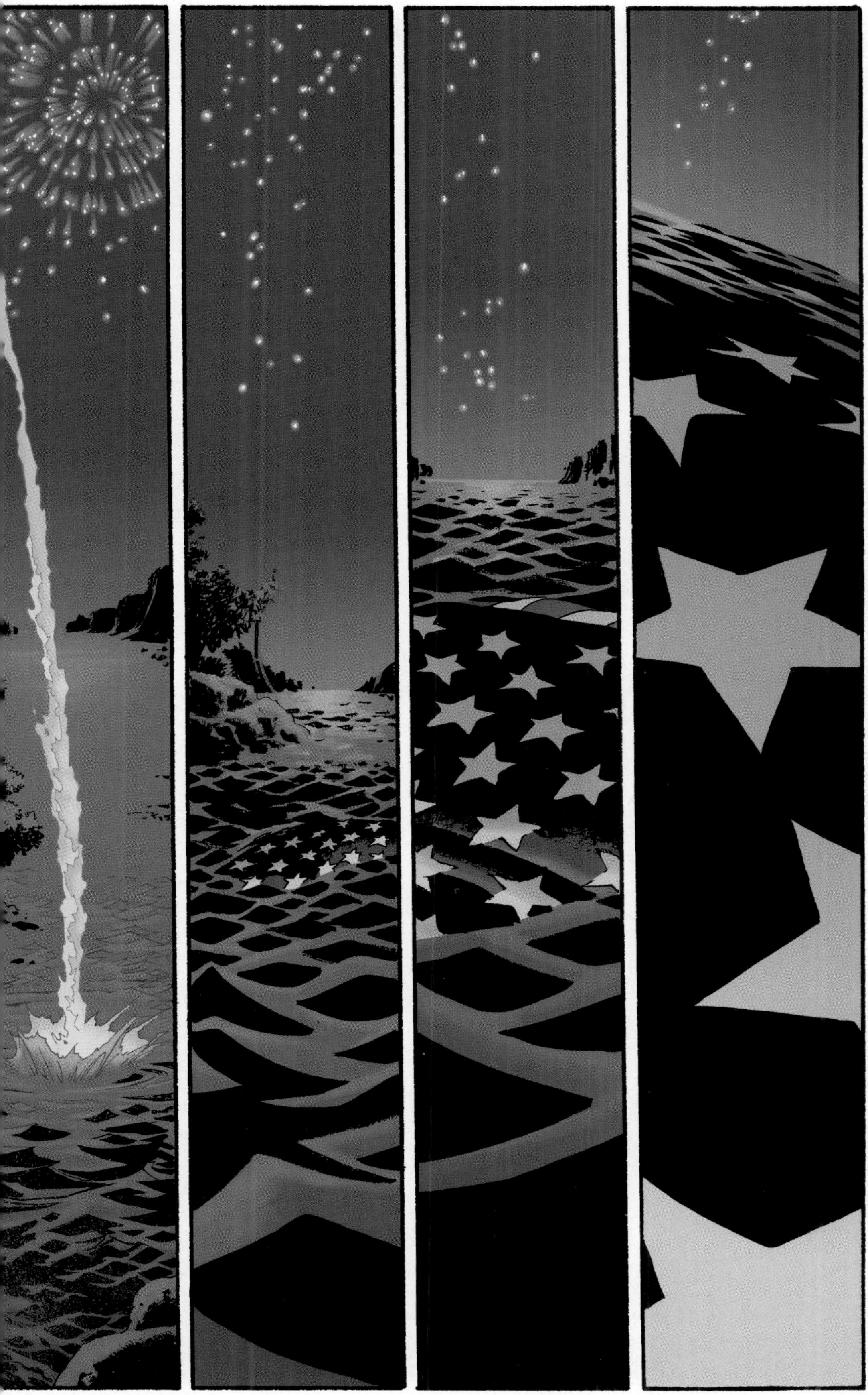

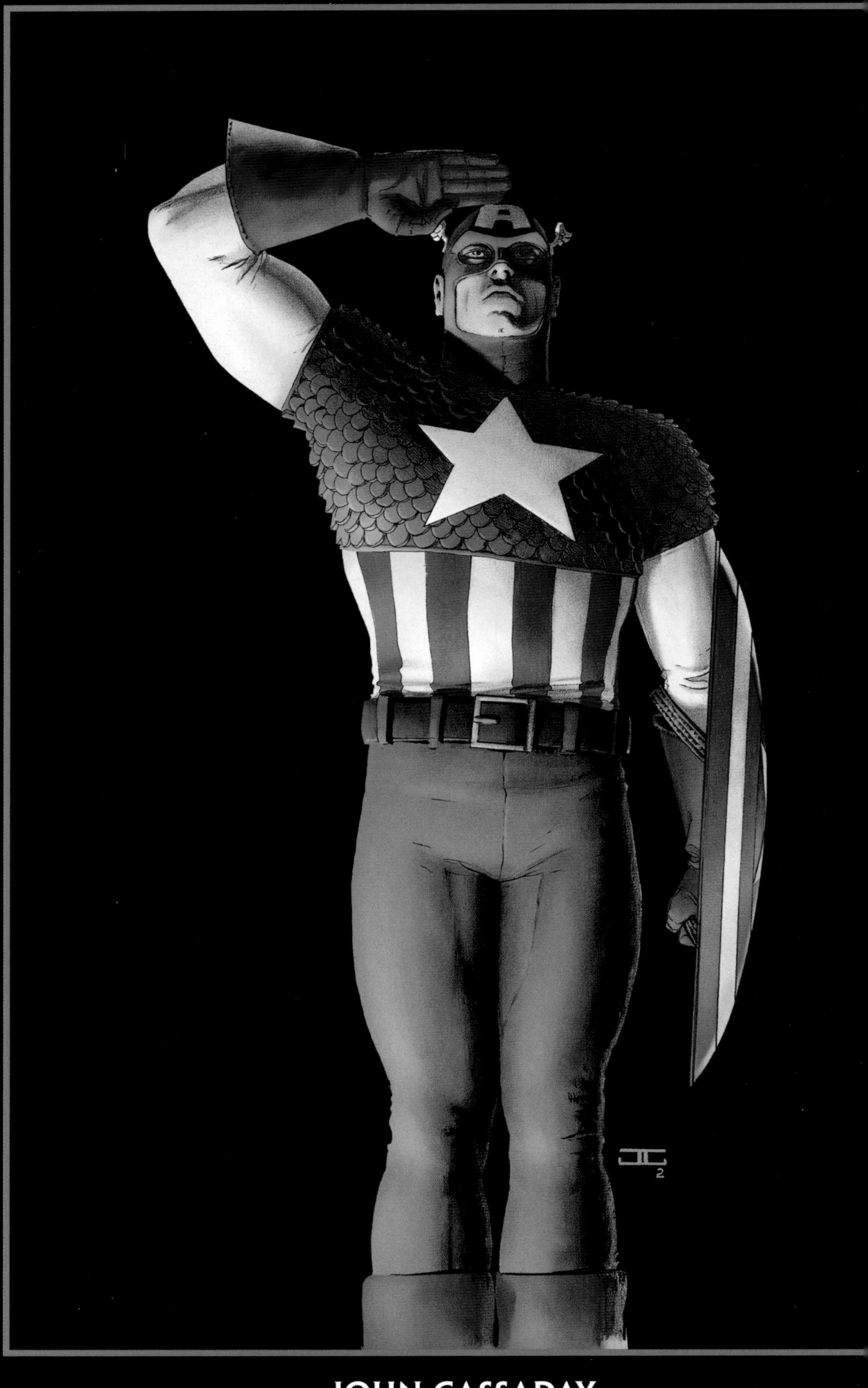

JOHN CASSADAY
Wizard #133 cover

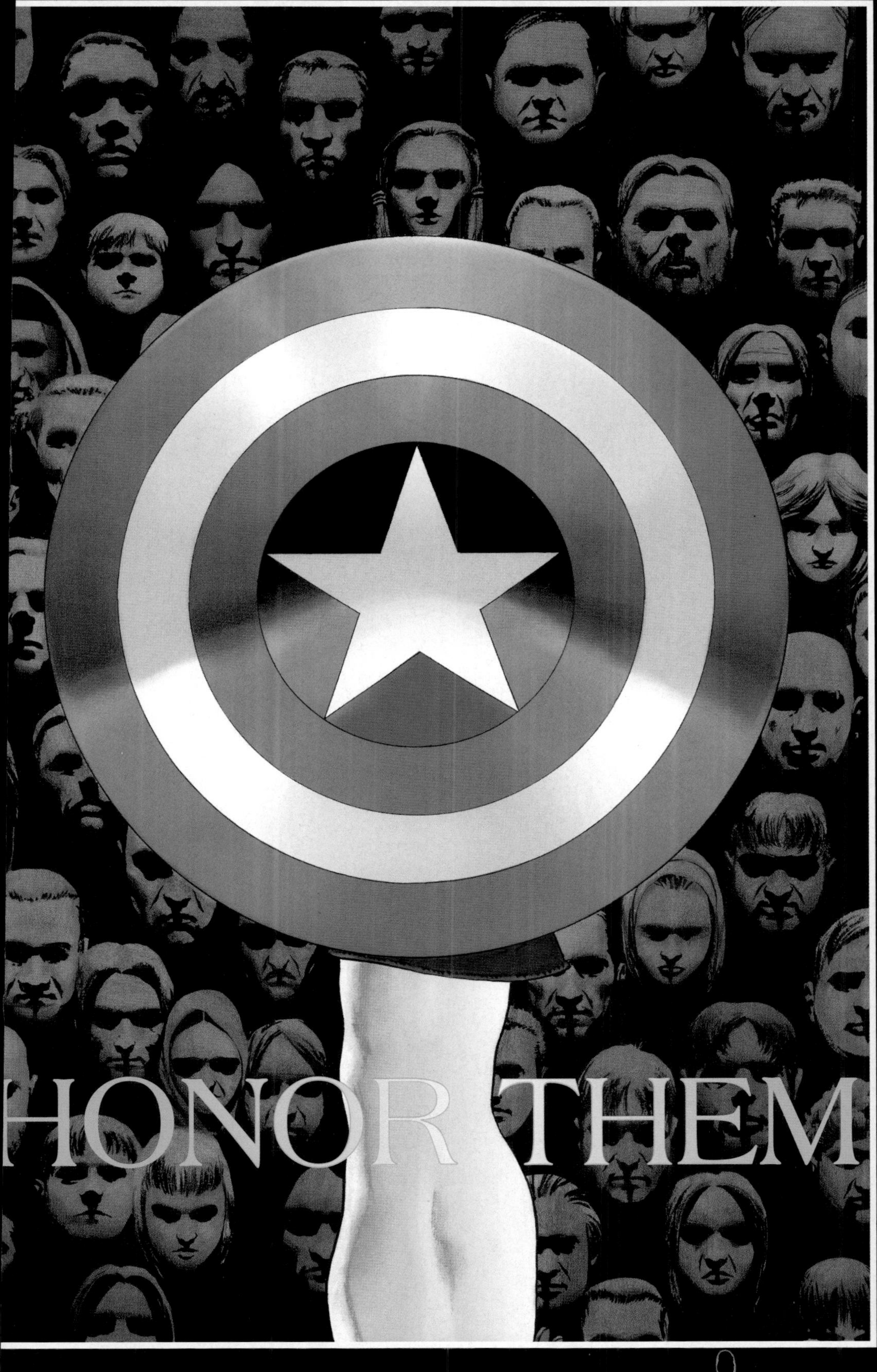

HONOR THEM

5 WARLORDS, PART 2: ABOVE THE LAW

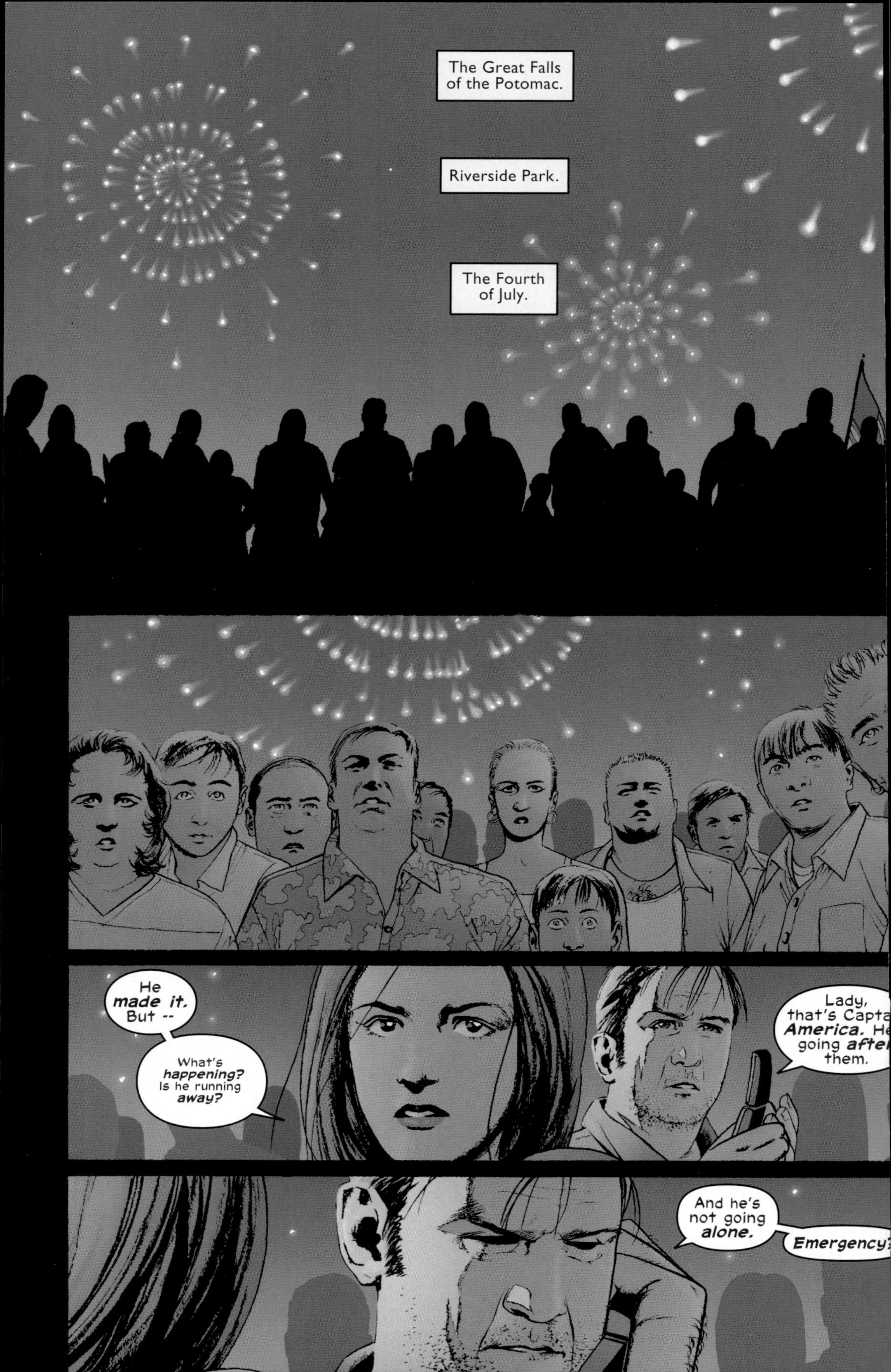

The Great Falls of the Potomac.
Riverside Park.
The Fourth of July.
He made it. But --
What's happening? Is he running away?
Lady, that's Capta America. He going afte them.
And he's not going alone.
Emergency?

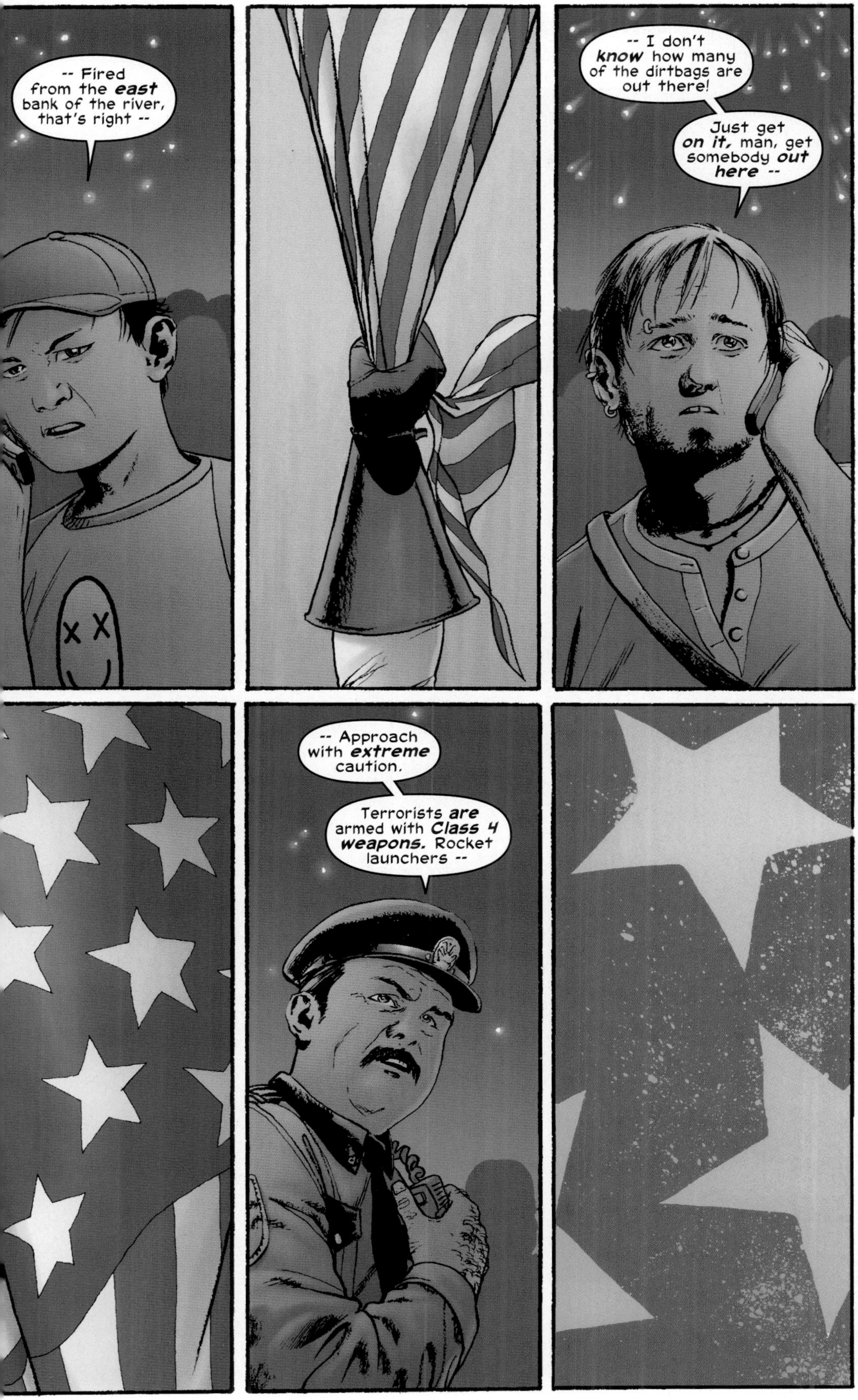
-- Fired from the east bank of the river, that's right --
-- I don't know how many of the dirtbags are out there!
Just get on it, man, get somebody out here --
-- Approach with extreme caution.
Terrorists are armed with Class 4 weapons. Rocket launchers --

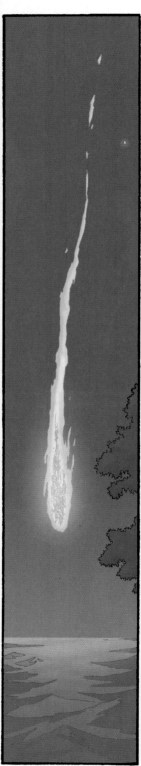

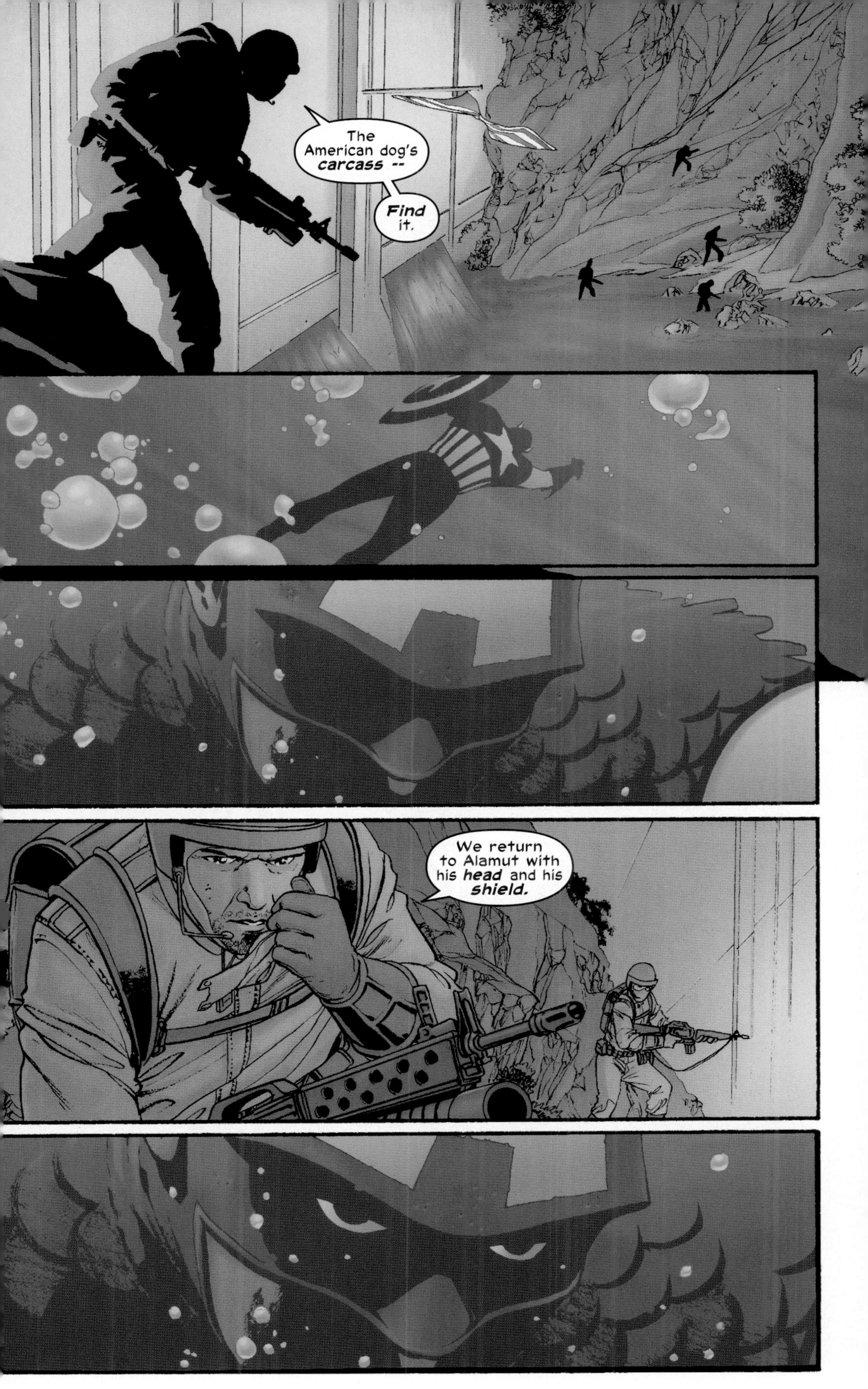

The American dog's *carcass* --
Find it.
We return to Alamut with his *head* and his *shield.*

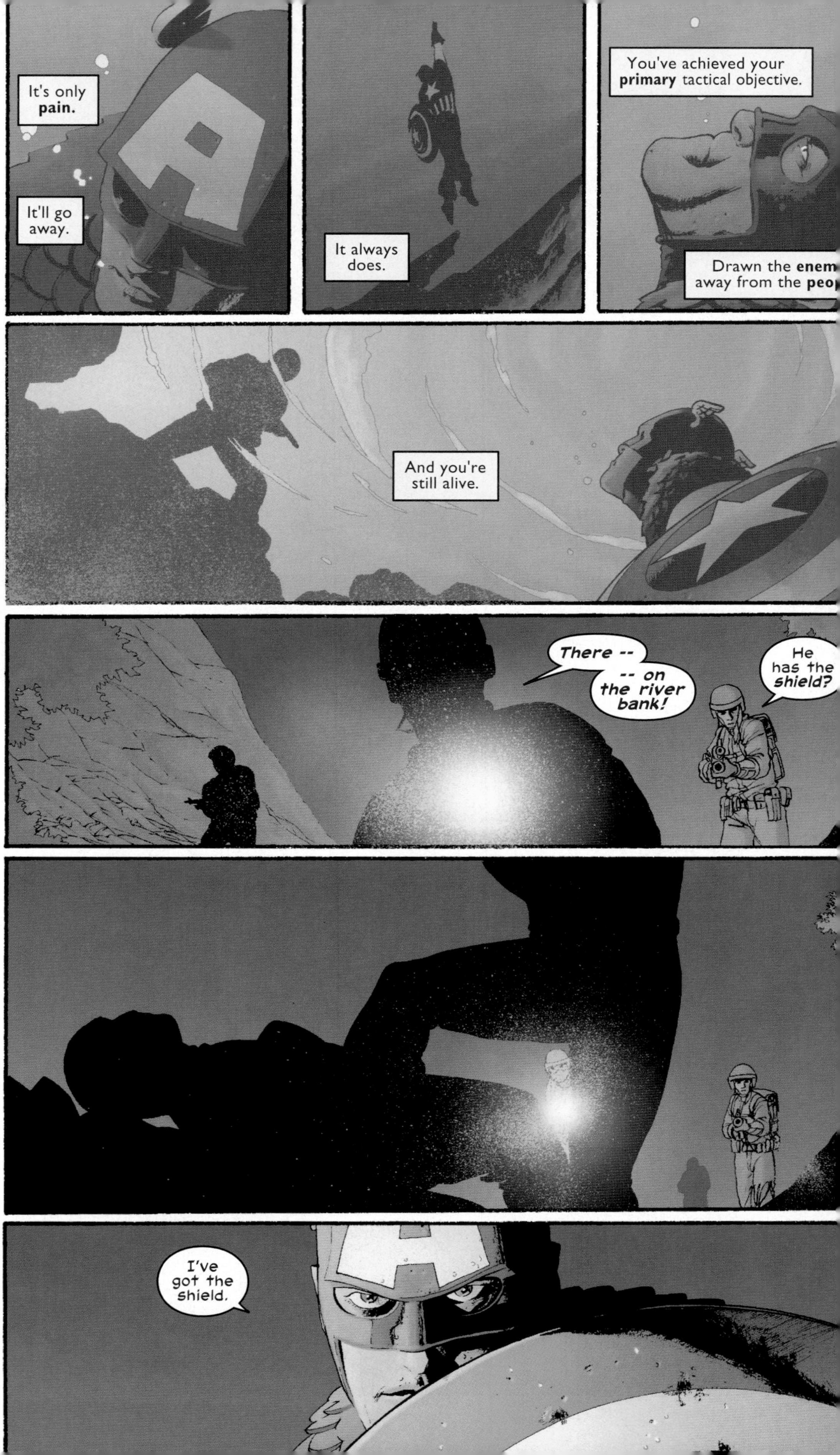
It's only **pain.**
It'll go away.
It always does.
You've achieved your **primary** tactical objective.
And you're still alive.
There --
-- on the river bank!
He has the shield?
I've got the shield.

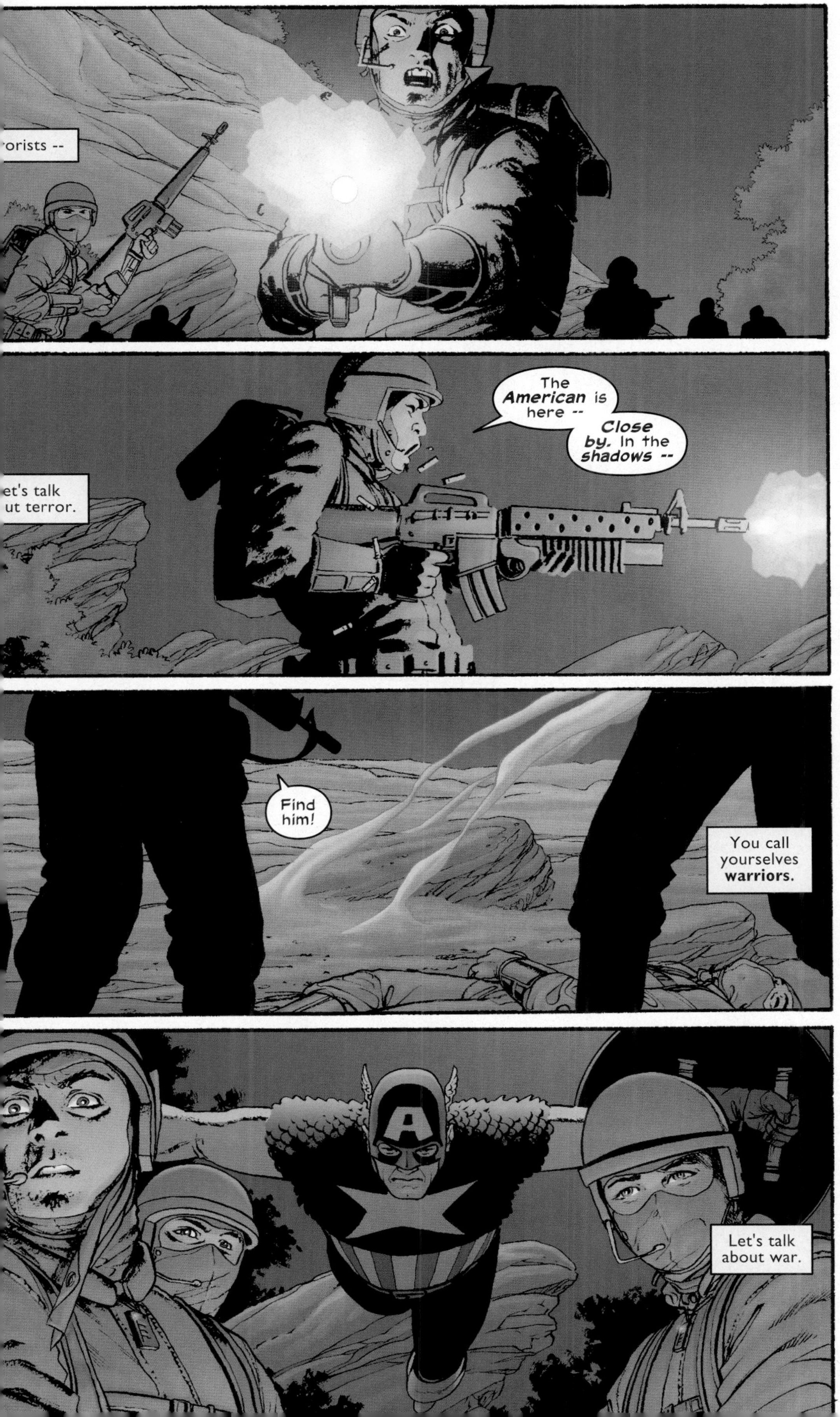

orists --
The American is here --
Close by. In the shadows --
et's talk
ut terror.
Find him!
You call yourselves warriors.
Let's talk about war.

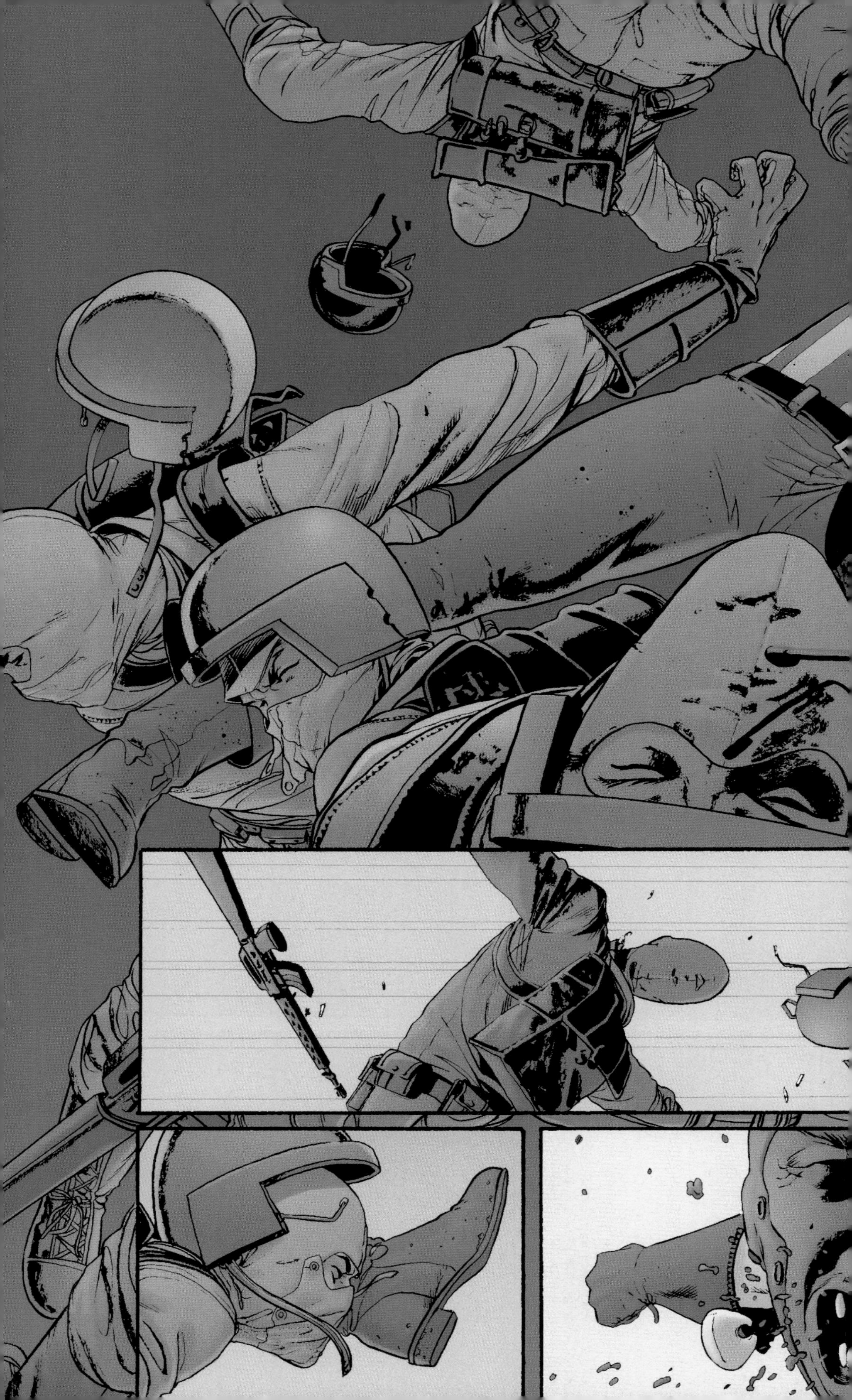

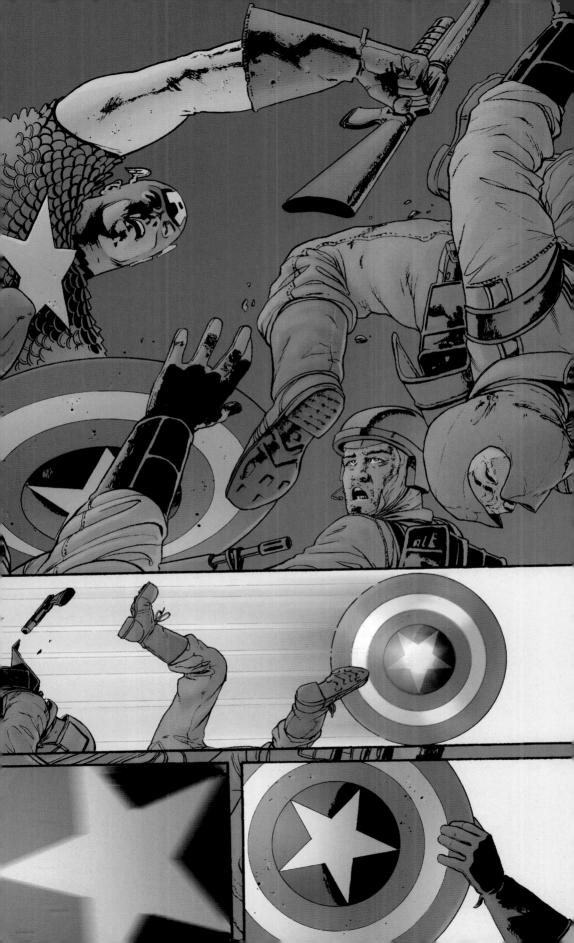

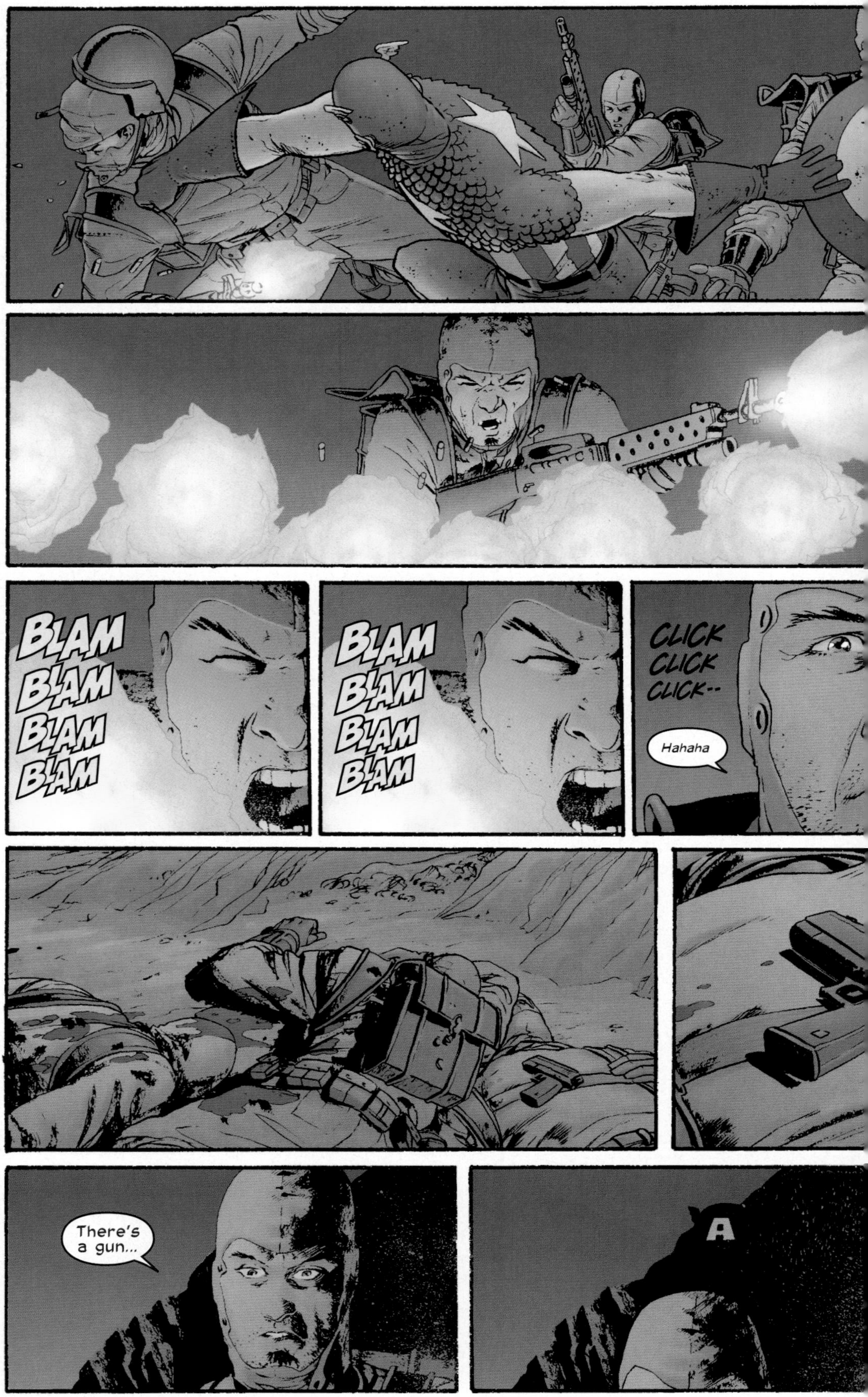
BLAM
BLAM
BLAM
BLAM
BLAM
BLAM
BLAM
BLAM
CLICK
CLICK
CLICK--
Hahaha
There's a gun...

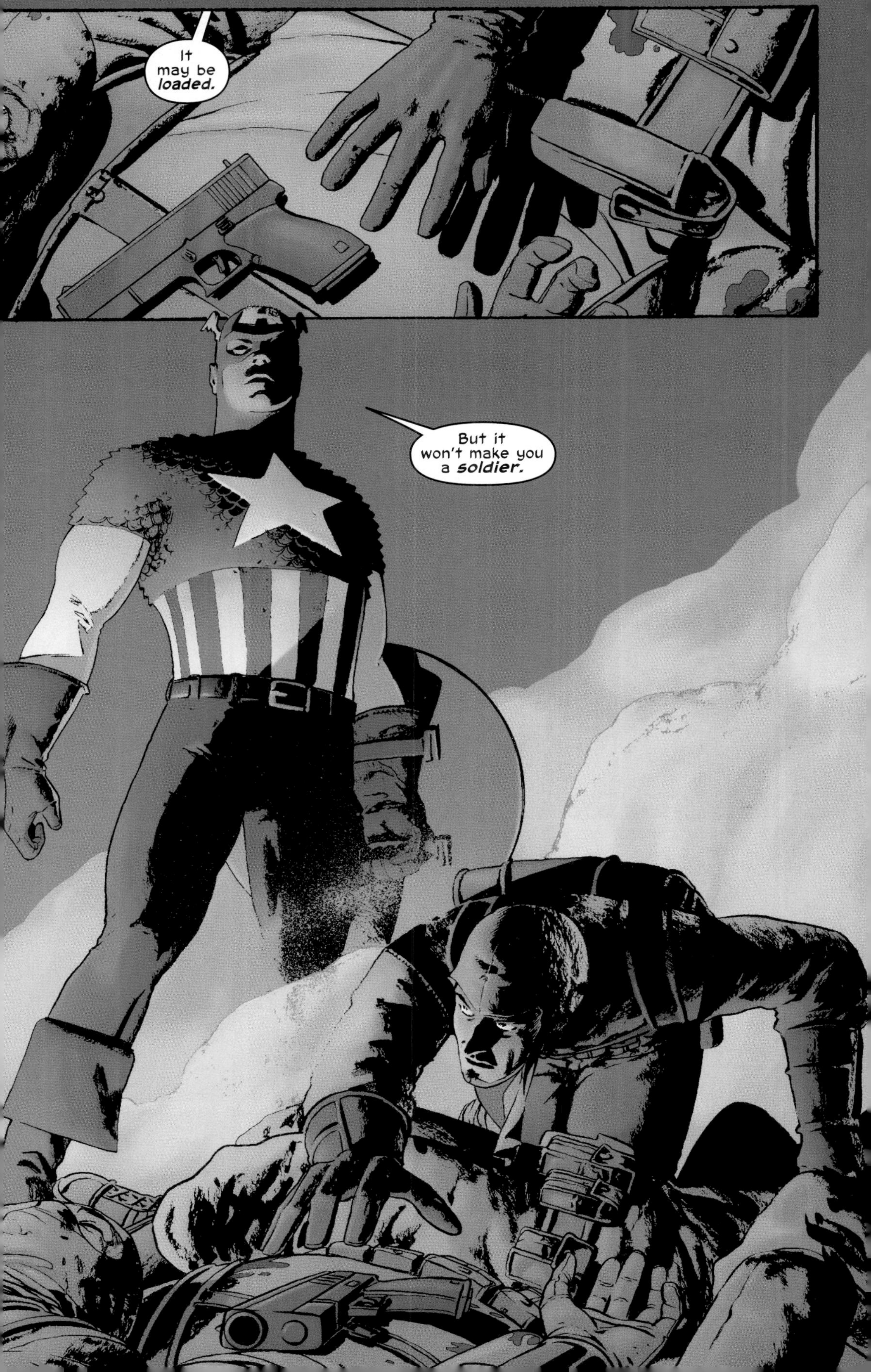
It may be *loaded.*
But it won't make you a *soldier.*

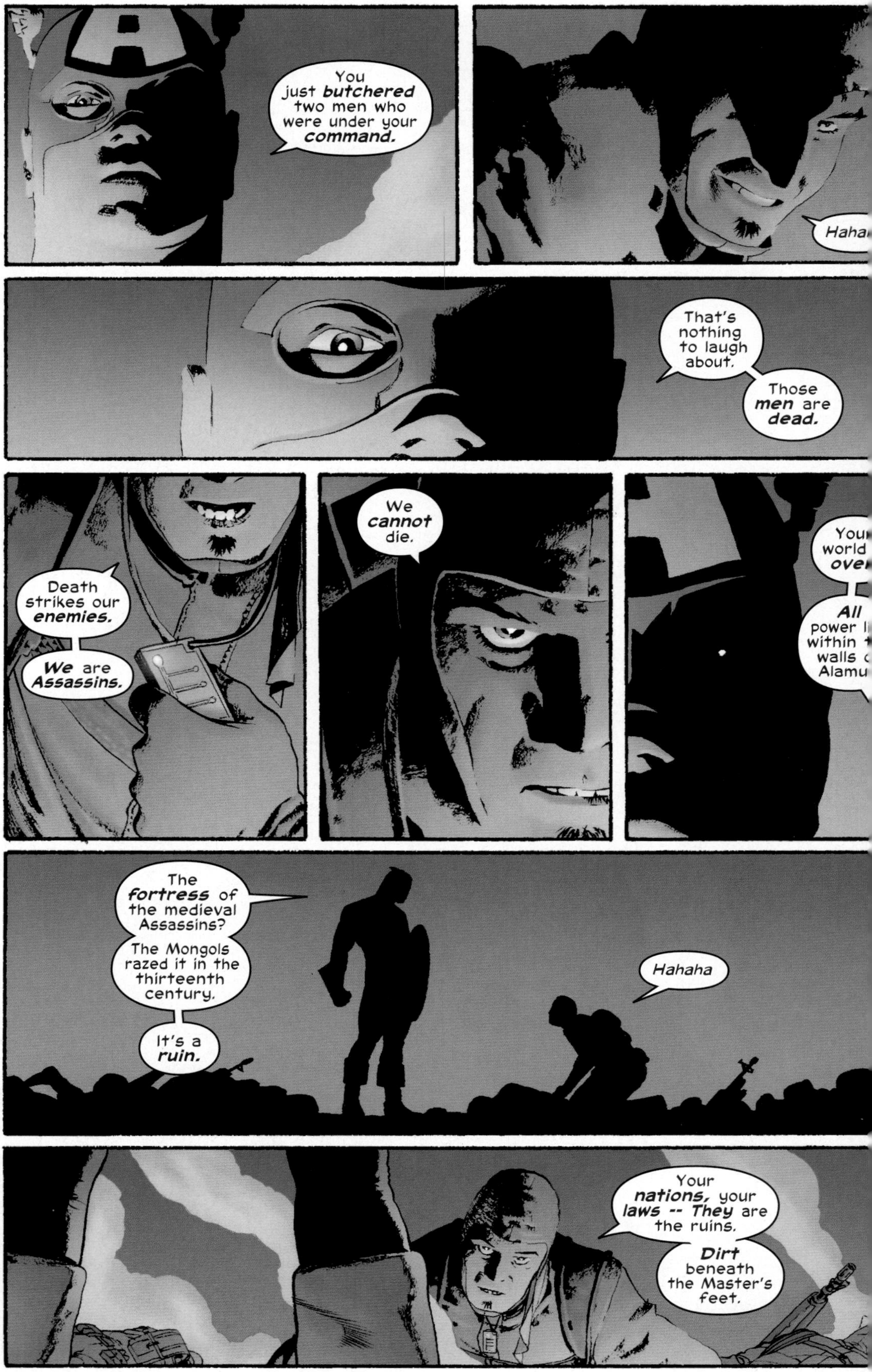

You just butchered two men who were under your command.
Haha
That's nothing to laugh about.
Those men are dead.
Death strikes our enemies.
We are Assassins.
We cannot die.
world
All power within walls
The fortress of the medieval Assassins?
The Mongols razed it in the thirteenth century.
It's a ruin.
Hahaha
Your nations, your laws -- They are the ruins.
Dirt beneath the Master's feet.

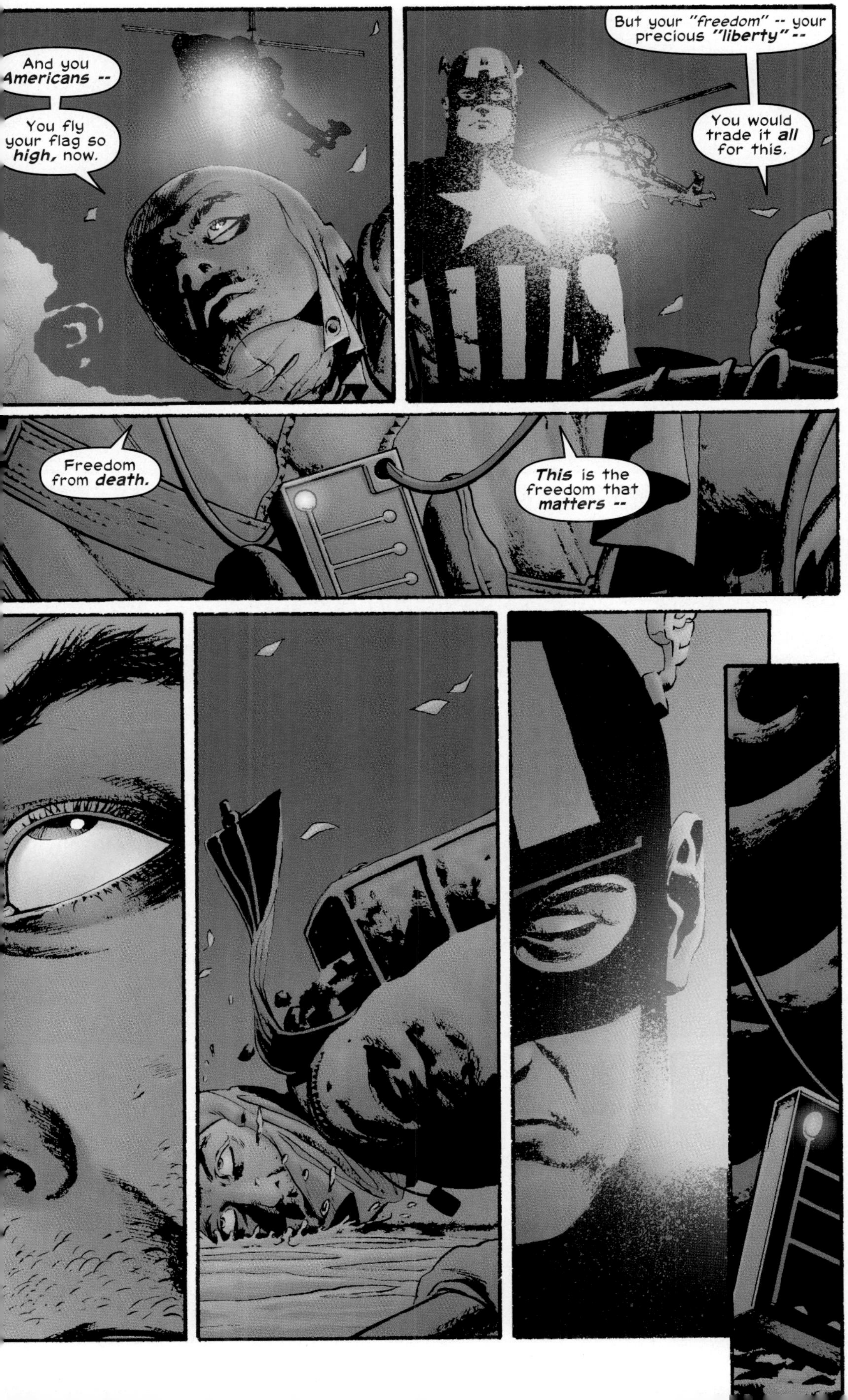
And you *Americans* --
You fly your flag so *high,* now.
But your *"freedom"* -- your precious *"liberty"* --
You would trade it *all* for this.
Freedom from *death.*
This is the freedom that *matters* --

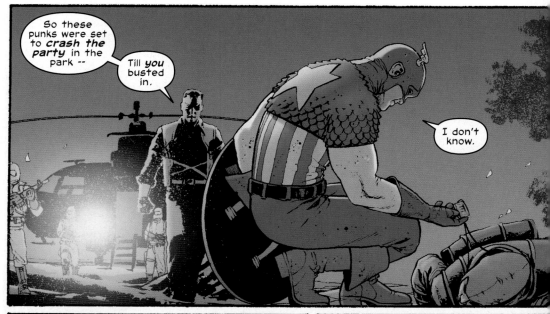

So these punks were set to *crash the party* in the park --

Till *you* busted in.

I don't know.

What have you been *doing* all this time -- reading him his *rights?*

You want to *know* what the game plan was, just *ask* --

Cap...

He's *dead.*

I didn't kill him.

Did *this?*

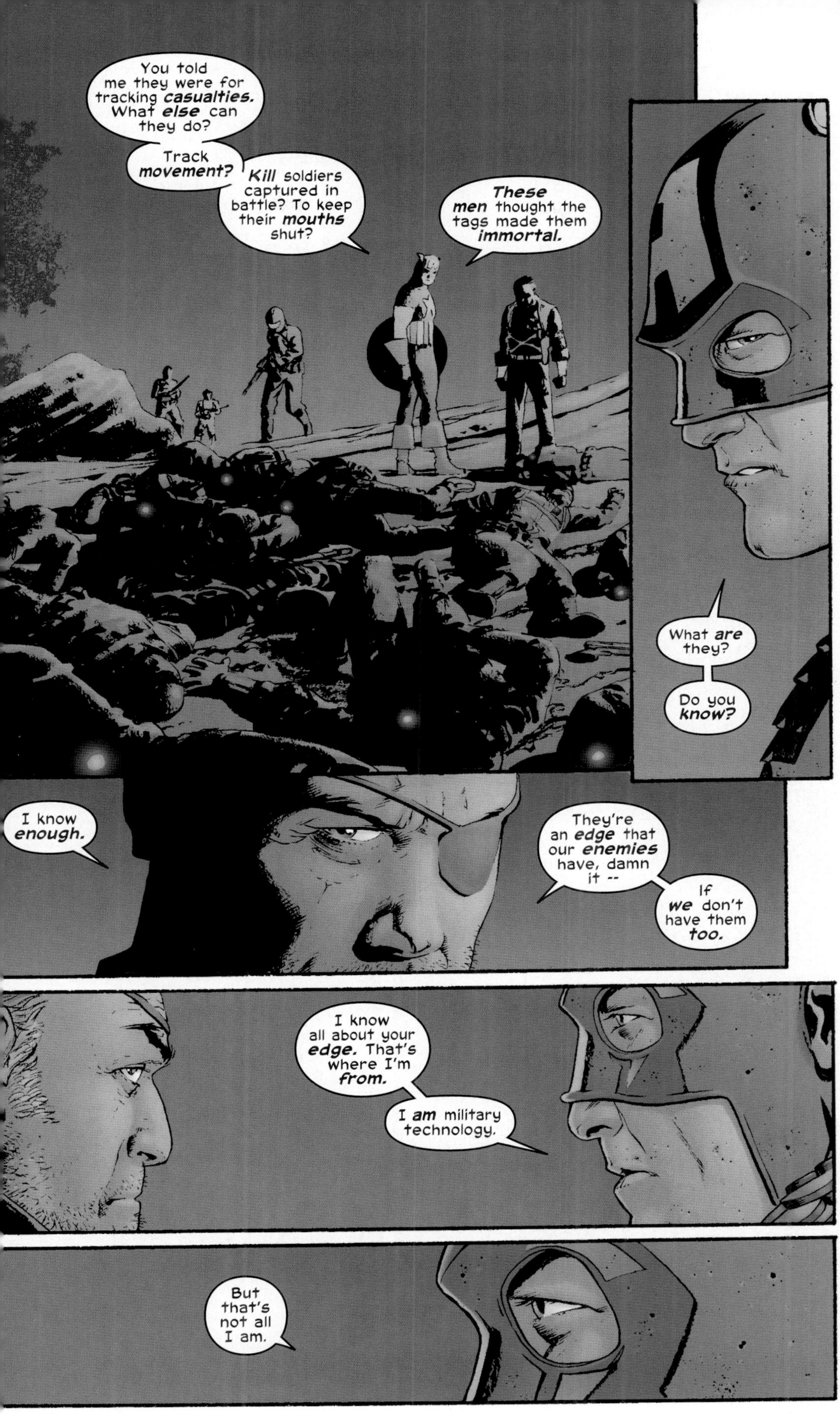
You told me they were for tracking *casualties.* What *else* can they do?
Track *movement?*
Kill soldiers captured in battle? To keep their *mouths* shut?
These men thought the tags made them *immortal.*
What *are* they?
Do you *know?*
I know *enough.*
They're an *edge* that our *enemies* have, damn it --
If *we* don't have them *too.*
I know all about your *edge.* That's where I'm *from.*
I *am* military technology.
But that's not all I am.

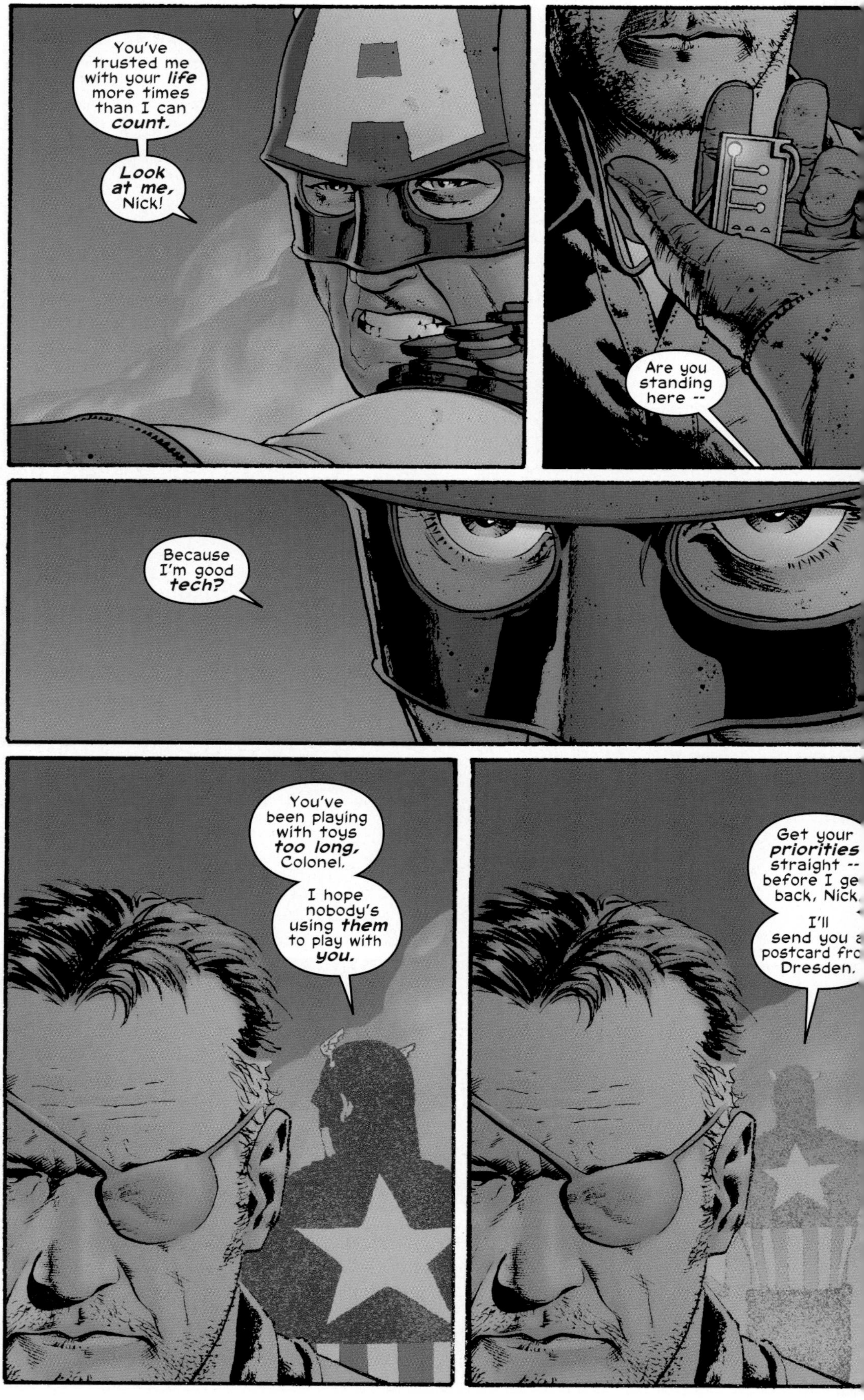
You've trusted me with your *life* more times than I can *count.*
Look at me, Nick!
Are you standing here --
Because I'm good *tech?*
You've been playing with toys *too long,* Colonel.
I hope nobody's using *them* to play with *you.*
Get your *priorities* straight -- before I ge back, Nick.
I'll send you a postcard fro Dresden.

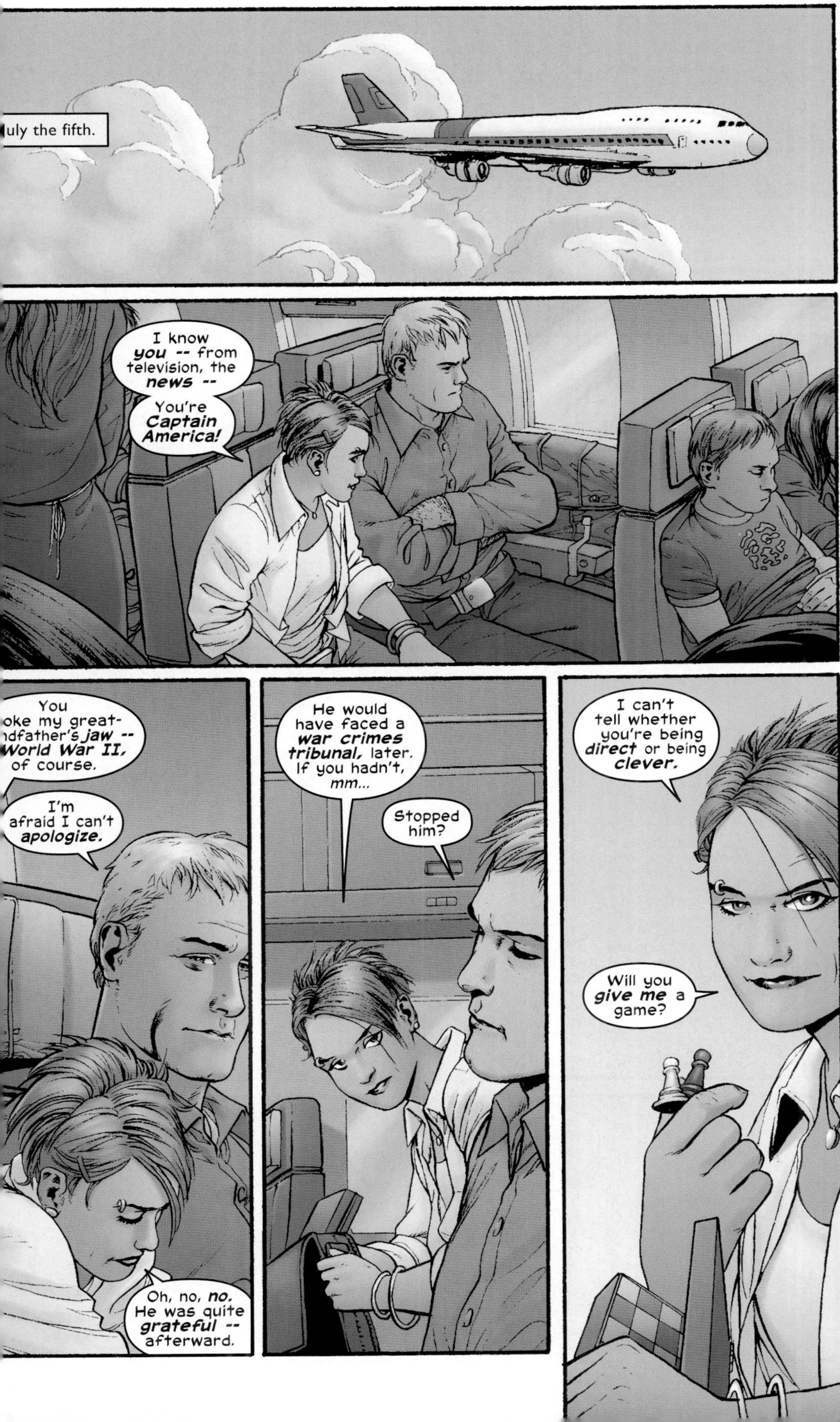

uly the fifth.
I know you -- from television, the news --
You're Captain America!
You oke my great- ndfather's jaw -- World War II, of course.
I'm afraid I can't apologize.
Oh, no, no. He was quite grateful -- afterward.
He would have faced a war crimes tribunal, later. If you hadn't, mm...
Stopped him?
I can't tell whether you're being direct or being clever.
Will you give me a game?

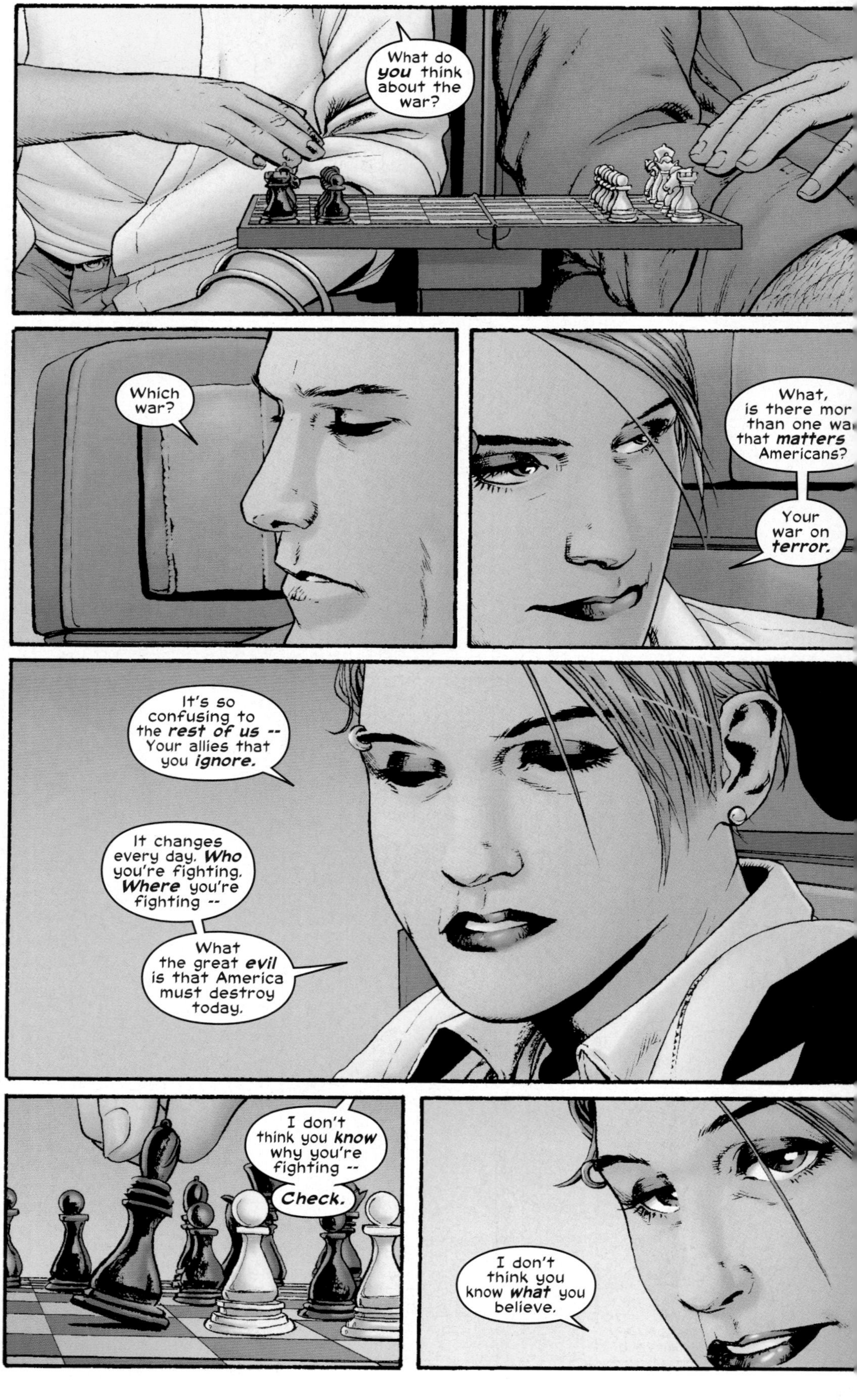

What do *you* think about the war?
Which war?
What, is there mor than one wa that *matters* Americans?
Your war on *terror.*
It's so confusing to the *rest of us* -- Your allies that you *ignore.*
It changes every day. *Who* you're fighting. *Where* you're fighting --
What the great *evil* is that America must destroy today.
I don't think you *know* why you're fighting --
Check.
I don't think you know *what* you believe.

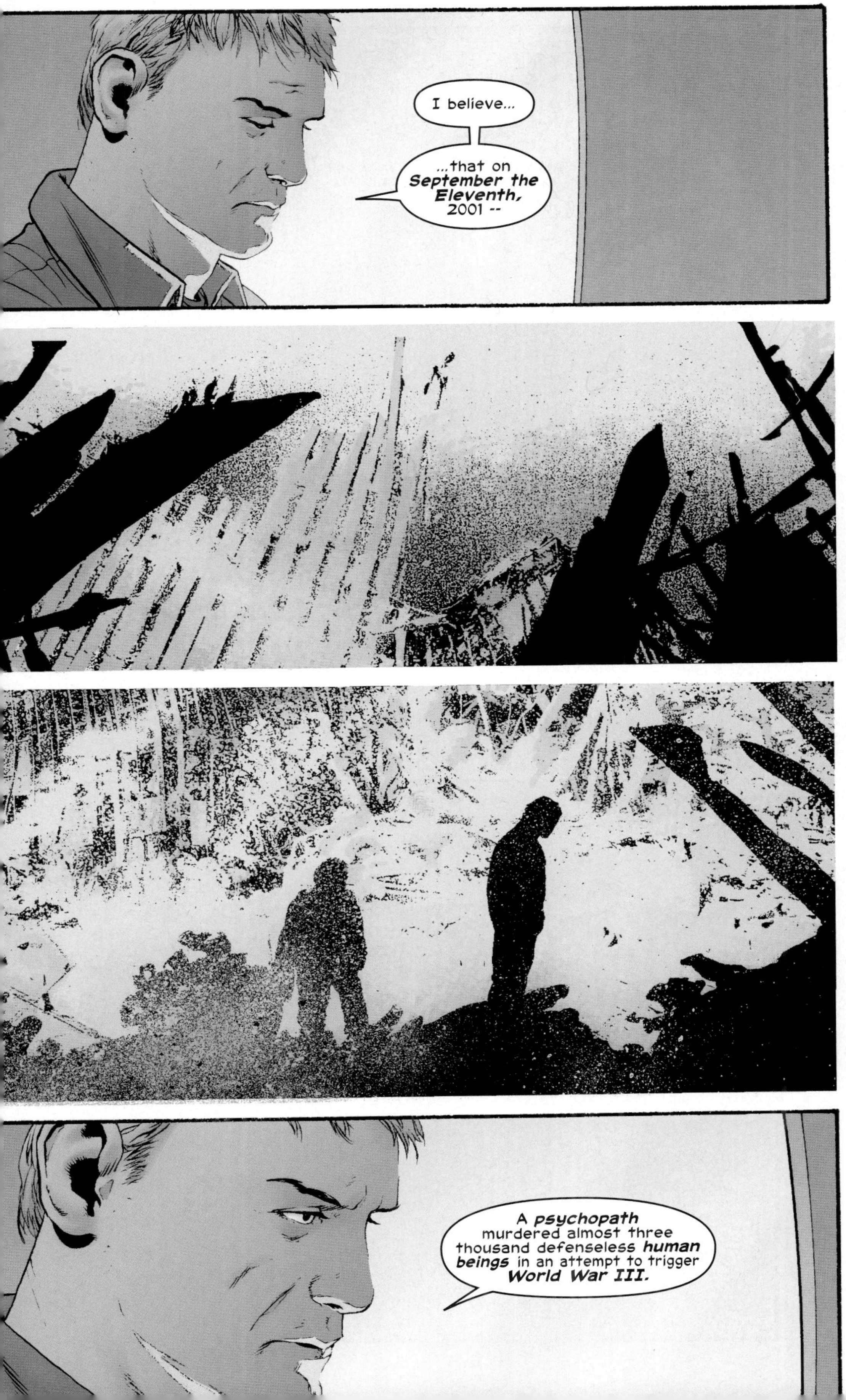
I believe...
...that on *September the Eleventh,* 2001 --
A *psychopath* murdered almost three thousand defenseless *human beings* in an attempt to trigger *World War III.*

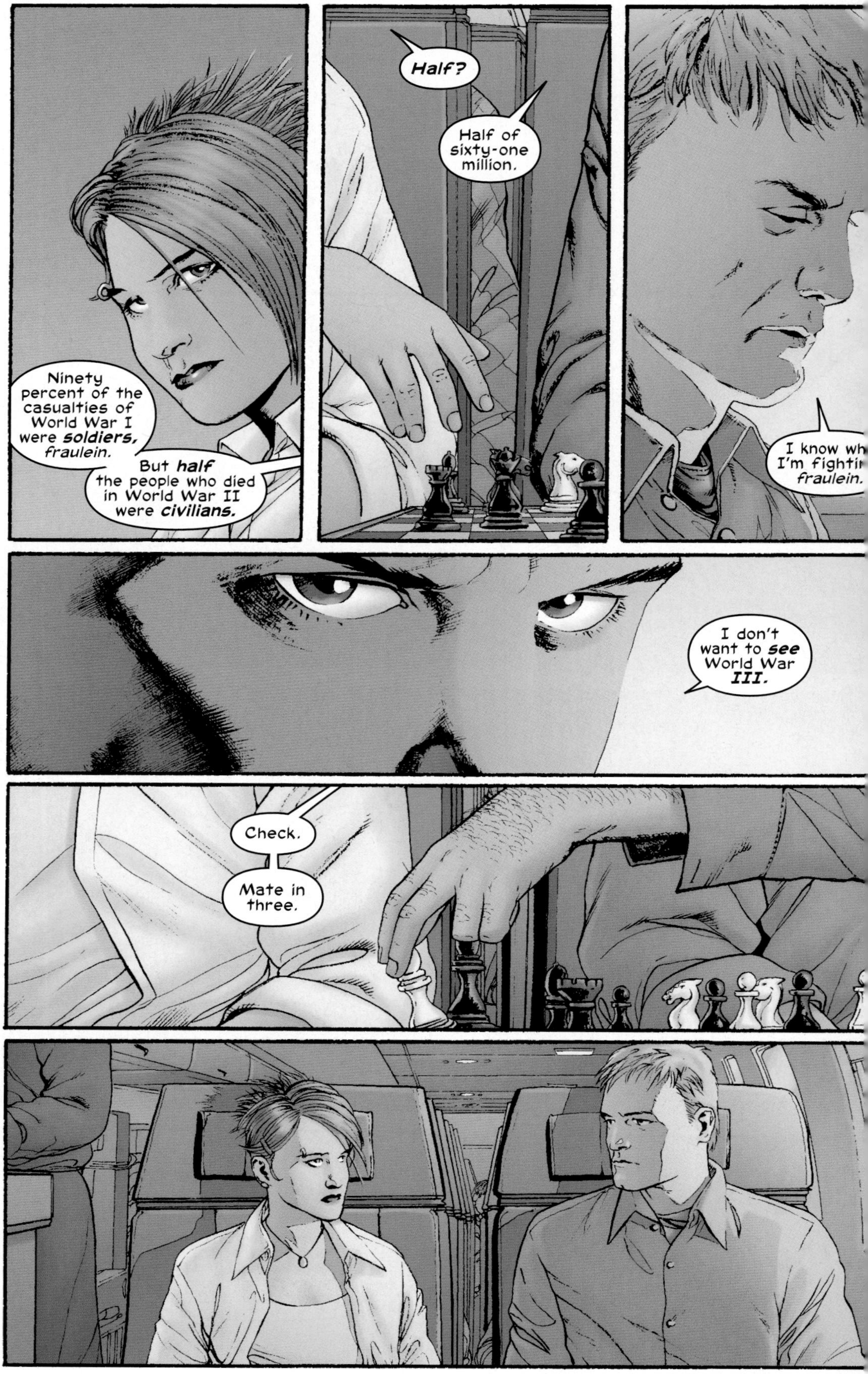
Ninety percent of the casualties of World War I were soldiers, fraulein.
But half the people who died in World War II were civilians.
Half?
Half of sixty-one million.
I don't want to see World War III.
Check.
Mate in three.

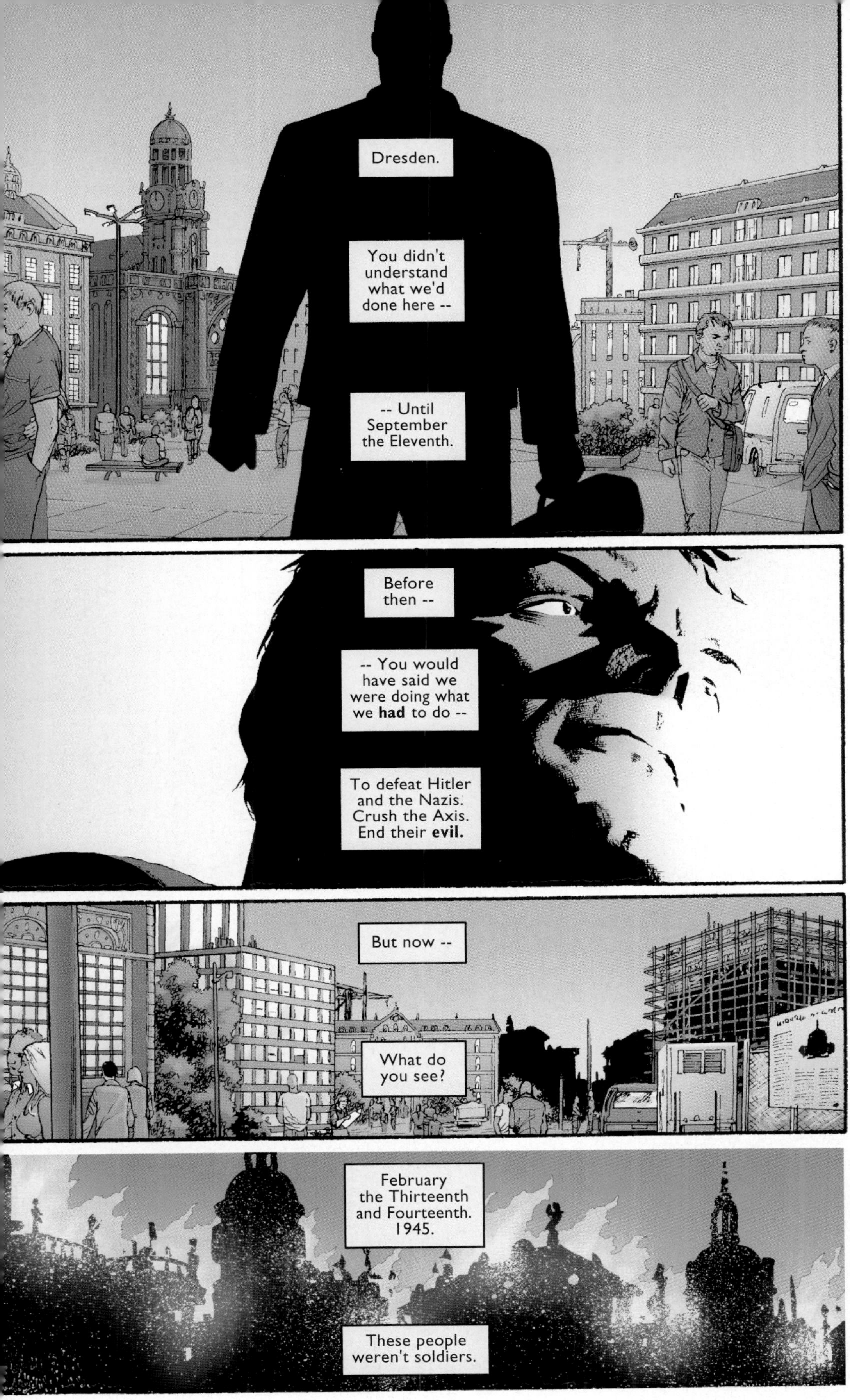
Dresden.
You didn't understand what we'd done here --
-- Until September the Eleventh.
Before then --
-- You would have said we were doing what we **had** to do --
To defeat Hitler and the Nazis. Crush the Axis. End their **evil.**
But now --
What do you see?
February the Thirteenth and Fourteenth. 1945.
These people weren't soldiers.

But they died.

They huddled
in the dark.

Trapped.

While the fire
raged above them.

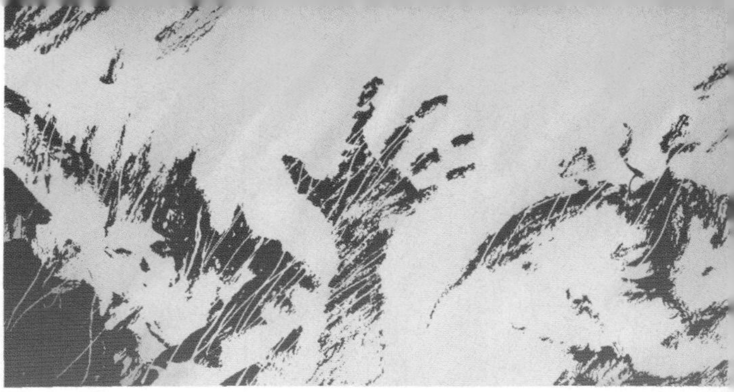

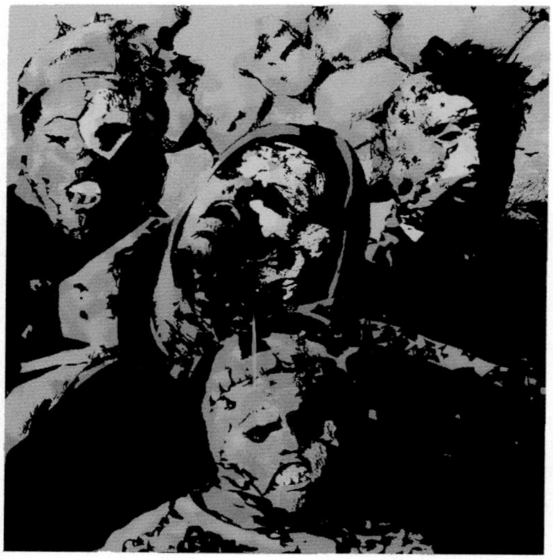

Faces pressed to
the broken walls
that locked them in.

Clawing at the cold
earth until it grew
too hot to touch.

And when there was
nothing left to breathe
there in the dark, they died.

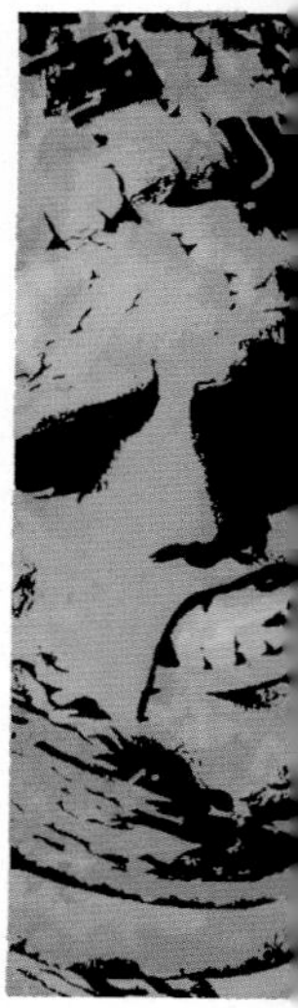

The city's firemen
fought the blaze for
days before they
could begin the
search for survivors.

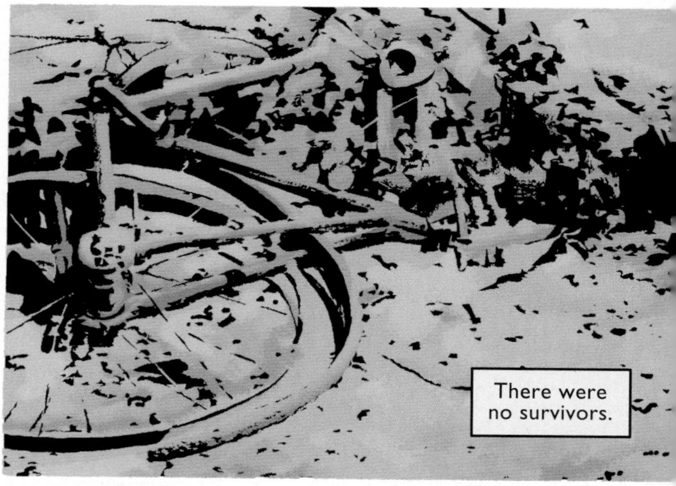
There were
no survivors.

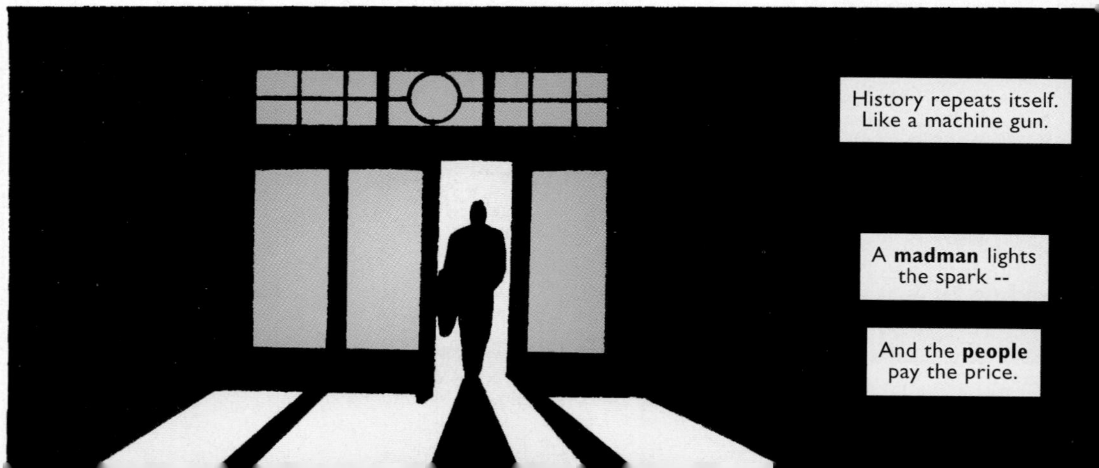
History repeats itself.
Like a machine gun.
A **madman** lights
the spark --
And the **people**
pay the price.

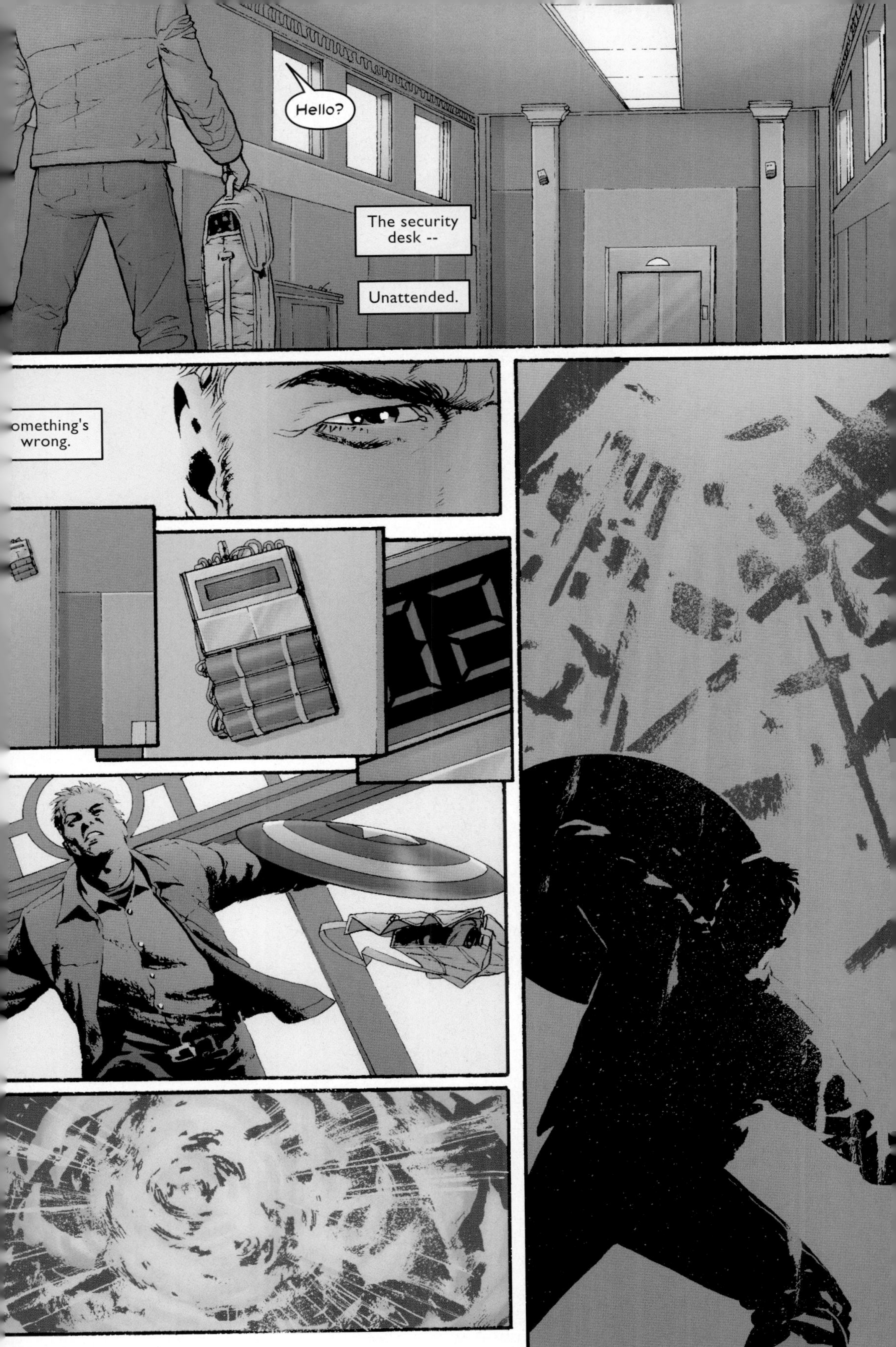
Hello?
The security desk --
Unattended.
omething's wrong.

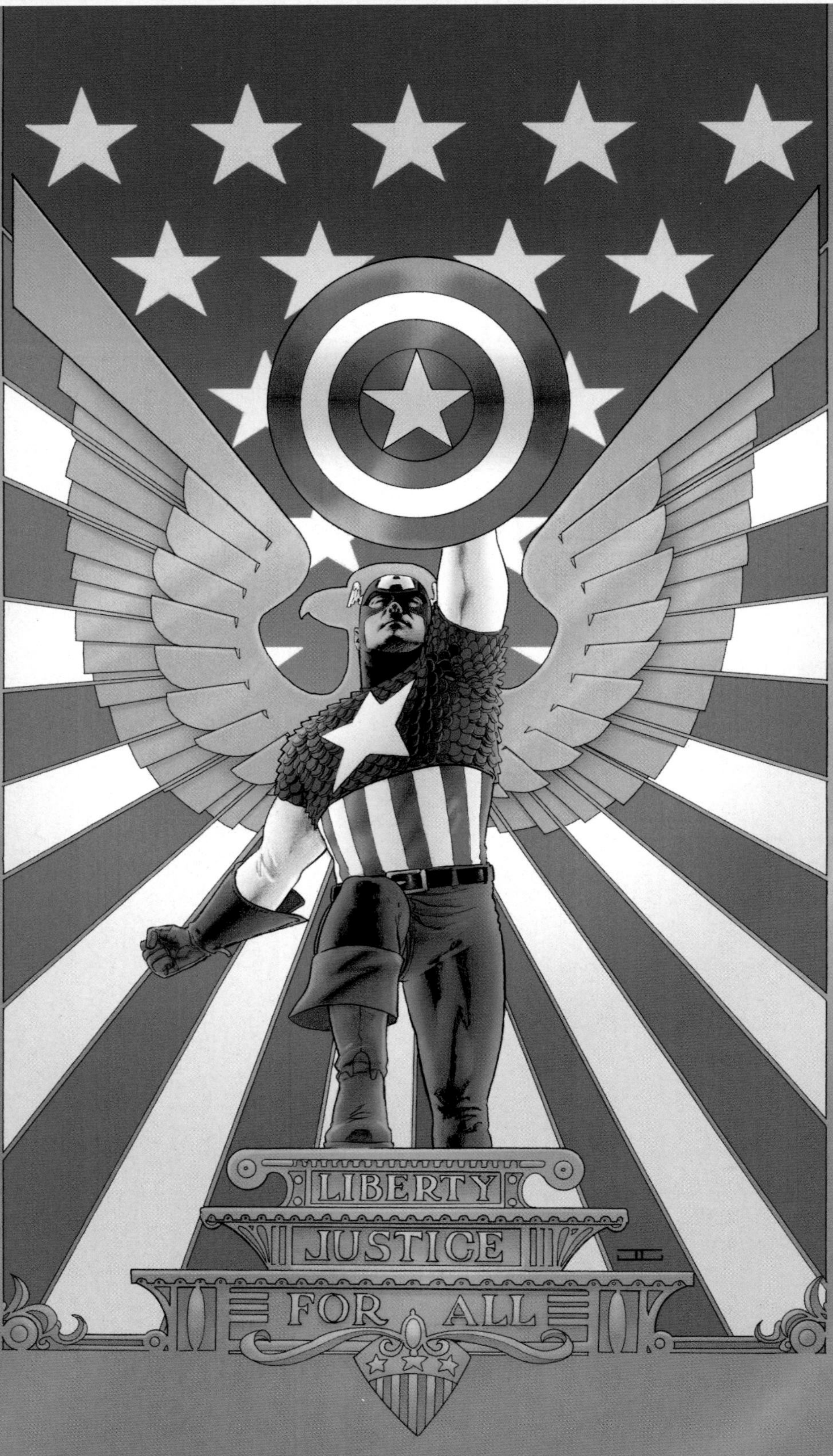
LIBERTY
JUSTICE
FOR ALL

6 WARLORDS, PART 3

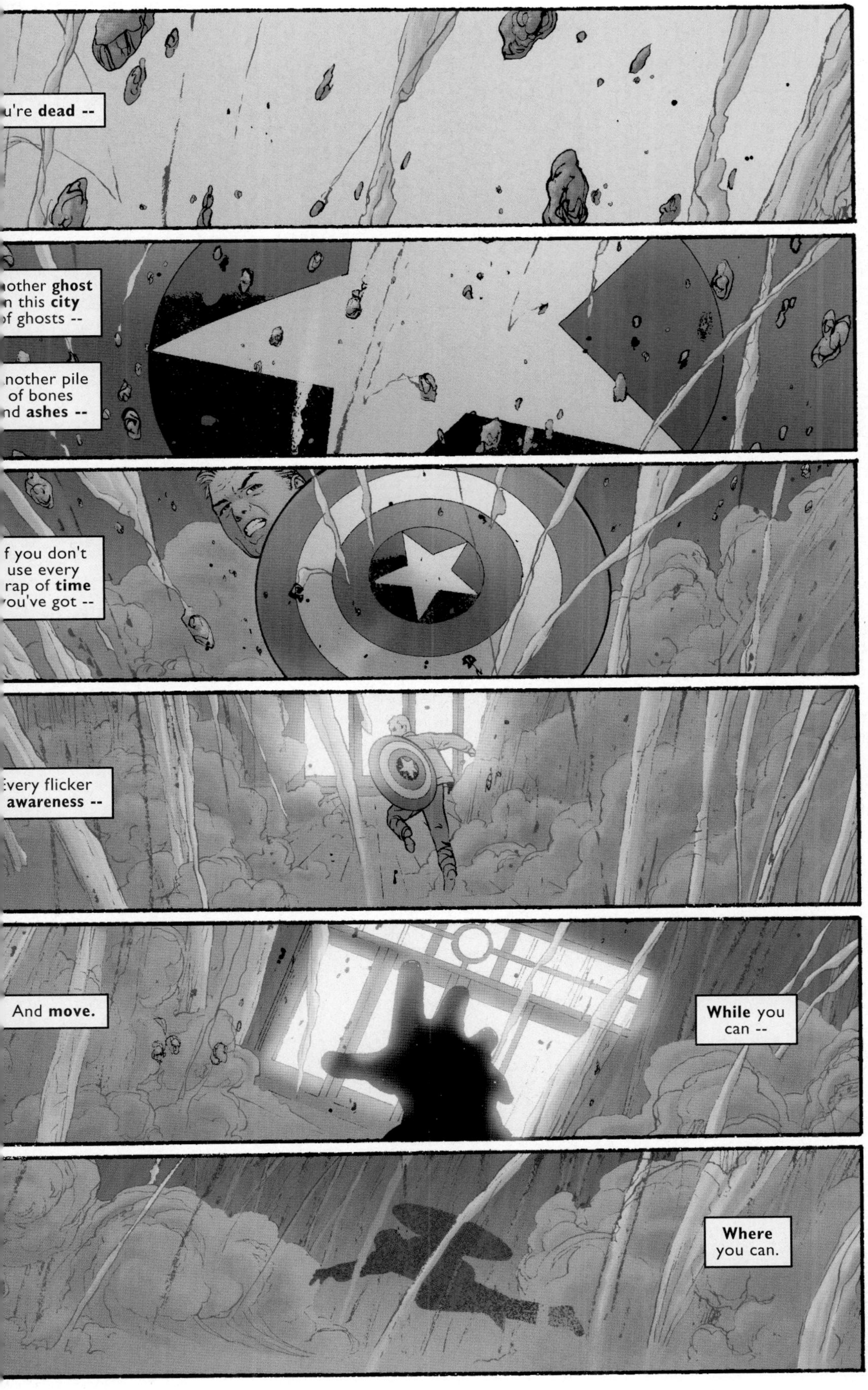
u're dead --
nother ghost n this city of ghosts --
nother pile of bones nd ashes --
f you don't use every rap of time ou've got --
very flicker awareness --
And move.
While you can --
Where you can.

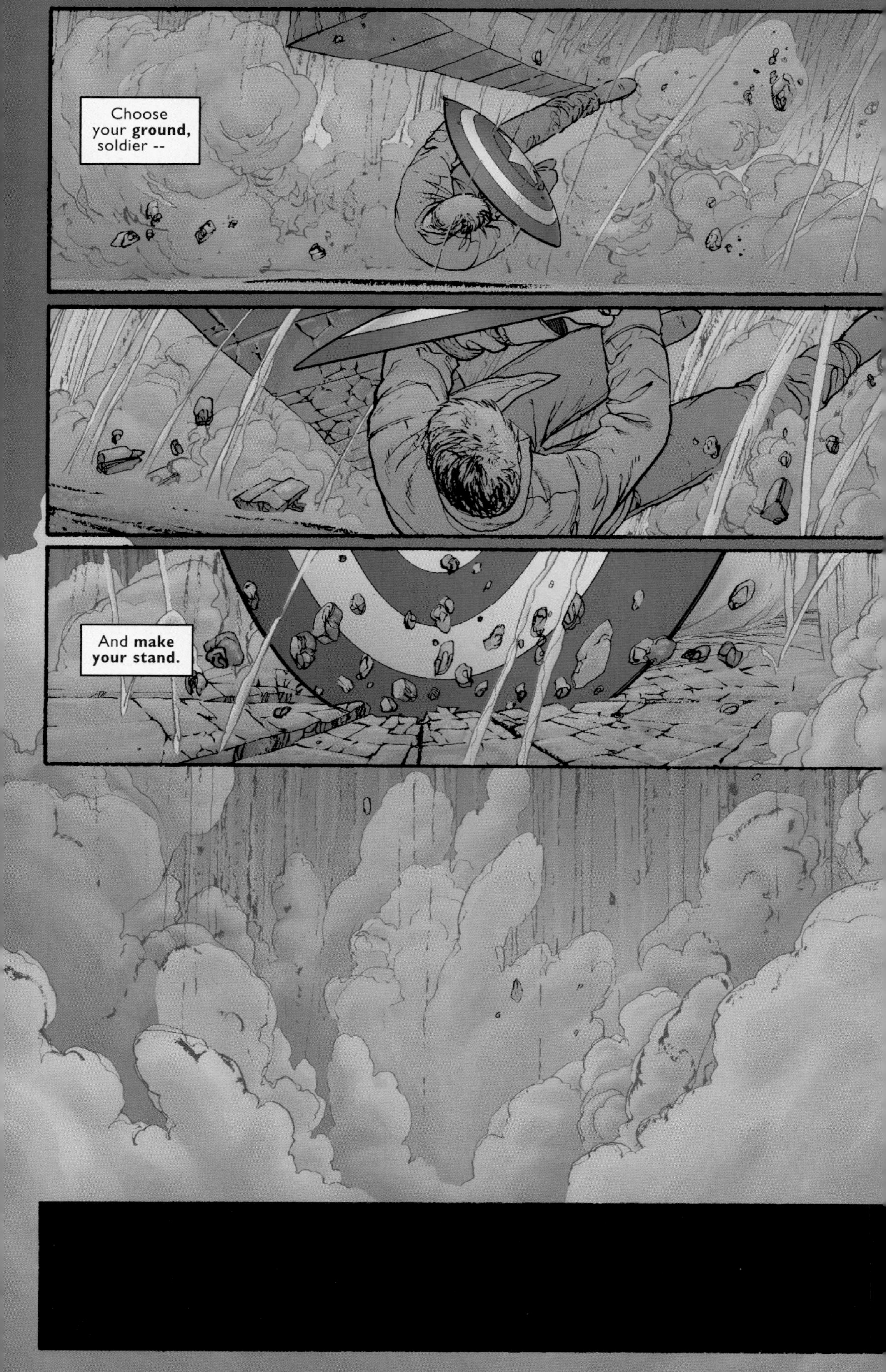
Choose your ground, soldier --
And make your stand.

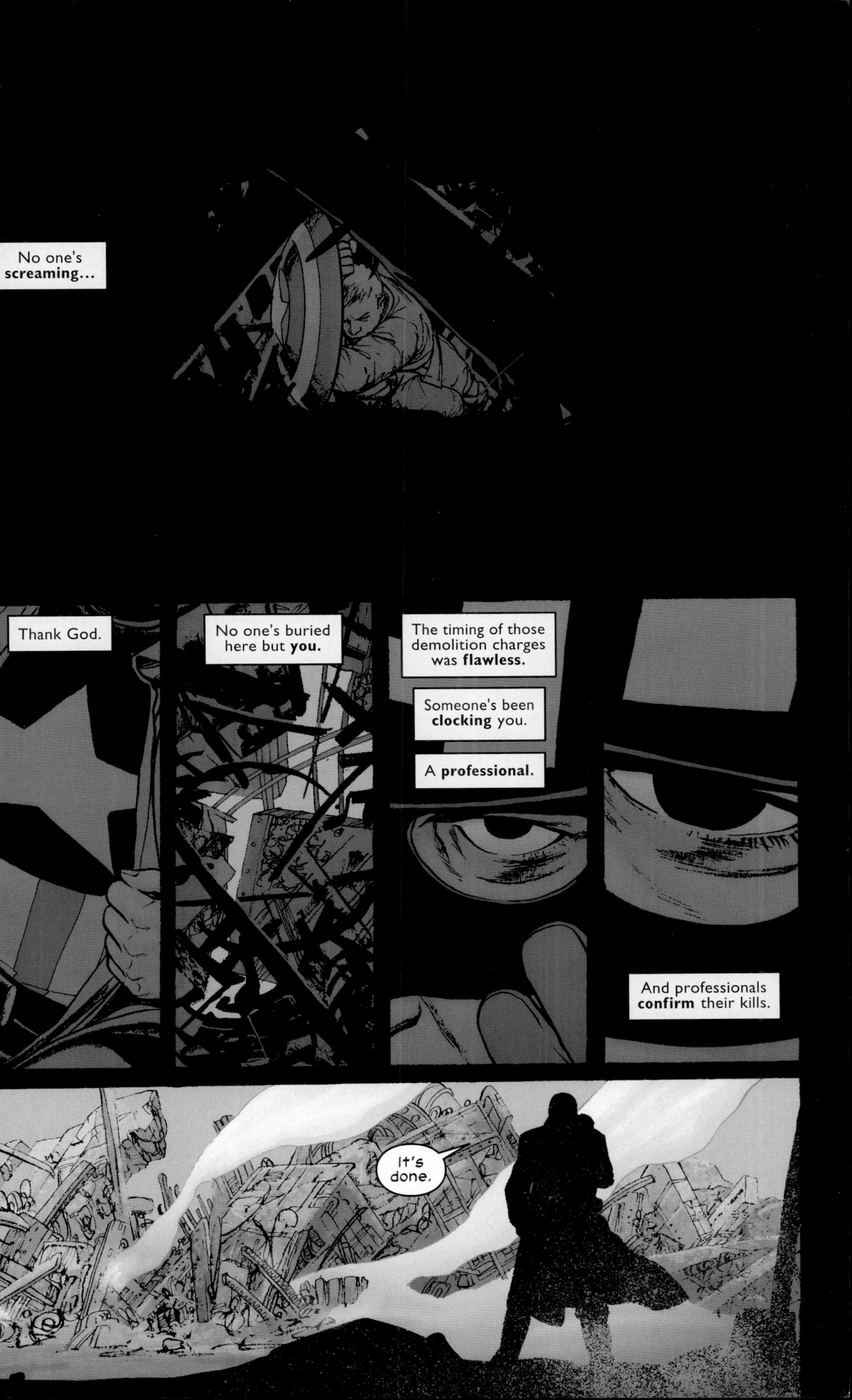
No one's **screaming...**
Thank God.
No one's buried here but **you.**
The timing of those demolition charges was **flawless.**
Someone's been **clocking** you.
A **professional.**
And professionals **confirm** their kills.
It's done.

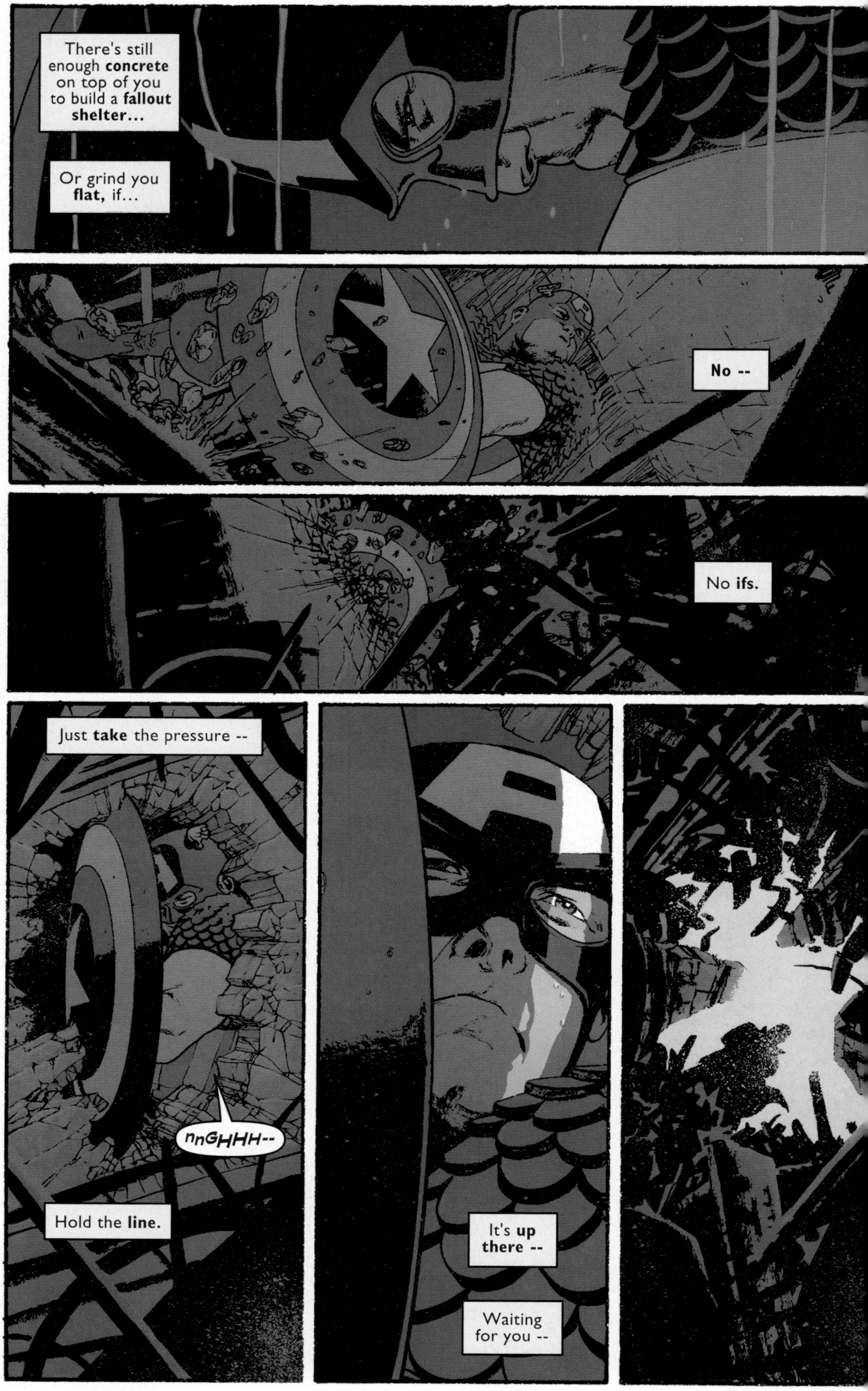

There's still enough **concrete** on top of you to build a **fallout shelter...**
Or grind you **flat,** if...
No --
No **ifs.**
Just **take** the pressure --
nnGHHH--
Hold the **line.**
It's **up there --**
Waiting for you --

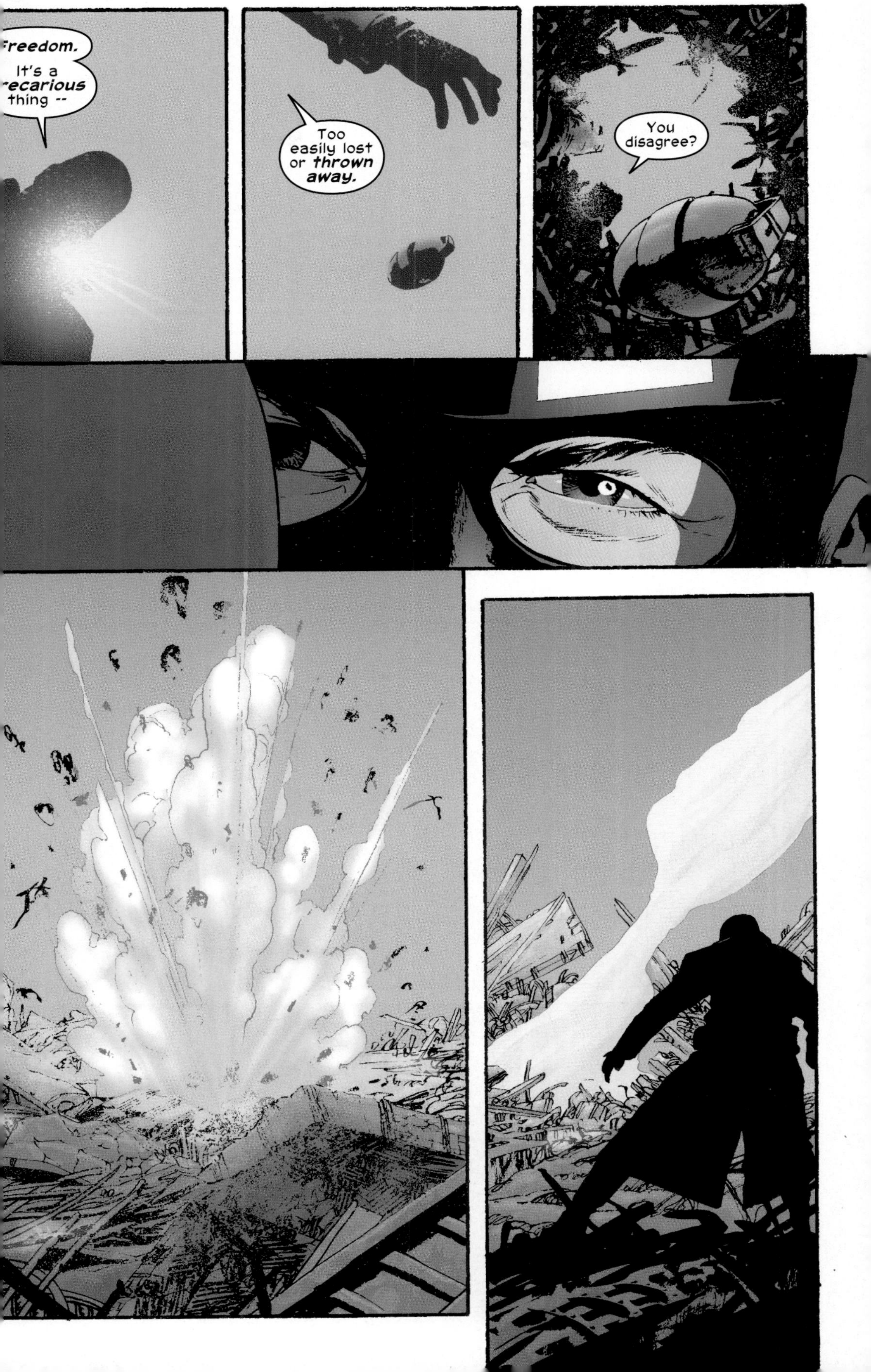
Freedom.
It's a recarious thing --
Too easily lost or thrown away.
You disagree?

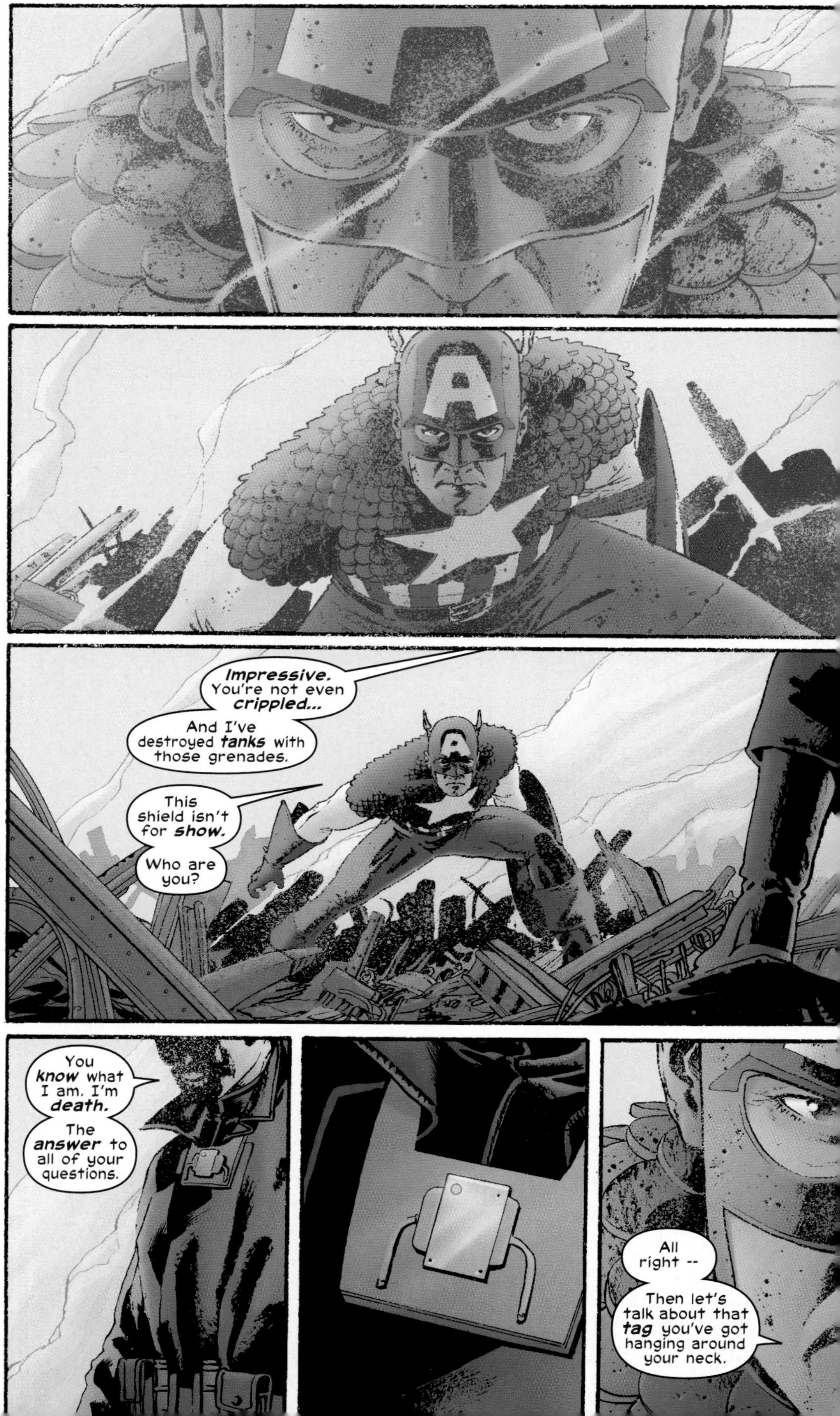

Impressive. You're not even crippled...
And I've destroyed tanks with those grenades.
This shield isn't for show.
Who are you?
You know what I am. I'm death.
The answer to all of your questions.
All right --
Then let's talk about that tag you've got hanging around your neck.

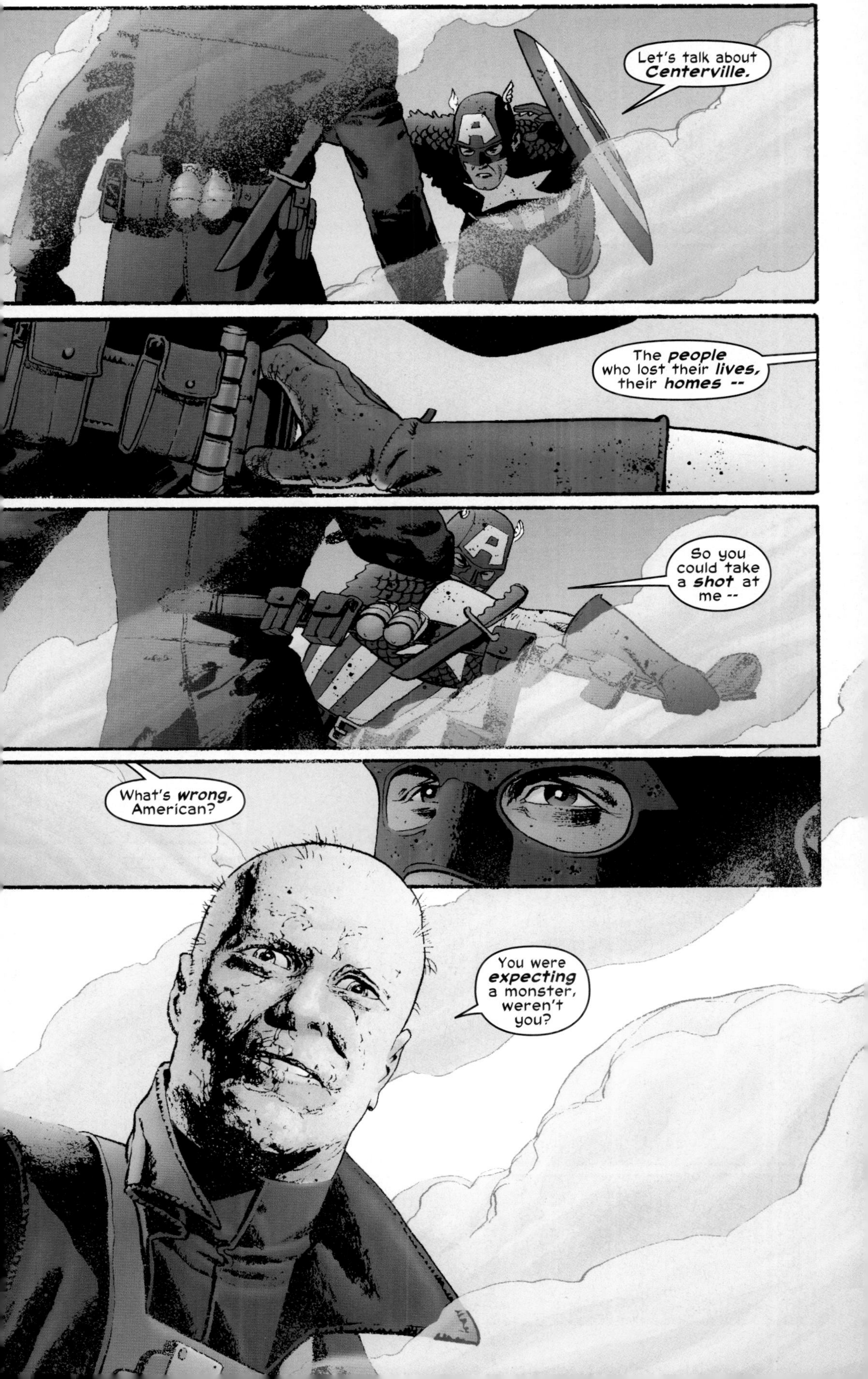
Let's talk about *Centerville.*
The *people* who lost their *lives,* their *homes* --
So you could take a *shot* at me --
What's *wrong,* American?
You were *expecting* a monster, weren't you?

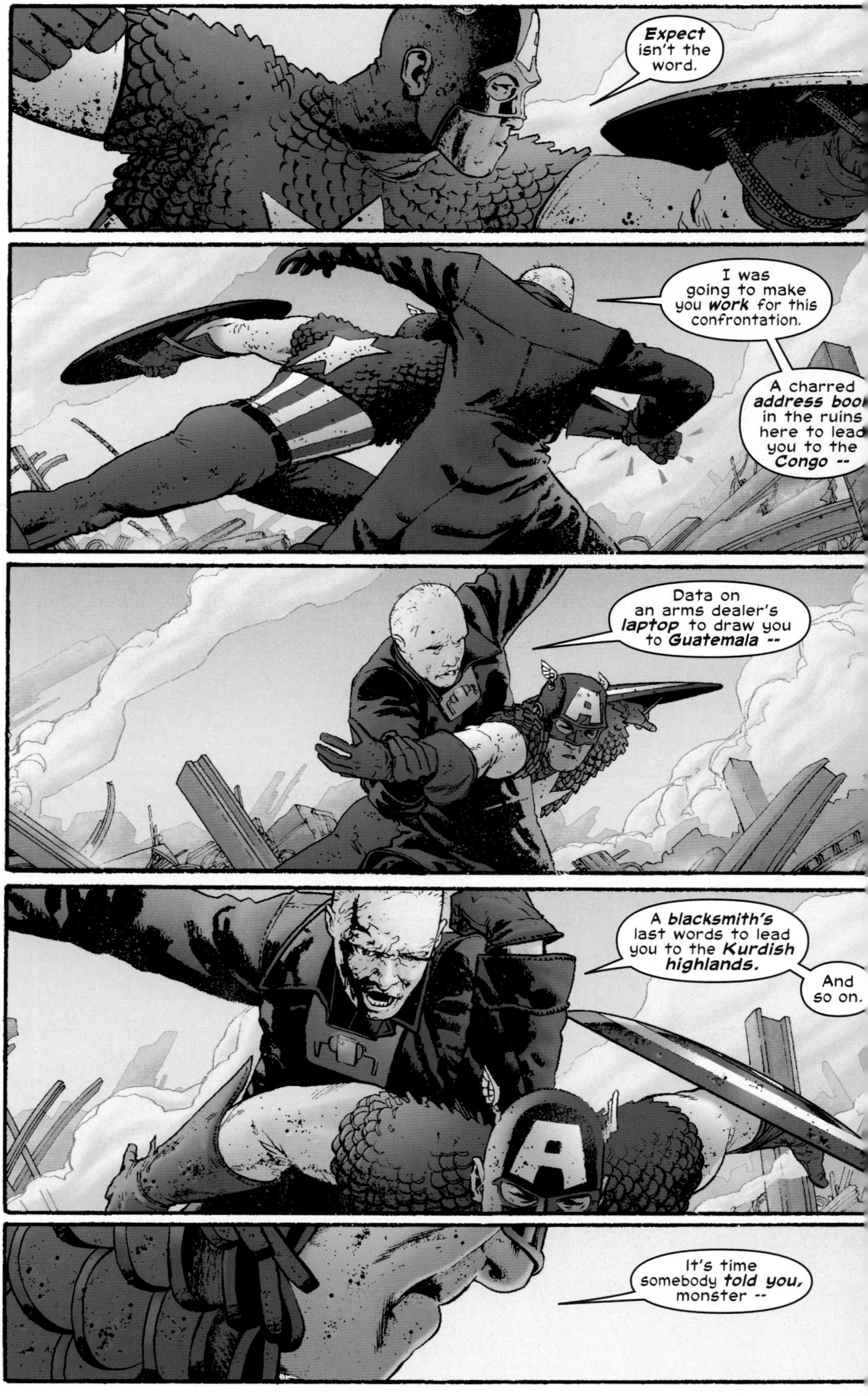

Expect isn't the word.
I was going to make you work for this confrontation.
A charred address boo in the ruins here to lead you to the Congo --
Data on an arms dealer's laptop to draw you to Guatemala --
A blacksmith's last words to lead you to the Kurdish highlands.
And so on.
It's time somebody told you, monster --

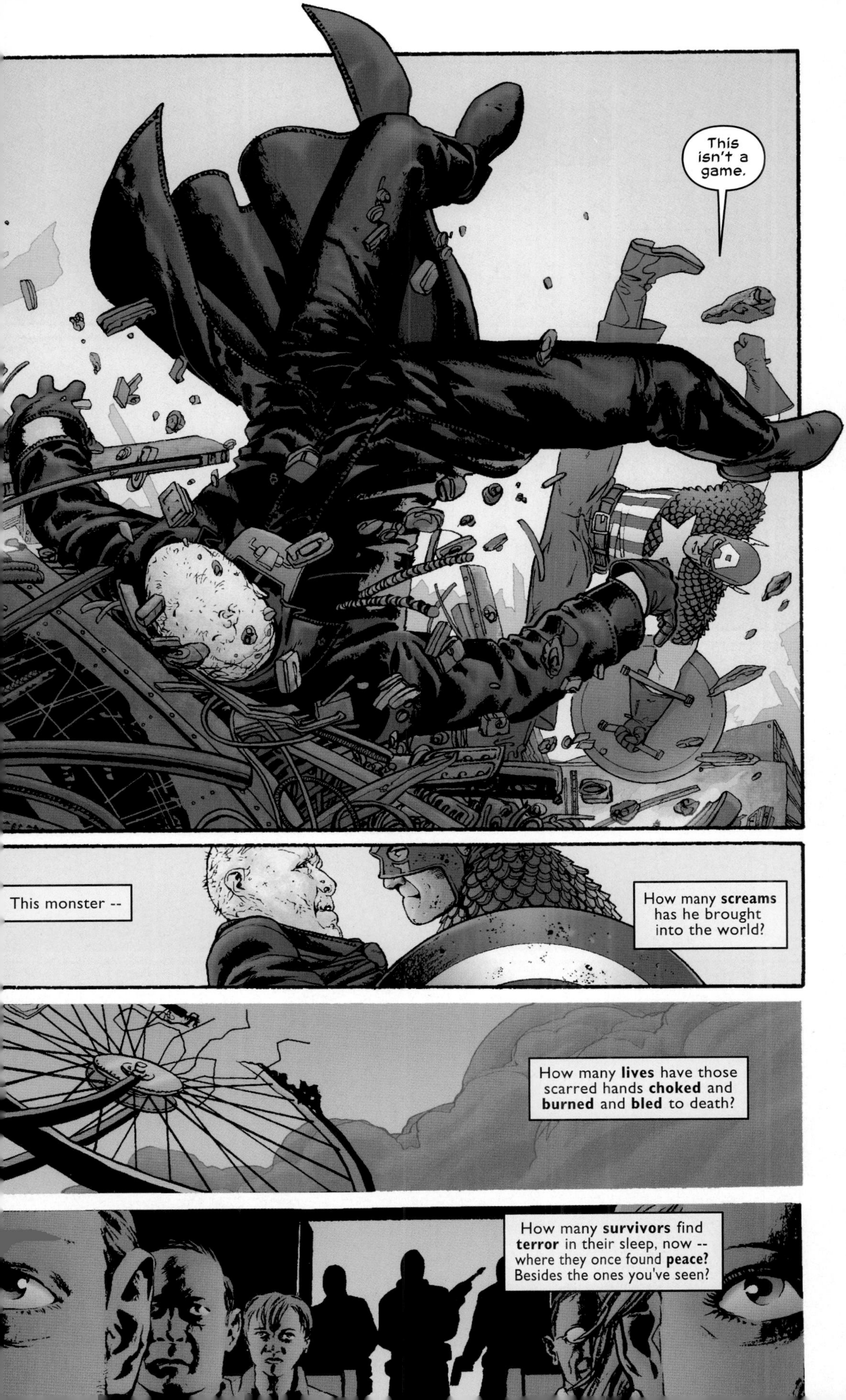

This isn't a game.
This monster --
How many **screams** has he brought into the world?
How many **lives** have those scarred hands **choked** and **burned** and **bled** to death?
How many **survivors** find **terror** in their sleep, now -- where they once found **peace?** Besides the ones you've seen?

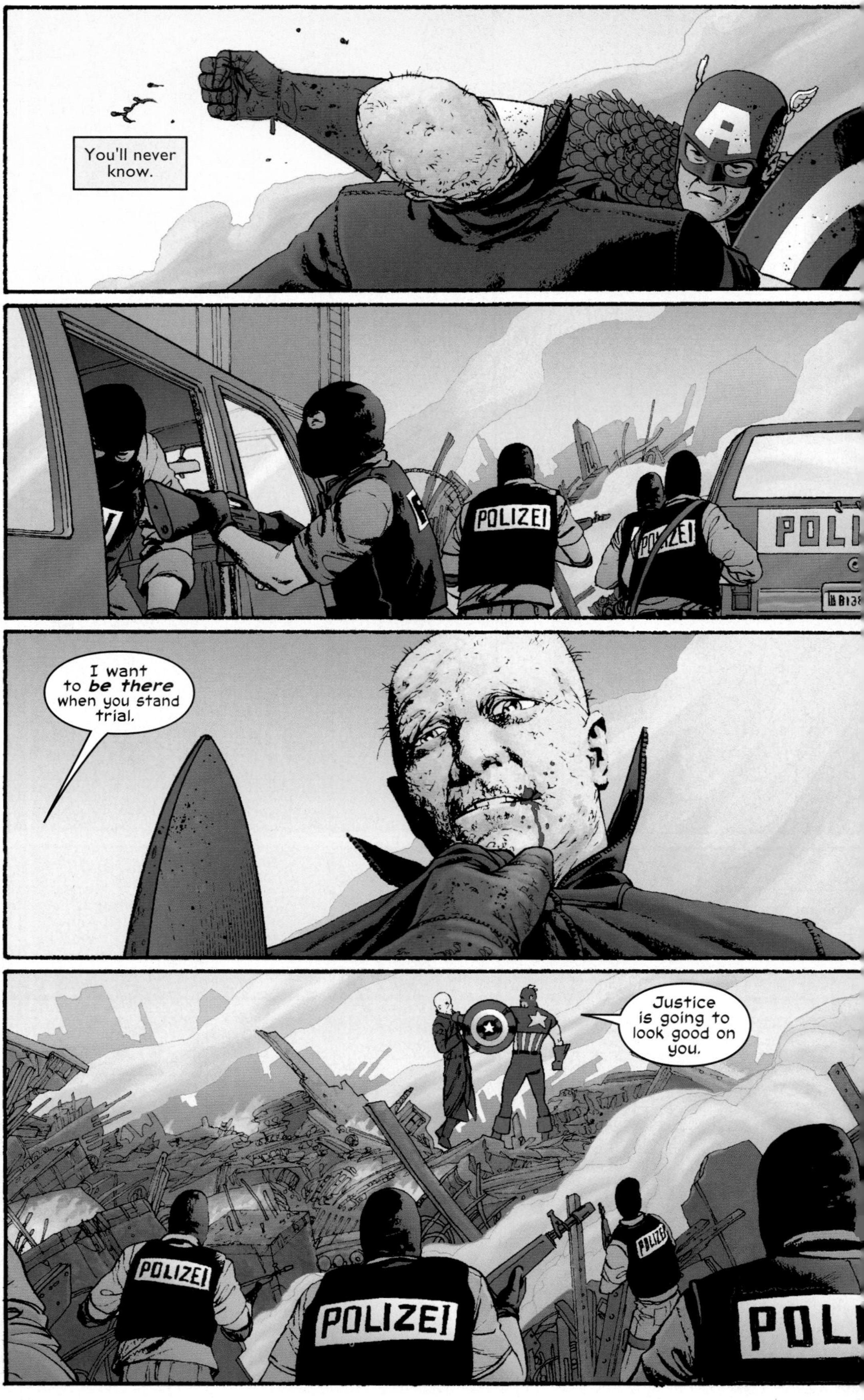
You'll never know.
POLIZEI
POLIZEI
POLI
I want to **be there** when you stand trial.
Justice is going to look good on you.
POLIZEI
POLIZEI
POLIZEI
POLI

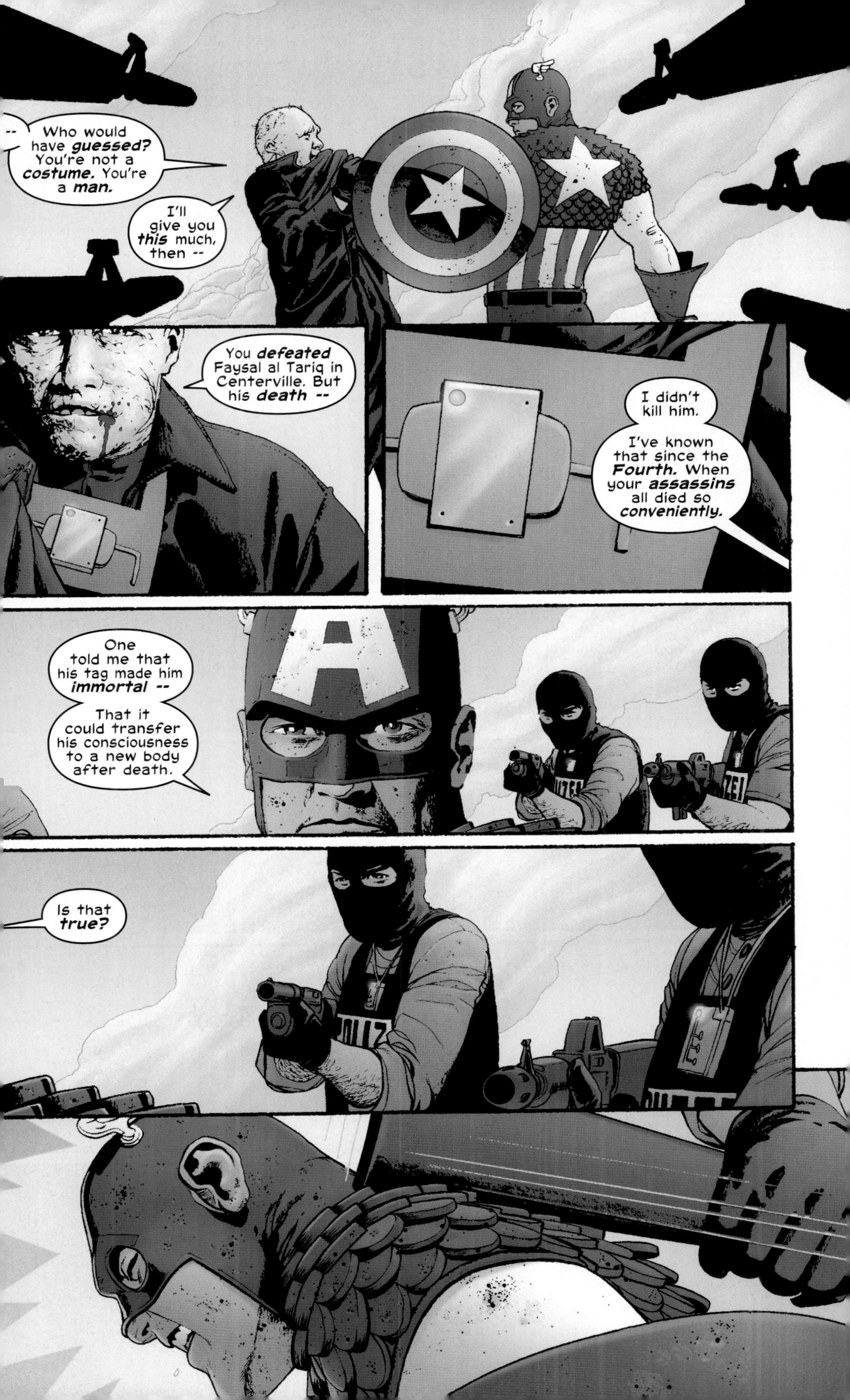
-- Who would have guessed? You're not a costume. You're a man.
I'll give you this much, then --
You defeated Faysal al Tariq in Centerville. But his death --
I didn't kill him.
I've known that since the Fourth. When your assassins all died so conveniently.
One told me that his tag made him immortal --
That it could transfer his consciousness to a new body after death.
Is that true?

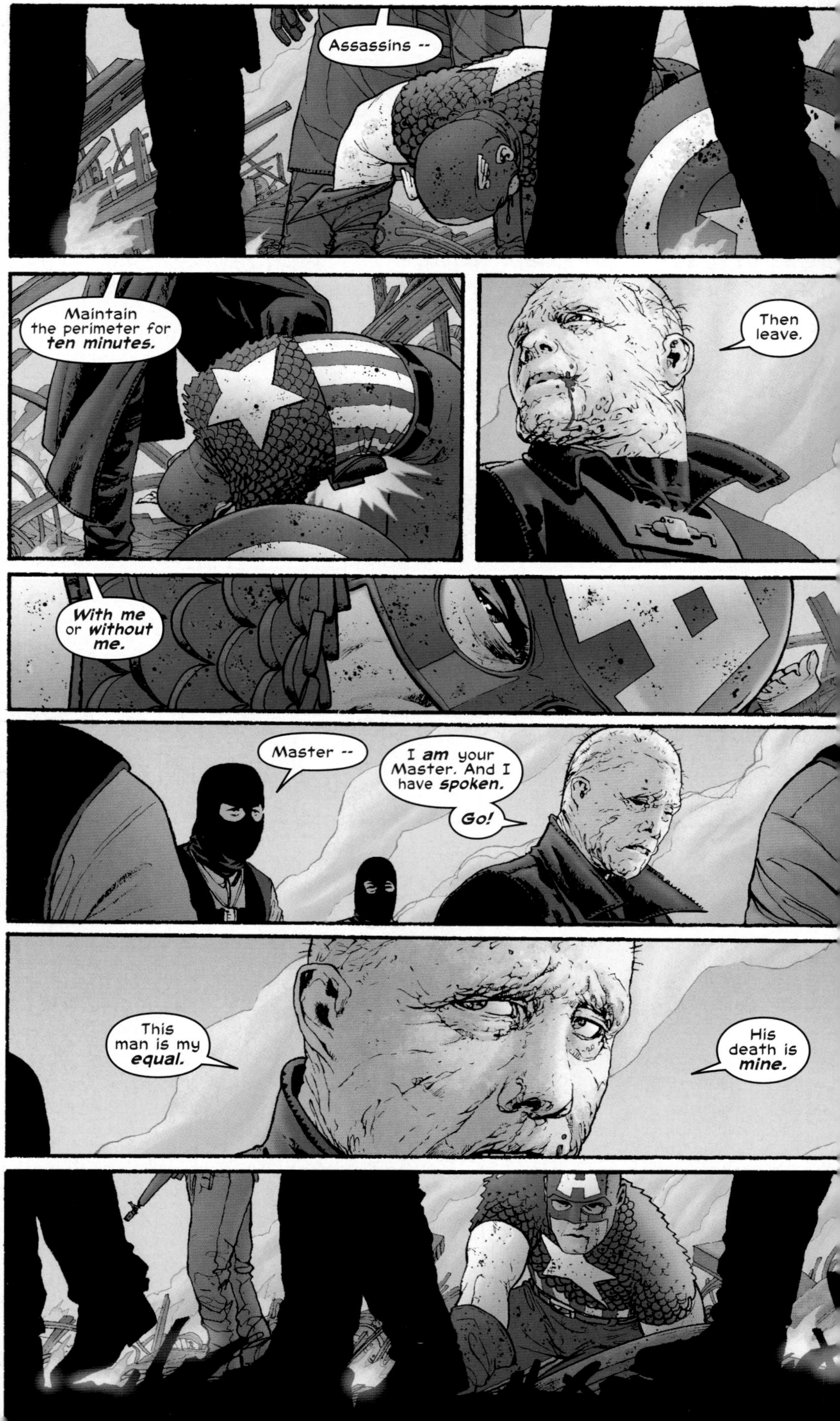
Assassins --
Maintain the perimeter for *ten minutes.*
Then leave.
With me or *without me.*
Master --
I *am* your Master. And I have *spoken.*
Go!
This man is my *equal.*
His death is *mine.*

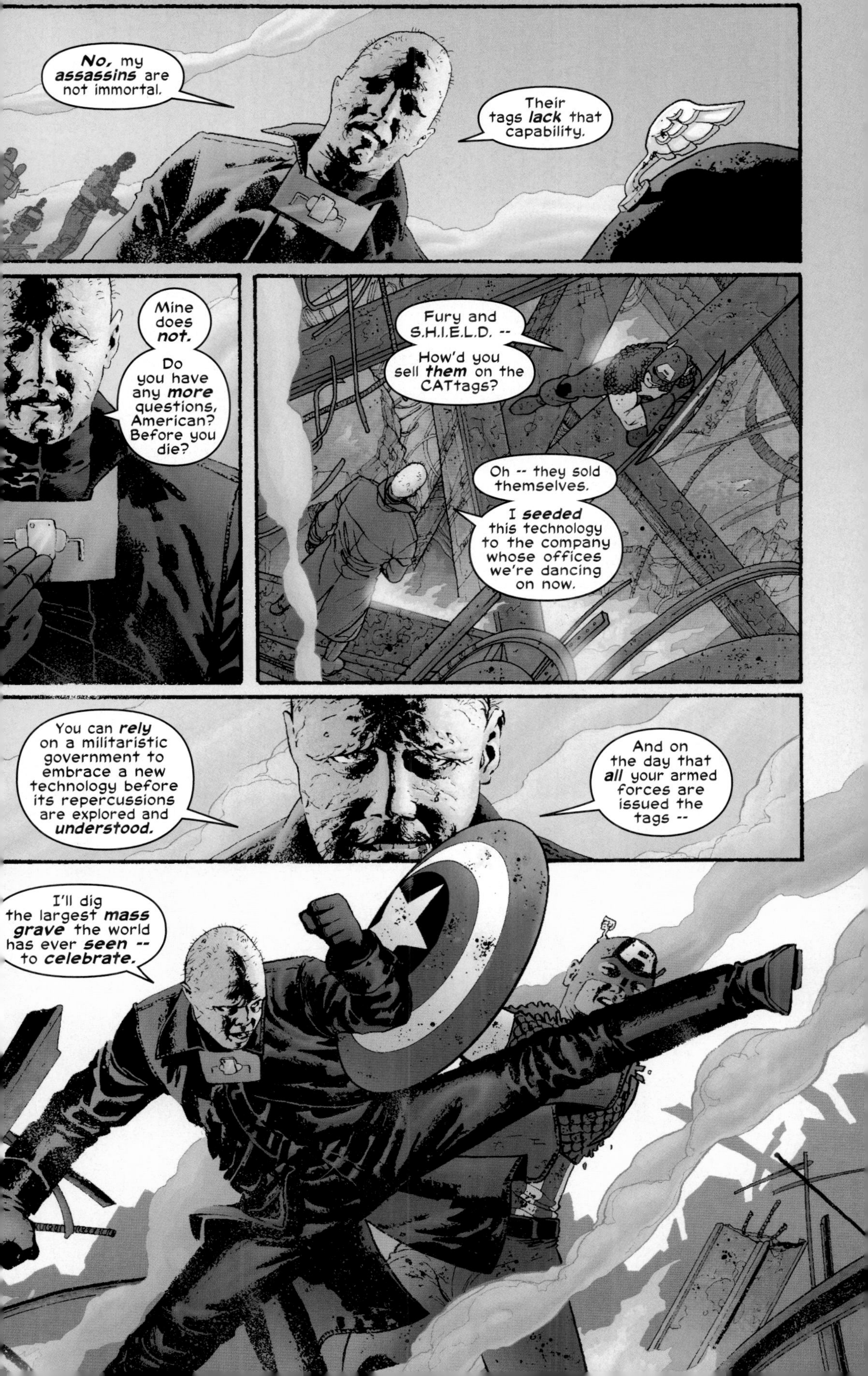
No, my assassins are not immortal.
Their tags lack that capability.
Mine does not.
Do you have any more questions, American? Before you die?
Fury and S.H.I.E.L.D. --
How'd you sell them on the CATtags?
Oh -- they sold themselves.
I seeded this technology to the company whose offices we're dancing on now.
You can rely on a militaristic government to embrace a new technology before its repercussions are explored and understood.
And on the day that all your armed forces are issued the tags --
I'll dig the largest mass grave the world has ever seen -- to celebrate.

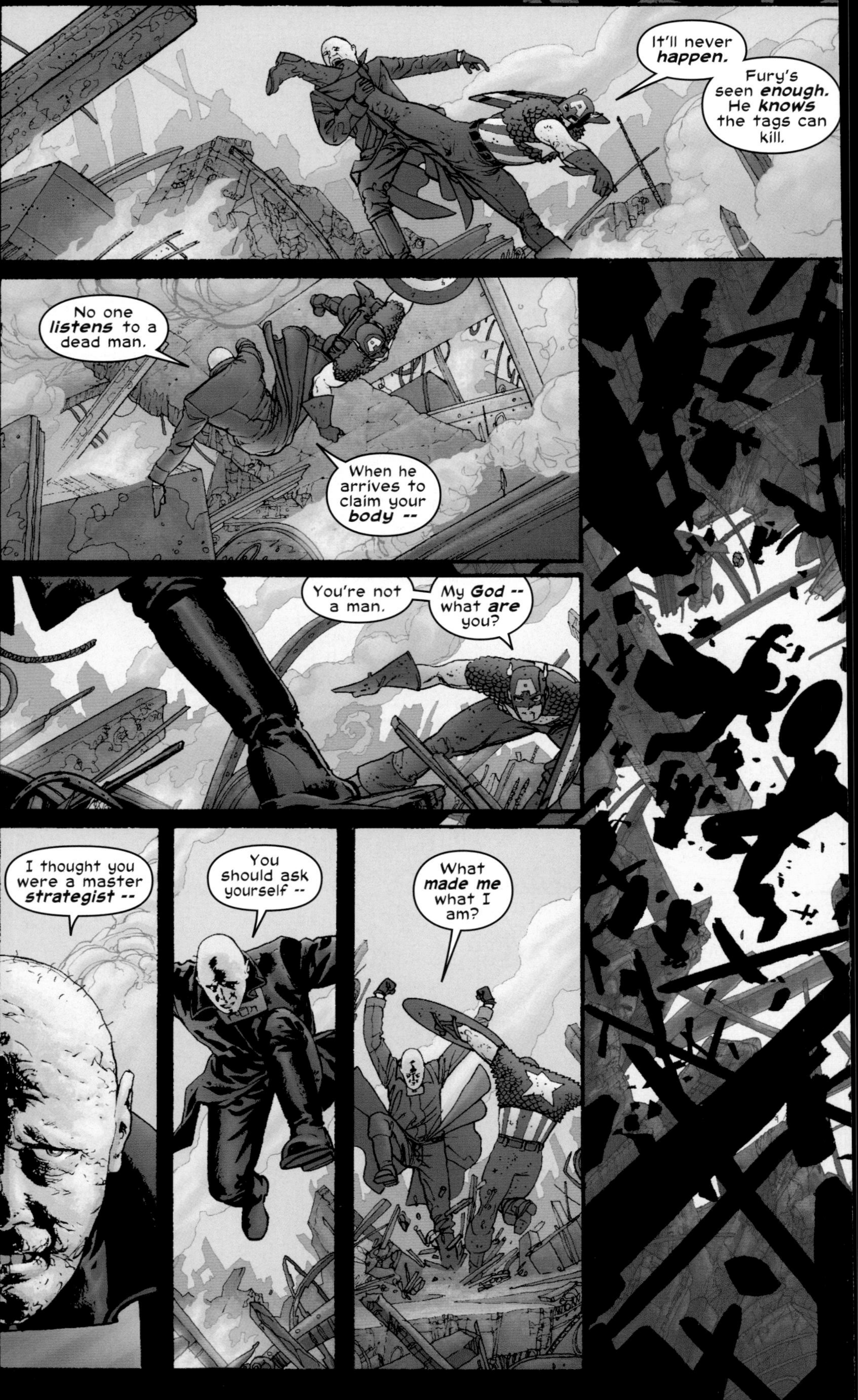
It'll never happen.
Fury's seen enough. He knows the tags can kill.
No one listens to a dead man.
When he arrives to claim your body --
You're not a man.
My God -- what are you?
I thought you were a master strategist --
You should ask yourself --
What made me what I am?

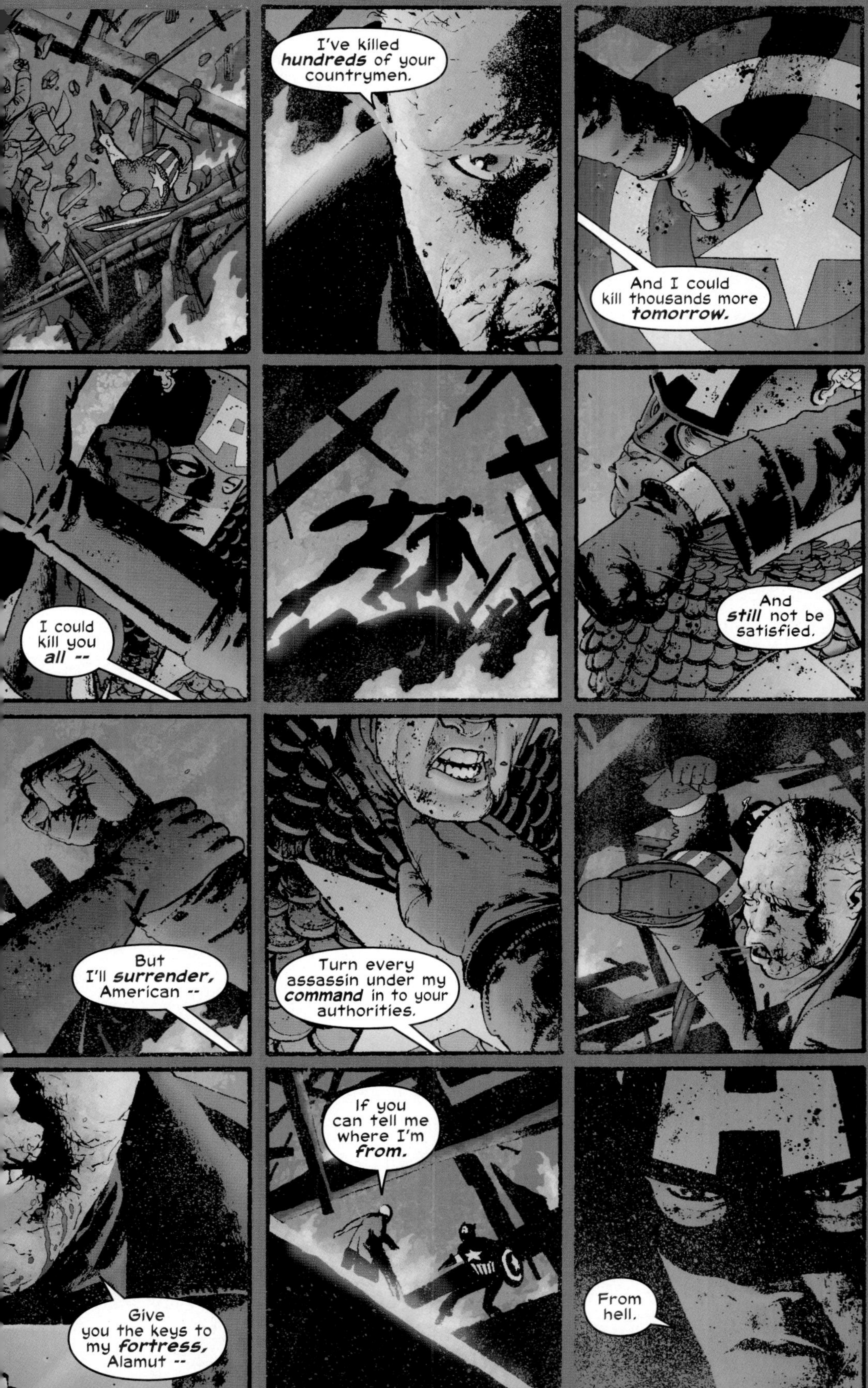
I've killed hundreds of your countrymen.
And I could kill thousands more tomorrow.
I could kill you all --
And still not be satisfied.
But I'll surrender, American --
Turn every assassin under my command in to your authorities.
Give you the keys to my fortress, Alamut --
If you can tell me where I'm from.
From hell.

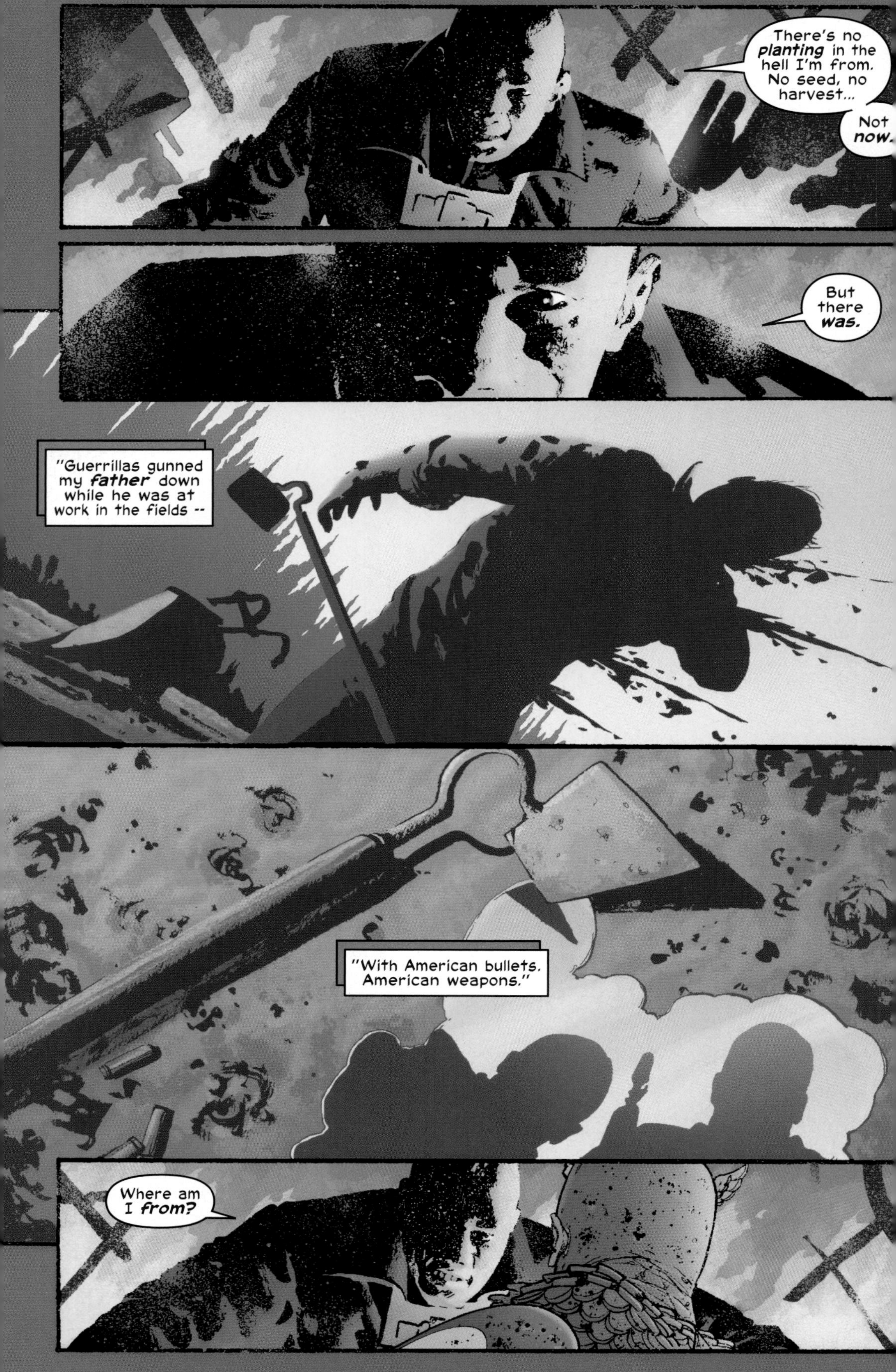
There's no planting in the hell I'm from. No seed, no harvest...
Not now.
But there was.
"Guerrillas gunned my father down while he was at work in the fields --
"With American bullets. American weapons."
Where am I from?

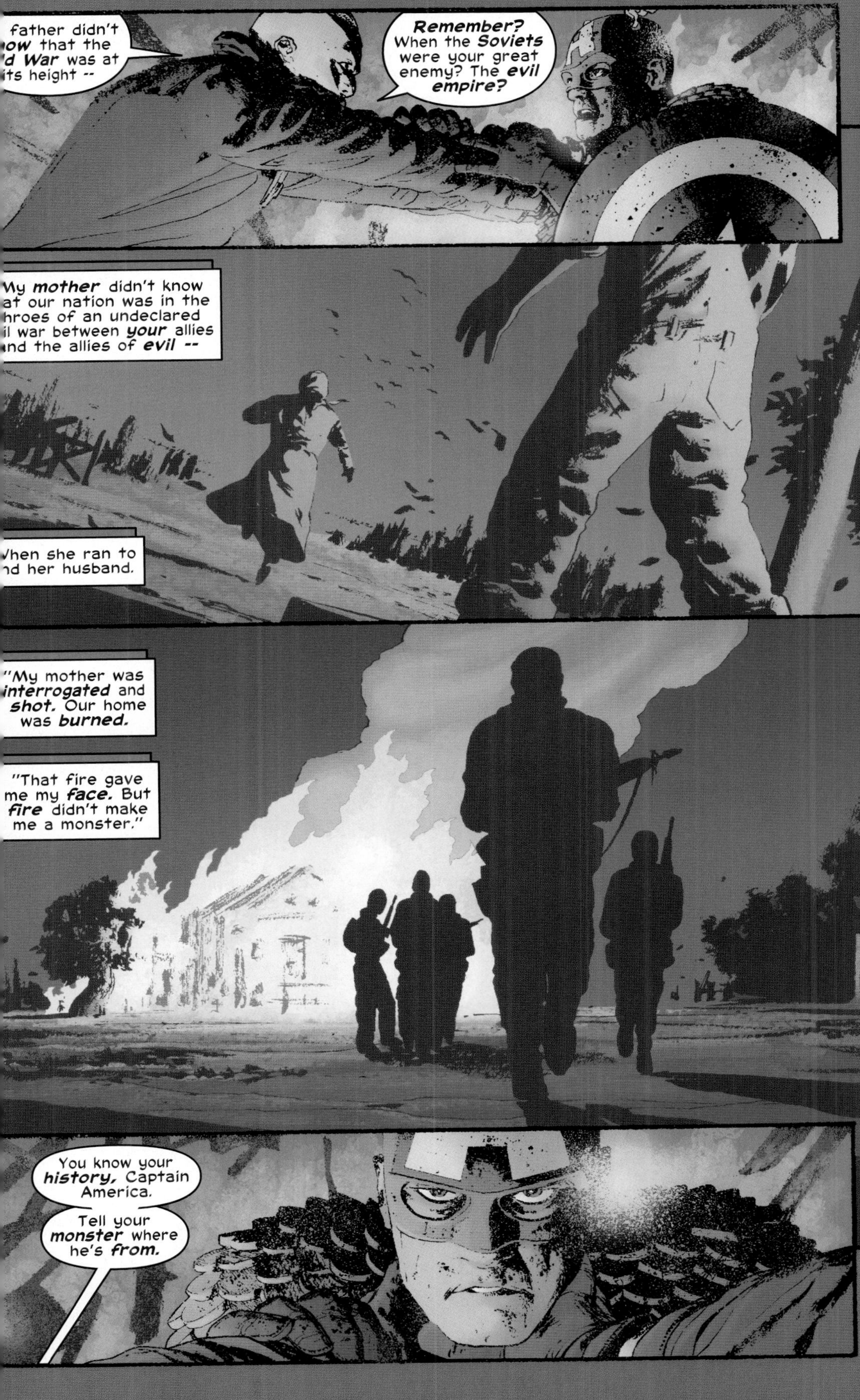
father didn't ow that the d War was at its height --
Remember? When the Soviets were your great enemy? The evil empire?
My mother didn't know at our nation was in the hroes of an undeclared il war between your allies nd the allies of evil --
When she ran to nd her husband.
"My mother was interrogated and shot. Our home was burned.
"That fire gave me my face. But fire didn't make me a monster."
You know your history, Captain America.
Tell your monster where he's from.

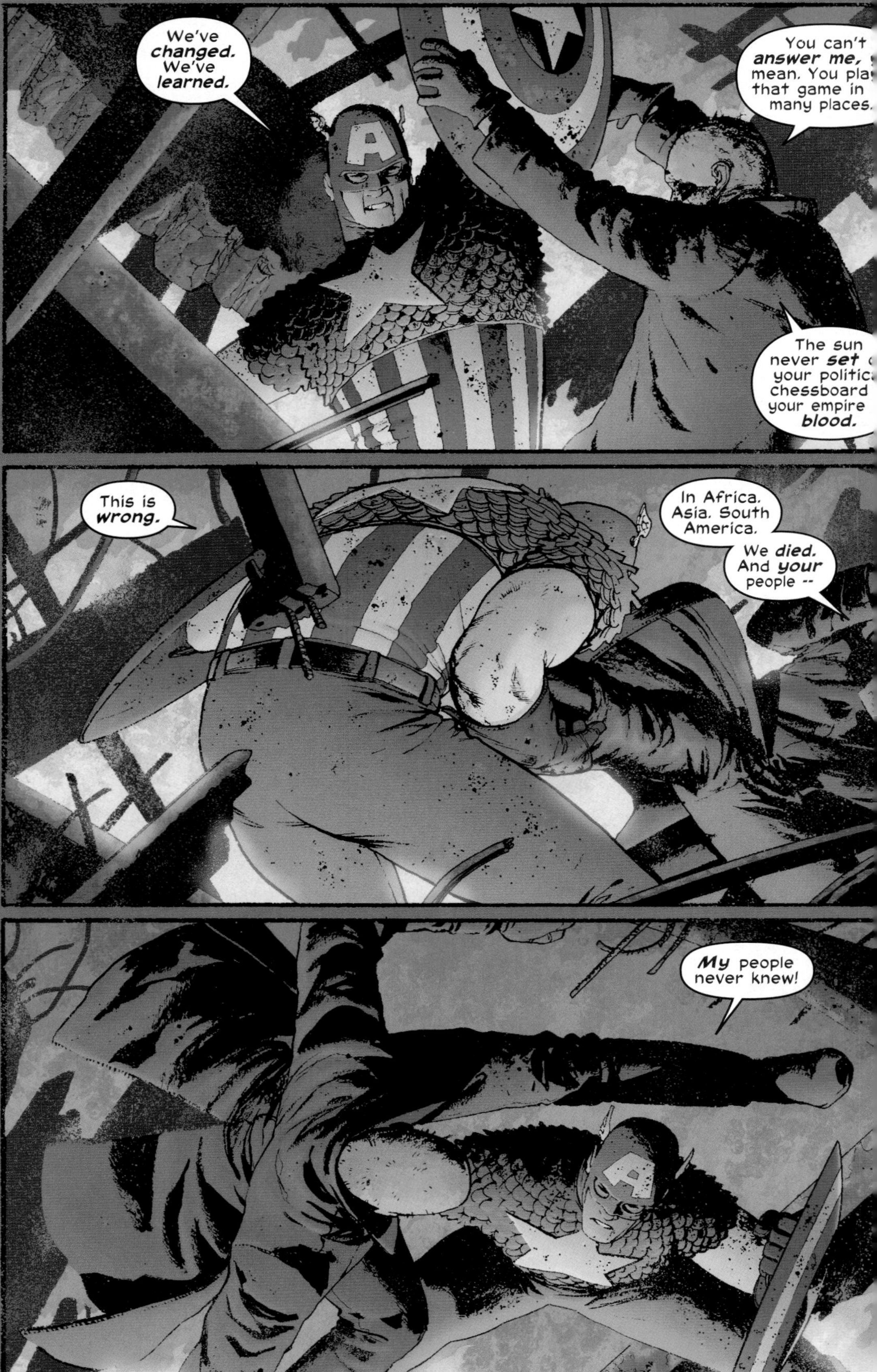
We've changed. We've learned.
You can't answer me, mean. You pla that game in many places.
The sun never set your politic chessboard your empire blood.
This is wrong.
In Africa. Asia. South America.
We died. And your people --
My people never knew!

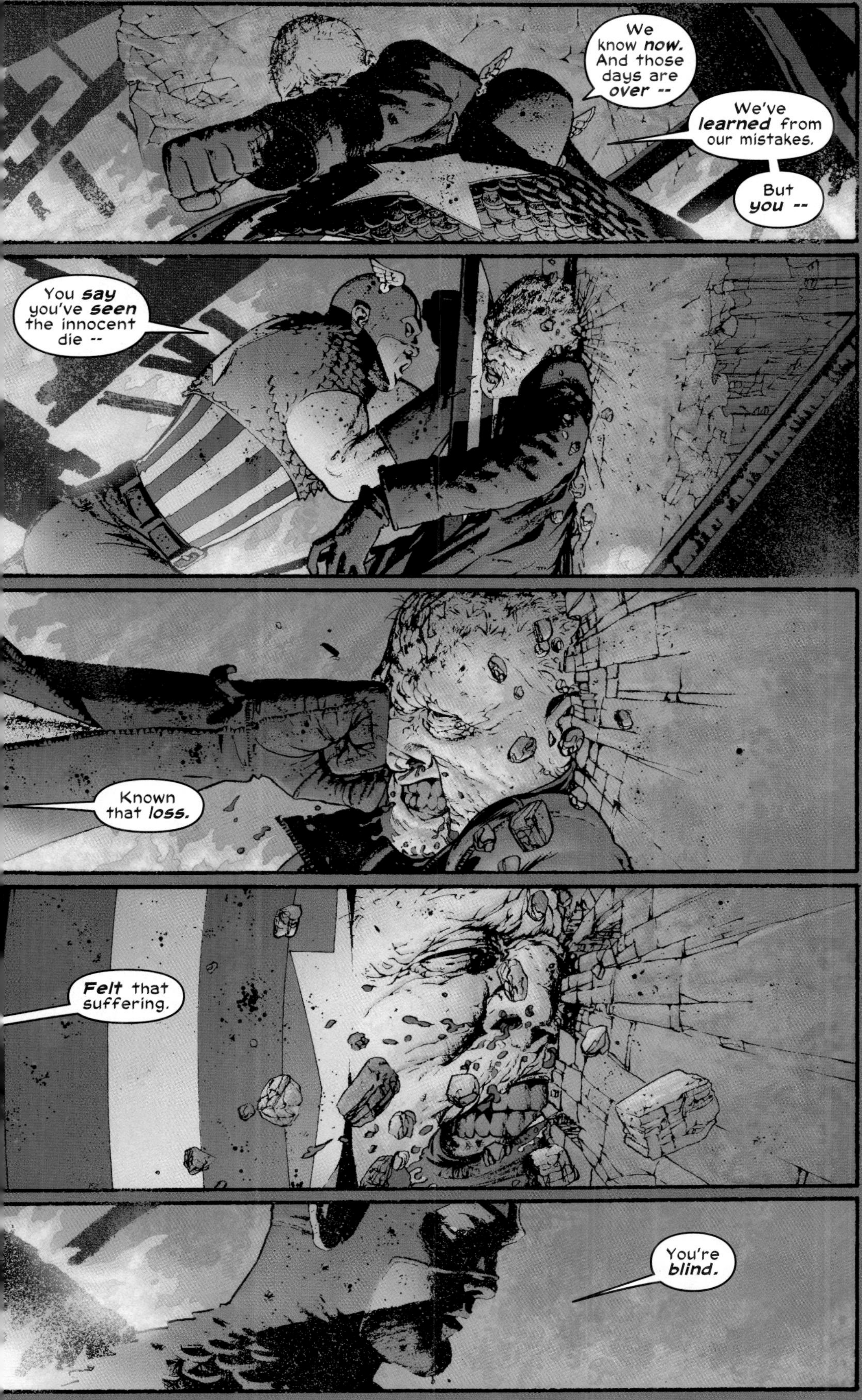
We know *now.* And those days are *over --*
We've *learned* from our mistakes.
But *you --*
You *say* you've *seen* the innocent die --
Known that *loss.*
Felt that suffering.
You're *blind.*

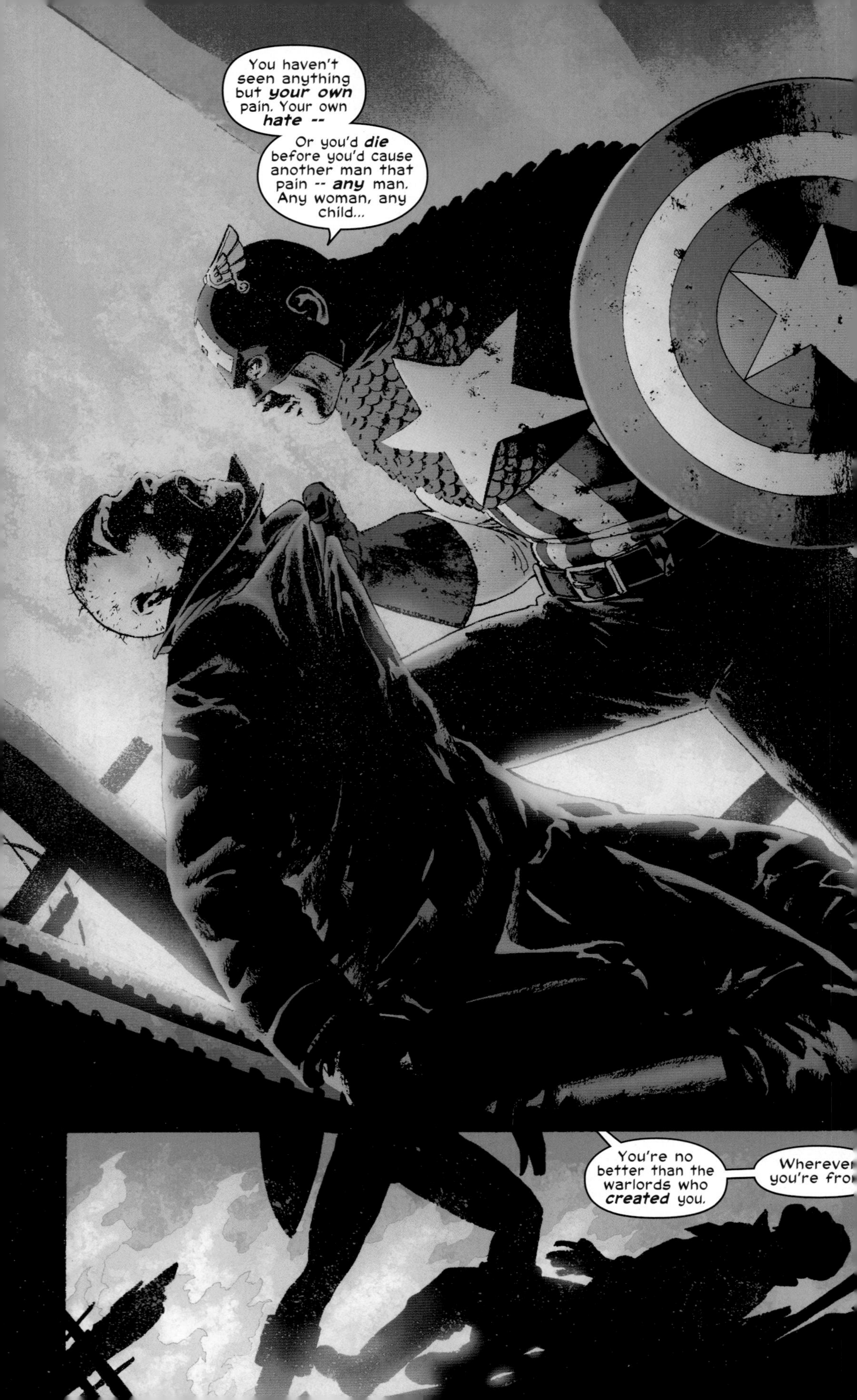
You haven't seen anything but **your own** pain. Your own **hate --**
Or you'd **die** before you'd cause another man that pain -- **any** man. Any woman, any child...
You're no better than the warlords who **created** you.

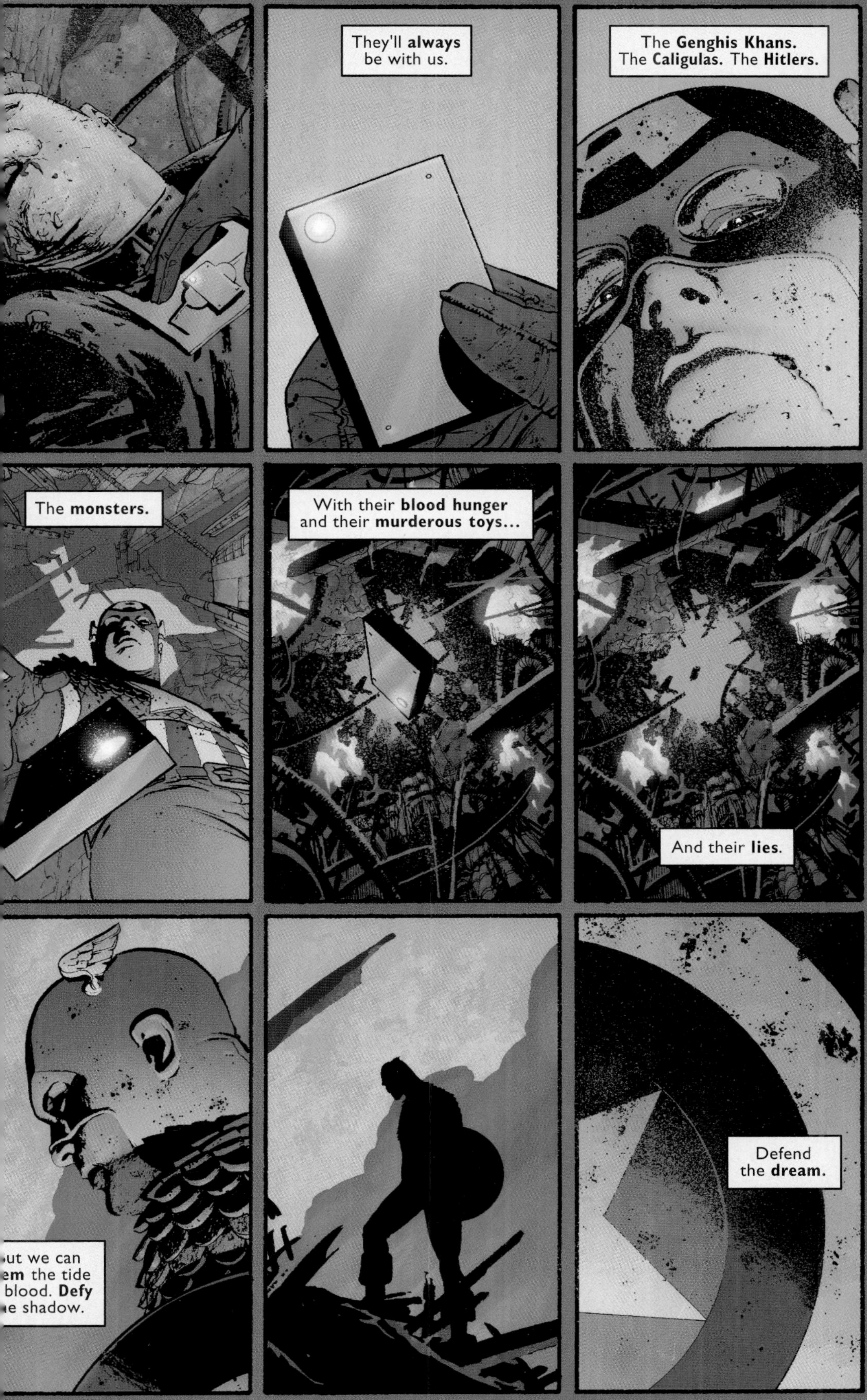
They'll always be with us.
The Genghis Khans. The Caligulas. The Hitlers.
The monsters.
With their blood hunger and their murderous toys...
And their lies.
ut we can
em the tide
blood. Defy
e shadow.
Defend the dream.

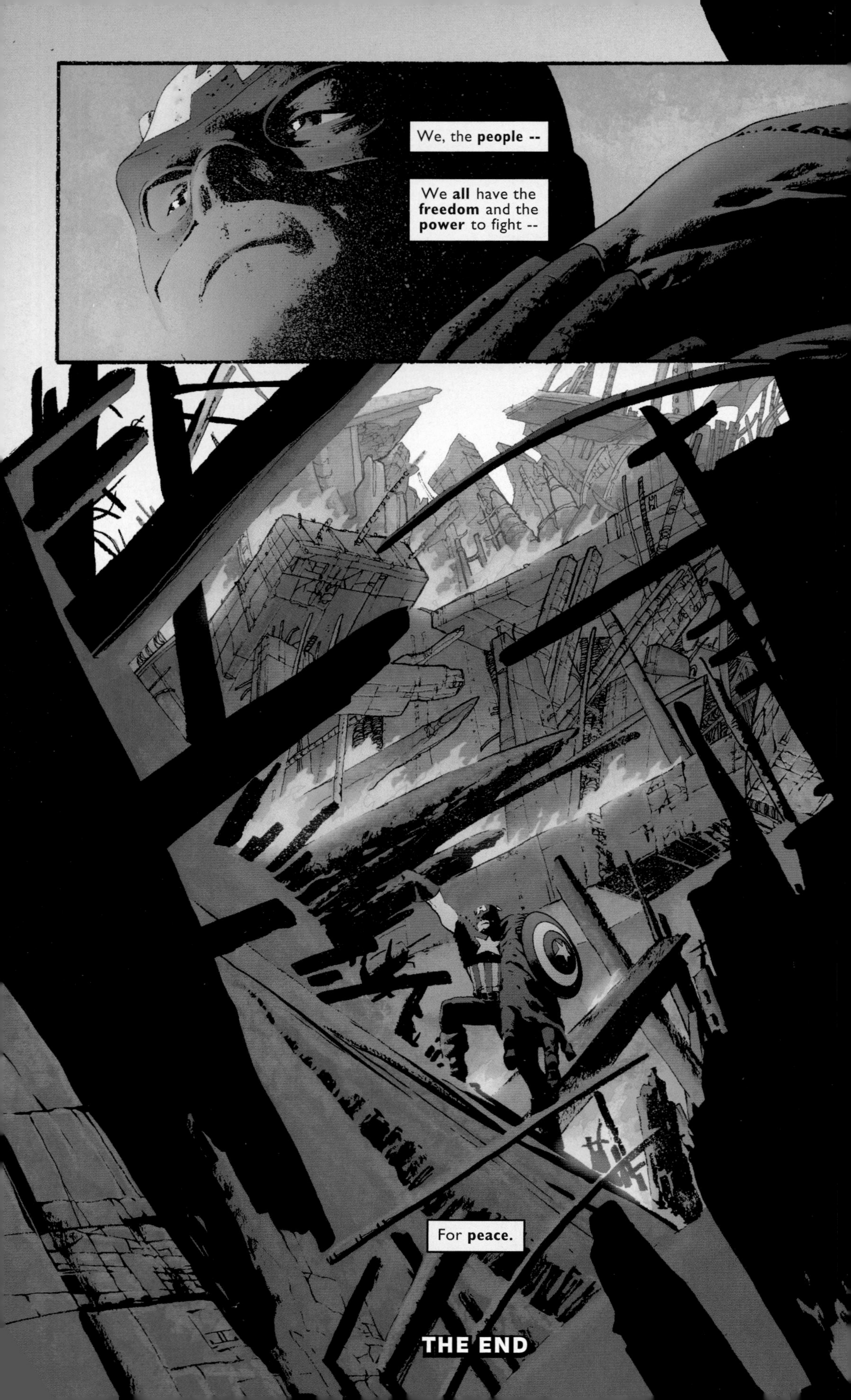
We, the **people --**
We **all** have the **freedom** and the **power** to fight --
For **peace.**
THE END

LOSS OF INNOCENCE

AN INTRODUCTION BY **MAX ALLAN COLLINS**

If you threw a dart at a map of America, aiming for the middle, you might well puncture my hometown—Muscatine, Iowa, where I still live. Muscatine is the kind of town that the Centerville of this graphic novel represents. Middle America. The Heartland. A great place to live, if only they didn't play country-western music in just about every restaurant and bar. On the other hand, the cost of living is low, the schools are great and my wife and I have our families here.

In a very real way, however, I also live in New York—Manhattan. As a freelance writer, my business associates—agent, editors, publishers—are almost exclusively located on that famous island. Just as movies are Hollywood, publishing is New York, and that includes much bigtime comics. On September 11, 2001, my reaction to the tragedies was heightened by a real sense that my other hometown—where many of my friends live—had been attacked in an all-out act of war.

I had one phone call get out to me, from my agent—about two days after the Twin Towers fell. And about three days after that, the cyber responses to my ARE YOU ALL RIGHT emails began to trickle in. Several of my publishers were within a few blocks of the Towers. As I waited to hear, I was terrified and felt helpless. These emotions were felt keenly all throughout this nation.

As so often happens in my life, an irony soon presented itself: I was just about to begin a novel called **The Lusitania Murders**, the fourth in a series of historical mysteries in which a fictional whodunit is built around and into a real disaster. I'd done the *Titanic*, the *Hindenburg* and, mostly recently, Pearl Harbor. The sinking of the *Lusitania* is generally considered by historians to be the first modern instance of civilians taking the brunt of an attack, of a large-scale act of war....

And so the soul-searching began. I found myself questioning the whole notion of writing entertainment built around disasters; hell, I found myself questioning the whole notion of writing entertainment. I've spoken to many writers of fiction—particularly genre fiction—and have found almost all of them were asking themselves the same question.

This shared moment of doubt proved to be relatively brief. While I never quite bought the specious notion that "we gotta play the big football game or else they win!" I did wonder how audiences would react to the kind of violent, action-oriented storytelling I often pursue. Of course, before long, it became clear—thank you, David Letterman; God bless you, Conan O'Brien—that we wanted to laugh again; from that nationwide realization flowed a renewed need for the kind of escapist entertainment most of us crave and perhaps even need.

The hero-driven comic book—particularly, the super hero variety—faced perhaps the greatest post-9/11 pop culture challenge of all. In the first place, super heroes grew out of a simpler time—the Depression—and most of the costumed crusaders, Captain America included, were designed to satisfy the tastes and needs of kids. Not little kids, but junior high school and high school kids. Many of that first generation of comic book readers went to war, and took their love and interest in comic books with them (and brought it home with them, too). And, of course, many super heroes fought the Nazis and Japanese in a war that—among kids of all ages, anyway—seemed so simple and straightforward, good guys vs. bad guys.

Captain America grew out of that era and such notions. The Jack Kirby and Joe Simon creation had a grittiness, however, that set it apart from the clean-cut Superman, the cartoonier Captain Marvel and even the noir-ish Batman. Simon and Kirby trumped the Joker with the Red Skull—disturbing images indicating the world of comic book super heroes was just beginning to lose a certain innocence.

It has been a great challenge through the years to keep a character like Captain America fresh and relevant. It would be easy for such a character to seem foolish, such a concept to appear naive, as times change and readers grow more sophisticated. But various talented writers and artists have managed this feat over the years—my favorite remains Jim Steranko's version, the Nick Fury-shared shadow of which falls benignly over the terrific reinvention in the pages ahead.

Writer John Ney Rieber and artist John Cassaday may have faced the most formidable of all modern Captain America challenges in attempting to take this classic character of a simpler time into the smoky aftermath of September 11th. They succeed heroically and not by stooping to jingoistic nonsense, nor do they make it seem foolish that a costumed hero like Cap is walking around a devastated Ground Zero...though, for a time, Cap himself chooses not to wear that costume.

The team achieves this in part by doing good work. Rieber's story moves swiftly, and his sparing captions and dialogue show both restraint and power. Cassaday's art is similarly swift, and the design and draftsmanship are flat-out beautiful. If the forward movement of the script and layout didn't propel the reader through the story like a hurled knife, Cassaday's artwork might be distractingly handsome...but the narrative helps the reader resist stopping to gawk, encouraging instead keeping pace with the tale. (Few who read this work will not go back through its pages afterward, however, to linger over Cassaday's artistry.)

What is even more remarkable is this story's courage and ability to examine the complexities of the issues that accompany terrorism... specifically, not to duck the things America has done to feed the hatred that led to the attacks. That is not to say Rieber offers justification for terrorism. Rather, he insists that we examine the root causes in a more complicated, grown-up manner than one might expect from a super hero comic book. This book is in color, after all, not black and white—and one of the most dominant and troubling colors here is gray.

I applaud the creators of this 21st-century Captain America tale. They demonstrate that great characters, forged in more innocent times, can survive and thrive in the post-9/11 world... at least when a creative team like this one defies the odds and heroically takes on the challenge.

Like somebody we all know. At least, we do here in Centerville.

MAX ALLAN COLLINS is the author of the graphic novel **Road to Perdition** *(illustrated by Richard Piers-Rayner), upon which the Tom Hanks/Sam Mendes film is based. His many novels include the Shamus Award-winning* **Nathan Heller** *historical mysteries, and his comics work includes fifteen years scripting the* **Dick Tracy** *syndicated strip. In his native Iowa, he has written and directed three independent films, most recently* **Real Time: Siege at Lucas Street Market**.

May we never forget the truth that was so clear to us that day:

That we are one.

And may our hearts and hands continue to work together to create
an enduring memorial to the victims and the heroes of that day:

A world where hate can find no room to grow.

John Ney Rieber

For my fellow New Yorkers,
who have suffered much
and struggle for faith still.

John Cassaday

All proceeds from the sale of original art from issue #1 will be donated by the artist to the families of NYC firefighters lost responding on 9/11 from Engine 40/Ladder 35.

Creator dedications from *Captain America: The New Deal Hardcover*